SAFARI PRESS

Bwana Babu Kwaheri

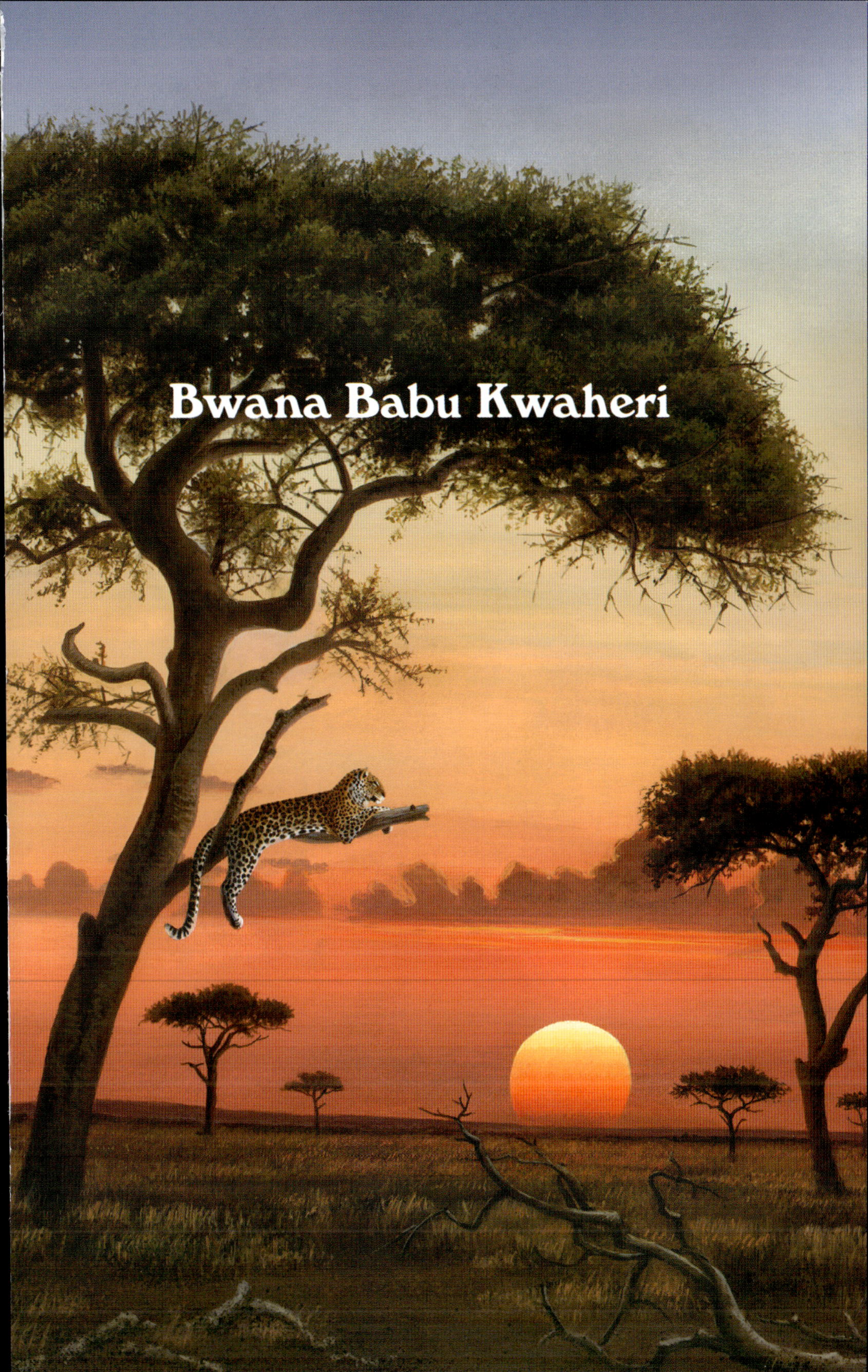

Young bull elephant feeding on camelthorn pods.

Bwana Babu Kwaheri

by

Joseph C. Greenfield Jr.

Forewords
by
Joey O'Bannon and William S. Jarrett

Safari Press

Greenfield Jr., Joseph C.

First edition

Safari Press Inc.

2011, Long Beach, California

ISBN 978-1-57157-382-7

Library of Congress Catalog Card Number: 2010928900

10 9 8 7 6 5 4 3 2 1

Printed in China

Readers wishing to receive the Safari Press catalog, featuring many fine books on big-game hunting, wingshooting, and sporting firearms, should write to Safari Press Inc., P.O. Box 3095, Long Beach, CA 90803, USA, Tel: (714) 894-9080 or visit our Web site at www.safaripress.com.

This book is dedicated to Africa. Perhaps my enchantment can be partially understood from the following:

Why Africa?

Why am I drawn to Africa
Like a firefly to a light?
I've listed many reasons,
But none of them seem right.

I've seen and heard the African bush:
A land unchanged by years.
Where beauty and danger lie side by side,
To love as well as fear.

I'm enthralled when hunting dangerous game
By horn, tusk and claw.
But all these sights and thrills,
Can't fathom Africa's draw.

So what's the magnet of Africa
That grips and holds me fast?
I know. After a million years,
I've come home, at last.

Table of Contents

Foreword to *Bwana Babu Kwaheri*

I am uniquely qualified to contribute a foreword for *Bwana Babu Kwaheri.* Dr. Greenfield and I have trained a number of pointer bird dogs and hunted bobwhite quail together for twenty-five years. During this time, we have developed a warm personal friendship. In 1996, I accompanied him on his first safari to Africa and have been with him on ten of his twelve safaris, functioning as the primary professional hunter on seven.

In fact, I talked Doc into breaking the mold as a one-species bird hunter in order to hunt dangerous game in Africa. What I did not accomplish was to change his attitude toward becoming a big-game hunter. Doc is still a quail hunter at heart. However, he has extended his love for a side-by-side double shotgun to a Holland & Holland .465 double rifle. Using this weapon, he has successfully hunted a number of Africa's dangerous game. He recently completed a quest for the Big Five. Paradoxically, he has not developed an interest in hunting other African game, including the large and beautiful antelope. In fact, I have seen him kill both record-book-size hartebeest and wildebeest for lion bait, but then show no interest in even having a picture taken to document these kills. In this regard, he is quite different from all of the other clients with whom I have hunted in Africa. In short, Doc "ain't" a big-game hunter.

During these safaris, Doc developed a keen insight into the workings and abilities of a number of native trackers. From his perspective, watching pointers perform is the essence of quail hunting. In a similar fashion, observing the trackers skillfully follow spoor is more exciting than the actual killing of dangerous game. Doc has developed a close friendship with a number of these individuals, especially Makanyanga.

Together, Doc and I have killed two elephants, two lions, over a dozen trophy-size Cape buffaloes, and a leopard. On three occasions, our encounters with Cape buffalo have been hair-raising, documenting their well-deserved reputation as dangerous game. All of these adventures have been meticulously (frequently humorously) described in this volume. In addition, a number of different facets of African hunting, as well as Africa itself, have been covered.

I count myself very lucky to have been able to share most of these adventures with Doc. He recently decided that his African safaris "will be no more." What will the future bring? Undoubtedly, we will continue to share our passion for hunting bobwhite quail with pointer bird dogs!

Joey O'Bannon
J&R Outfitters
Indiantown, Florida
2009

Foreword to *Bwana Babu*

I've never been on an African safari, but I've known several outdoor writers who have. They all concur that those who hunt dangerous big-game animals represent a breed apart. They delight in the challenge of the hunt, of course, but they relish equally the companionships that are formed along the way, especially among their guides and trackers. Dr. Joseph Greenfield Jr. has experienced all of this and more.

In addition to hunting big game in Africa, he has long been an avid hunter of quail, as evidenced by his recently published book on that subject, *A Quail Hunter's Odyssey*. I first met Joe Greenfield a few years ago in the course of editing two articles, taken from his book on quail hunting, in the *Shooter's Bible*. His accounts of chasing these elusive birds all afforded a different dimension to Joe's life as a hunter. An engaging sense of humor emerges in those pages, an element that has doubtless served him well in the past.

What his readers should also know about the author is his long and highly successful career as one of the top heart specialists in the country. Dr. Greenfield began his medical career in 1956 at Duke University Medical Center where he has been a James B. Duke Distinguished Professor of Medicine since 1981 and was chairman of the Department of Medicine from 1983 to 1995. His many research papers and medical publications all attest to a life full of great accomplishments. Against this background of high-level achievements, it's not surprising that Dr. Greenfield should find success in Africa as well.

In addition to the recounting of his exploits in the hunting fields of Africa, what I like particularly about *Bwana Babu* are, for beginners, the poems that follow each chapter. I can't recall any other hunting book of its kind that features such gems created by the author himself. The stories and poems of *Bwana Babu* are also complemented by colorful photos taken by the author during his seven trips to Africa.

Close attention should, in my opinion, be placed especially on the chapter presenting a brief biography of Makanyanga, a peerless tracker and, in fact, a "living legend," along with Alex Walker, an outstanding big-game guide. The story of these two close friends and hunting companions, both of whose paths have crossed Joe Greenfield's, tells much about the recent history of the African safari and its murky future.

So sit back and enjoy your trip to the game fields of Africa and relive the lively experiences of a man who has succeeded in fashioning two careers that are at once diverse, challenging, and, in many respects, lifesaving.

William S. Jarrett, editor
Shooter's Bible (1985–2002)
Southbury, Connecticut
2005

Acknowledgments

My African adventures are a direct product of my long and close friendship with Joey O'Bannon. He "twisted my arm" to make the first safari and has hunted with me on ten of the twelve. On several occasions, his quick actions kept me from serious injury, or worse. Joey outlined the salient features of our hunting relationship in his Foreword. To him I am forever grateful.

Alex Walker was instrumental in making many of the early adventures possible. Barry Burchell, the professional hunter on three of the last safaris, is an outstanding guide and individual.

I am deeply indebted to a number of the trackers who have "opened the door" for me to African hunting: Simon, Pius, Singi, Doudi, Sampson, Martin, Moshile, Corporal, Alex, and especially Makanyanga. Makanyanga's skills are without equal. Also, I consider him to be a close personal friend.

Bucky Flowers, an outstanding taxidermist, mounted and designed the display of the trophies.

William S. Jarrett provided a Foreword and was instrumental in bringing the initial manuscript to publication.

The outstanding efforts of a number of colleagues have been essential in the preparation of this book:

Lesa M. Hall rejuvenated many of the photographs.

William Coke Ariail III painstakingly formatted many of the photographs from videotape.

Bettie C. Houston skillfully prepared multiple revisions of the manuscript.

Judith C. Rembert provided essential advice regarding the content and style of the manuscript as well as carefully editing the text.

Clive Kay's exceptional artwork greatly enhanced this presentation.

Finally, I am indebted to both Jacque Neufeld and Ludo Wurfbain for making possible the publication of this material.

To Set the Stage

Chapter I

I am a dyed-in-the-wool bobwhite quail hunter, having pursued this sport for more than sixty-five years.[1] A precipitous decrease in the quail population in the mid 1980s made it necessary to look outside my home state of North Carolina to pursue my passion. In the course of this quest, I met Joey O'Bannon, the owner of J&R Outfitters in LaBelle, Florida, and began hunting on his preserve. Joey and I developed a warm, lasting friendship. We have hunted quail together approximately thirty days per year for the past twenty-five years, both at LaBelle and more recently near Indiantown, Florida.

So why, at age sixty-five, did I decide to try big-game hunting in East Africa? The answer is simple: Joey persuaded me to go. He can talk me into anything!

Since quail hunting is seasonal, Joey had begun guiding a number of his clients on plains-game safaris to South Africa. During one of these expeditions, he worked with Graham Jones, a professional hunter who also conducted safaris in Tanzania for both plains game and Cape buffalo. Joey, who wanted to expand his hunting options, decided to hunt with Graham in Tanzania. He convinced me that hunting Cape buffalo in the Serengeti would be a

[1]Greenfield Jr., Joseph C. *A Quail Hunter's Odyssey.* Long Beach: Safari Press, 2009.

new and exciting experience. With a great deal of trepidation, I gave it a try. Joey was right. Buffalo hunting was much more challenging than I had anticipated. I was bitten and severely infected by the "African hunting bug," so much so that I have returned for a total of twelve safaris.

My initial foray was to hunt Cape buffalo. A somewhat circuitous set of circumstances on my next two safaris enabled me to hunt both elephant and lion. I became thoroughly enthralled by every aspect of hunting these magnificent animals, especially Cape buffalo. Recently, I hunted leopard twice and completed my quest for the Big Five by darting a rhinoceros.

I've chosen to present the stories of my multiple excursions into the Dark Continent in chronological order, relying on voluminous contemporary notes to write about these "exploits." Each description of a specific safari was written at the conclusion of it, so there is an elapsed time of thirteen years between the first and last account.

The reader will identify a significant transformation in my outlook from the initial to the last trip. I've gradually changed from a quail hunter, who looked with disdain on big-game shooting, to an enthusiastic pursuer of dangerous game. I have not, however, become a convert to hunting the spectacular African plains game. I have shot several trophy-quality antelope for lion bait or camp meat, but I did not enjoy these experiences. I have also concluded that bird shooting in Africa ain't for me. The participation of my pointer bird dogs is a must for my bird-hunting enjoyment.

A major factor contributing to my enjoyment of hunting dangerous game has been the opportunity to observe at close hand the outstanding capabilities of a number of native trackers. They introduced me to an entirely new aspect of hunting. I owe all of them, especially Makanyanga, an enormous debt.

I have attempted in these machinations not only to describe the hunting sequences but also to elucidate my compulsive preparations for each safari. I have included a broad overview of the contributions of the safari industry to both the welfare of the local inhabitants and to the preservation of Africa's rich fauna and flora. In presenting a panorama of African hunting, several chapters deal with subjects other than the direct pursuit of dangerous game.

The tales recounted are, at least, a semiaccurate description of what went on. (Truthfully, nothing has been played down.) I have struggled not to project myself as either "a know-it-all" or "a great white hunter" of dangerous game. As a sign of respect (I hope), I was dubbed *Bwana Babu* (grandfather) by the usually perceptive Tanzanian staff. While hunting dangerous game and completing my quest for the Big Five, I have managed not only to survive but to thoroughly enjoy a number of extraordinarily exciting experiences in present-day Africa. My cup is full.

My future fortunes will be turned exclusively toward my first love: pointer bird dogs and bobwhite quail hunting. It is time for me to say "farewell" to Africa. My African adventures will always be a significant part of my essence—but the curtain has fallen. Africa, *Kwaheri.*

But for now, come and relive these adventures with me.

Bwana Babu

To be known as *Bwana Babu*
I'm told is a sign of respect.
Is Swahili so different from English:
Grandfather doesn't mean—old wreck?

Well, I'll take them at their word
'Cause the trackers are fond of me.
Even when my pace is so slow,
Our quarry has time to flee.

When trying to quietly slip
Through brush or silently walk,
I make so much racket
That I usually ruin the stalk.

Bwana Babu Kwaheri

As a woodsman I'm less than terrific.
My eyes have grown weak and dim.
Game easily spotted by all,
Alas—I still don't see 'em!

So what if I'm noisy and slow?
Spotting animals, I miss quite a few.
But as long as I can hunt with these men
I'm proud to be called *Bwana Babu.*

The Serengeti, Butterflies and Buffaloes

Chapter II

During my fifty-year hunting career, I had been content to spend my time pursuing bobwhite quail and never had considered going on an African safari to hunt big game. In fact, I had found my prior experience with American big game, white-tailed deer, less than exciting—similar to shooting a neighbor's billy goat. However, Joey O'Bannon, who owns J&R Outfitters in Indiantown, Florida, persuaded me to give Africa a try. Joey and I had hunted quail together for ten years and were close friends.

To expand his outfitting business, Joey had spent the last four or five summers guiding clients on plains-game safaris on several large South African game ranches. There he had worked with professional hunter Graham Jones, a former member of the South African armed forces, who was planning to guide several safaris to Tanzania during the next season. I met Graham in Florida at Joey's hunting preserve in early February 1996.

His description of Cape buffalo hunting was very enticing. The hunting concession was located near Fort Ikoma, immortalized by Robert Ruark in his writings about Africa. After Joey agreed to accompany me on the hunt, I made a spur-of-the-moment decision to give hunting Cape buffalo a try.

For a number of years, I had enmeshed myself in the voluminous literature on African hunting, especially that pertaining to dangerous game. From the early explorers and ivory hunters to the recent safari guides, their tales provided a rich mosaic of African adventure. The more I reflected on my decision to hunt Cape buffalo, the more excited I became.

Never having been a world traveler, I obtained my first passport, along with a Tanzanian visa. For only $228, the nurse at the Duke Medical Center Travel Clinic administered the necessary immunizations (I passed on the Hepatitis A vaccination since I didn't plan to visit the local brothels), and she thoroughly indoctrinated me on the necessity of drinking only boiled or bottled liquids. Finally, I began taking the antimalaria drug Lariam a week prior to the trip.

When planning the safari, I indicated to Graham that I had little interest in plains game but looked forward to the opportunity to hunt Cape buffalo. I had read about the plethora of African upland game birds, so I discussed the feasibility of bird hunting with Graham. Since he gave me no encouragement, I didn't take a shotgun, a decision I later regretted.

Joey, who would be guiding in South Africa prior to my safari, brought the rifles: a .375 H&H Brno Magnum (for my use) and a newly purchased .470 NE Krieghoff Classic double rifle. Joey had obtained the Brno from Derek Evans, a well-respected professional hunter who had retired. This rifle had seen a lot of action. Derek had used it on the entire gamut of African game.

I flirted with the notion of taking my .465 NE Holland & Holland sidelock. Unfortunately, I learned the current value of this beautiful double rifle (approximately $35,000) and decided against taking the chance that it might be damaged or stolen. (One of the ironies of life is to learn that something you own is worth so much money that you become reluctant to use it.) I'd paid very little for the Holland twenty years ago, and I had fired it only once or twice, killing a few pine trees. For this trip, it rested in my gun safe, making it of little practical use. The Krieghoff was a serviceable rifle. When Joey tested it in Florida, it was also effective in killing pine trees as well as an occasional armadillo, but it fell far short as a high-class weapon when compared to the Holland.

I was glad that I had inquired about proper hunting attire. I learned that dark khaki or dark-colored clothing would be acceptable, but wearing camouflage is a definite mistake: The wearer might be misidentified as a terrorist and either arrested or shot. For damn sure, my camouflage clothing remained in the United States. Also, I was advised not to bother purchasing excessively expensive tsetse fly-proof clothing since these critters can bite through anything. Impregnating clothing with mosquito repellent works fine until washday. On safari, clothes are washed with lye soap daily, so forget the repellent. Although the caustic lye soap cleans exceptionally well, it turns worn garments into tatters, making new underwear and socks a necessity. In fact, after a few washings, colors will fade and holes will appear, even in new clothes.

To prepare for the trip, I reread a number of classic works about Cape buffalo hunting, as well as the detailed anthology, *Hunting the African Buffalo.*[1] I concluded that an exciting, and perhaps perilous, experience awaited me.

Although many of my world traveler friends were appalled that I didn't fly first or at least business class, I've always said that I travel coach because nothing cheaper is offered. I boarded the American Airlines jet carrying a video camera, clothes (I'd bought a Willis and Geiger safari jacket so that I would look the part), and enough antibiotics to treat every disease on the African continent.

Upon arrival in London, I adapted fairly well to the new language (trolley means baggage cart, lift means elevator) and had no trouble checking into the airport hotel. I used the twelve-hour layover in London to fulfill a longtime desire to visit the Purdey showroom. I had hunted quail with a vintage Purdey[2] 12-gauge shotgun for several years, and in 1995, a number of my colleagues presented me with a beautifully engraved Purdey shotgun—a real heirloom.

[1]Rikhoff, Jim. (Editor) *Hunting the African Buffalo.* Clinton, NJ: Amwell Press, 1984.

[2]Dallas, Donald. *Purdey Guns and Rifle Makers: The Definitive History.* London: Quiller Press, 2000.

I took a train to London's center, then a cab to Audley Street. When I arrived at Purdey's (established around 1802), I felt somewhat out of place without a coat and tie, feeling as though I more resembled a ragamuffin than the British lords who usually frequent this premier gun shop. The gentlemen at Purdey's were extremely gracious, showing me their guns and the world-famous "long room" (in which the firm's long and distinguished history is depicted). They spent several hours patiently correcting a large body of misinformation I'd acquired regarding their shotguns. At least there is one place on this modern earth where a longstanding commitment to excellence and pride of workmanship is still being maintained!

On the next leg of the journey, British Airways to Dar es Salaam, Tanzania, I enjoyed the company—when he wasn't snoring—of a garrulous Irish sailor. I arrived at Dar es Salaam, population more than a million, to find a bustling Indian Ocean seaport. I'd expected to be met at the airport by a physician staff member of the Muhimbili Hospital with whom the Duke Department of Medicine had an affiliation, but somehow we missed each other. I discovered that my baggage had been pilfered. (Fortunately, the only significant losses were a 35mm camera and sunglasses.)

I found a cab driver, a pleasant retired government worker, whose moribund vehicle coughed and wheezed like an asthmatic. He drove me to the hotel via a four-lane road full of potholes and lined with street vendors hawking myriad articles that no doubt included my camera and sunglasses. I rested in my room until 5 A.M. when the same driver took me back to the airport. His cab stalled three times; once I had to get out to help push, but we made it well in advance of departure time. Early arrival turned out to be a good thing. I learned the policy of Air Tanzania: When enough passengers show up to fill the plane, the plane departs, regardless of the posted departure time! And fill the plane they did. All the seats were stuffed with one or more passengers and the aisles occupied by luggage, chickens, and goats.

I arrived at the Kilimanjaro airport in Arusha and was met by a very nice lady employed by Hunters and Guides Safari Company (for whom Graham worked). She offered to drive me to the hotel, but the hotel also had dispatched a taxicab, so I went in that vehicle. Big mistake. The driver drove sixty mph over roads designed for oxcarts; in fact, the road was packed with oxcarts! The cab rides in Dar es Salaam and Arusha were by far the most dangerous parts of my journey. My hotel room featured a balcony overlooking an outside dining area. I had a skybox view of a long, loud, and lavish wedding reception that made sleep nearly impossible. It wasn't until these festivities ended at 3 A.M. that I finally got to sleep.

Joey had arrived from Johannesburg about 10 P.M. but was delayed at the Arusha airport trying to get our guns and ammunition through Customs. This lengthy process finally came to a satisfactory, if somewhat expensive, conclusion. He got to the hotel about 2 A.M. and managed to grab a few hours of sleep.

Our charter flight from Arusha to Fort Ikoma left early the next morning, loaded to the maximum with our equipment and paraphernalia for camp. For a moment I feared we would never leave the ground; in fact, we became airborne with about three inches of runway to spare!

A thick cloud cover rendered Mount Kilimanjaro invisible, but I did see the impressive Mount Meru. During the first part of the journey, we flew over a luxurious landscape covered with small farms, then a mountainous barren desert dotted with kraals belonging to the Masai, and finally over the Serengeti.

When we arrived at the airstrip at Fort Ikoma, the pilot had to buzz the field twice to scatter the wildebeest, gazelle, topi, and other "critters" before the plane could land. I had a strange feeling when I stepped off the plane—*déjà vu?* Somehow I knew that I had been here before and would return to Africa again and again!

Graham and his staff, which included two trackers, Hussein and Cosmos, met us. Hussein, the elder of the two, suffered from a wasting malady (probably tuberculosis) that resulted in a loss of voice and a "death warmed over" appearance. Cosmos, young and strong as a bull, functioned as a general factotum. As events progressed, however, the designation of these two as "trackers," especially Cosmos, was, to say the least, overdone. Graham drove us to camp in his new Toyota Land Cruiser, equipped with a comfortable seat behind the cab much like the rig I used when hunting quail in Florida.

We were the first group of the season. Graham and his wife, Ananda, had arrived just three days before, and the camp was only partially ready. The camp was designed to mimic those of classic British safaris and featured a well-furnished dining area, a cook shed, and individual sleeping tents. I was assigned a large tent with a concrete floor that had a sleeping area and a separate bathroom. The camp stood on the edge of an essentially dry riverbed containing a few scattered pools of water. However, plenty of water for use other than drinking was just two to three feet below the surface.

The hunting season opened the next morning, so we spent a part of the afternoon checking the accuracy of our rifles. Rifle practice went fine. I shot smoothly and accurately with the .375, but Graham's new .416 bolt-action rifle failed to feed cartridges from the magazine, meaning that my backup would be dependent on a single-shot rifle. We'd originally planned for Joey to videotape the hunt but shelved the idea. We needed him to carry the .470 and provide real backup. I would be glad that we made this decision.

The rest of the day I hunted butterflies (I've collected them since childhood) near the camp, an activity, I could tell, that Graham and his staff found very odd. Well, too bad. I figured that if Arthur H. Neumann,[3] one of Africa's legendary elephant hunters, also was a dedicated lepidopterist, I was in good company. To my surprise, the butterflies bore a marked similarity to those in the southern United States. Many of the same families are represented: swallowtails, whites, monarchs, blues, and skippers.

Since fresh lion pugmarks (tracks) were evident in the sand outside my tent, Joey, armed with the .470, accompanied my butterfly hunting excursions, undoubtedly a first, since butterflies aren't generally

[3]Neumann, Arthur H. *Elephant Hunting in East Equatorial Africa.* London: Rowland Ward, Ltd., 1898.

listed as dangerous. I found the dry riverbed to be a favorite home of butterflies, primarily due to areas of moist sand. Unfortunately, wounded or sick animals also seek this terrain, making it especially important to be prepared to deal with a dangerous situation.

While collecting butterflies, I was introduced to a ubiquitous African pest: the tsetse fly. I had read about them, of course, and had used the recommended sprays to ward off mosquitoes and these critters. No luck! Tsetse flies seem to thrive on repellents and are tenacious, hard-shelled, and difficult to kill. They quickly bore a hole in one's skin, producing a bite at least as painful as that of the large horseflies found in the United States. Oh, well. Paradise must have some drawbacks!

After the evening shower, we were treated to a classic safari ritual: sundowners served near a smoky campfire, followed by a multicourse dinner lasting until 10 P.M. Not yet recovered from jet lag, I dozed through most of the first night's proceedings. Thereafter this ritual became enjoyable, in spite of the incessant chatter from one of the owners of the safari company, who had invited himself to the camp.

The man assigned to my tent constantly hovered close-by and was extremely solicitous of my needs. He insisted on keeping a kerosene lamp lit, and, no matter how many times I blew it out, he restarted it. The fumes gave me a headache. I finally convinced him that I preferred the dark by removing the wick.

Before the trip I had attempted to master a few Swahili phrases, but language has never been one of my strong points. (I had a traumatic experience with German in college when the professor told me, "Originality in a language isn't appreciated." (Apparently I had stated in German that I had "shaken hands with a tree".) Trying to communicate in Swahili didn't work out, *asante sana* (thank you very much) and *jambo* (a greeting) being my limit. I relegated myself to using sign language. I'm sure my simple-minded attempts left the camp staff thinking I should be the one captured in the butterfly net.

I slept comfortably but was frequently awakened by the African night sounds: cavorting baboons, lions roaring in the distance,

Joey, the author, and Cosmos. This Cape buffalo was determined to give us a serious "health problem."

the shrill bark of zebras, and the dry rasp of a nearby leopard. I felt safe through all of this, knowing an armed guard patrolled the camp, until I learned the next day that the guard slept soundly while on duty. From then on, I kept a loaded rifle as a close nocturnal companion.

The next morning we loaded the guns and ourselves into the Toyota Land Cruiser. The temperature stood at sixty-five degrees, with the air clear and somewhat damp from a brief overnight rain. Although almost on the equator, we enjoyed a nearly ideal temperature because of the high altitude of 5,500 feet.

I chose a seat behind the cab to have a better view of the landscape. We rode through beautiful rolling countryside studded with acacia trees and covered with grass. As we passed near an acacia tree, I reached out to push one of the limbs away. Bad idea. I quickly withdrew my hand, which had been painfully impaled on a three-inch thorn. First lesson: Although they may be beautiful, most things in Africa prick, sting, scratch, or bite.

Most of the grass was brown, but many acres had been recently burned and had regrown in brilliant green. The nature of the terrain was pretty much as I expected from viewing a number of National Geographic specials about the Serengeti. However, nothing, absolutely nothing, in tourist books or television programming had prepared me for the unbelievable plethora of game species. The wildebeests were congregating in this area prior to their annual migration. In many areas it seemed I could have blindfolded myself, taken a shot at random, and likely have hit a wildebeest.

Although the wildebeest was the predominant game animal, Thomson and Grant gazelles, zebras, topis, and giraffes were present in great numbers. A large black object that I initially mistook for a buffalo came into view. When we got closer, this "buffalo" turned out to be a very large male ostrich.

A game scout in the employ of the Tanzanian government accompanied us, in theory because he knew the territory and the location of game. He was not up to snuff in either category. He was also charged with making sure that we didn't break the laws, but the only definitive action I saw this game scout take involved robbing an ostrich nest of eggs, a highly illegal undertaking. The game scout did manifest one impressive feature. Swahili flowed from his mouth faster and louder than from anyone I've met before or since. On one occasion, after a rapid-fire animated oration lasting five minutes, I asked Graham what he had said. Graham's translation was, "Drive about a hundred yards farther before crossing this ditch." We learned to ignore this game scout's worthless vocal outpourings.

We did not spot any buffaloes that morning, but about 4 P.M. we did see a pair of bulls that Graham judged not to be fully mature. While we drove toward them, four young lions appeared, and shortly thereafter we spied a large lioness about thirty yards from the Land Cruiser. The truck came between her and a herd of wildebeests, and the annoyed look on her face seemed to say, "Get out of my way so I can catch dinner."

The lion episode made one thing abundantly clear: Cosmos, a muscular young man, was deathly afraid of dangerous animals. Graham had designated Cosmos to be a tracker, but I learned that his "skills" were acquired while cooking in Dar es Salaam. Shortly after we saw the lion, the truck passed close to a low branch, which knocked Cosmos off. Although stunned, he hit the ground running at nearly Olympian speed to return to the safety of the truck. Needless to say, Cosmos didn't accompany us when stalking game.

After our noon lunch break the next day, I decided to hunt butterflies. I caught several and was actively pursuing another one when Graham shouted to remind me, "This is where we saw the lions yesterday." I quickly confined pursuing butterflies to the vicinity of the truck.

Shortly after renewing the hunt, we heard a distinct thumping sound coming from a nearby thicket. When we drove closer, we saw two male waterbucks fighting each other in a manner that appeared to be very hostile. We watched several minutes of serious sparring, when the smaller animal left the scene rapidly, apparently no worse for the experience.

The game scout gave us permission to kill a wildebeest for camp meat, which meant that I didn't have to pay the trophy fee. Graham identified a fairly large male, and I shot it from sixty or

The author and his first Cape buffalo. This "old dagga *boy" has an impressive boss.*

seventy yards. The wildebeest ran about a hundred yards before falling. Hussein performed the bloodletting ritual to make the meat edible for the Muslims in camp.

I'd seen a number of large impalas and made an out-of-character decision to try to collect one. The next day we came across several of these graceful antelopes. I shot a large male from about one hundred twenty yards. He moved just as I squeezed the trigger. The bullet hit too far back, and he escaped into thick brush. Our "trackers" made a halfhearted and unsuccessful attempt to follow the wounded animal (without leaving the truck). This unfortunate episode stifled any desire I had to hunt other antelope.

However, Joey indicated that he would like to procure a topi. This plan was fine with both me and the game scout. Trophy-size topis were numerous; in fact, the only difficulty Joey experienced was waiting until his quarry moved far enough away from the herd so that the bullet would hit only one animal. When it moved, he quickly connected with an excellent trophy topi. An added feature: Topi meat is a hell of a lot better to eat than wildebeest.

We drove near the village below the remaining structure of Fort Ikoma, built by the Germans prior to World War I. The village consisted primarily of thatch-covered wooden huts. Also evident were a few small houses, in various stages of disrepair, built of concrete blocks. A number of men "resting" under the shade trees waved at us. There were no women around. Most likely they were tending crops, gathering wood, hauling water, or taking care of the children. Parked nearby were several four-wheel-drive vehicles marked "Dusseldorf Zoo." Later I saw them filled to the brim with citizens riding back and forth on the pothole-studded roads, going nowhere. The village owns an electric generator (funded by the Germans), and many of the huts are lit up at night—to what purpose is not clear. There is little opportunity for employment except for the occasional safari company or the few jobs as policemen and guards in the Serengeti Park. My overall impression of the area was one of inactivity and poverty.

Later that afternoon we came across a small herd of buffaloes, but the lone bull was young and his boss "soft." Nearby I saw the results of poaching: a giraffe caught in a wire snare and partially butchered. The hyenas and vultures were rapidly clearing up what was left.

The following day, our fourth at the camp, I woke up early and took my Lariam. Typical doctor, I hadn't read the directions regarding the need to take the drug on a full stomach. (Previously I'd done so by chance). I wasn't prepared for the nausea and vomiting that occurred some twenty miles outside camp. Probably I should have given up on the day, but we kept going, and by 2 P.M. I felt much better, though somewhat dehydrated and dizzy. That was our hottest day, with the temperature about eighty-five degrees.

We spotted two large Cape buffalo bulls on the edge of a ravine and approached them through some fairly long grass. As we started the stalk, Joey whispered, "Have you read Capstick's *Death in the Long Grass?"*[4] That smart-ass question certainly enhanced my excitement. (Capstick's book gives grisly details of how numerous people met their deaths while hunting dangerous game; few, if any, animals are more deadly than the Cape buffalo.)

Hussein, Graham, Joey, and I walked slowly and cautiously in single file along a game trail. Suddenly, the two bulls, still as death, materialized thirty yards in front of us. Everything I'd read about the insolent, penetrating stare of a Cape buffalo seemed like gross understatement. Almost hypnotized, I gazed back.

Graham pushed me in front to shoot, but Hussein, trying to set up a three-pronged support for my rifle, was in the way. We resembled Curly, Larry, and Moe more than knowledgeable big-game hunters. (We should have carried out considerable practice with these "sticks" before we confronted the buffalo. I learned a good lesson.)

Just when things sorted out and I could have taken a shot, the buffalo decided they'd had enough people viewing. Emitting a snort of derision, they turned and cleared out. We ran after them

[4]Capstick, Peter Hathaway. *Death in the Long Grass.* New York: St. Martin's Press, 1977.

for thirty yards to the edge of the long grass. They broke into the open about a hundred yards away. By then I'd become so pumped with excitement, as well as feeling woozy from the Lariam, that I couldn't hold my rifle steady.

They stopped about one hundred yards off and stared at us for a moment, arrogant and mean. I didn't take a shot. We were on the edge of the Serengeti Game Park, so, theoretically, we couldn't follow a buffalo inside the park if I wounded it. I didn't regret my decision.

Reflecting on my first real encounter with Africa's "Black Death," I wonder why I didn't just thank everyone for the experience and proceed to hunt butterflies for the rest of the trip! Moreover, during the ride back to camp that night, herds of wildebeests, their eyes an eerie red in the headlights, seemed to think it great fun to stampede in our direction and run into the truck. I was learning a lot about the dangers of big-game hunting.

The next day we saw four cheetahs near a recent kill that was being consumed by vultures, the local garbage-control unit. The cheetahs strolled away, looking back at us apparently unconcerned. We didn't find any buffaloes, though signs of them were everywhere.

We did come across a fairly thick area about five miles from camp that fairly cried out for burning. Why not? We set the grass ablaze, proud of an environmental contribution that would make new grass possible. We gave it no more thought until arriving back at camp. During the day the wind direction had shifted, blowing the fire toward camp. Ananda became frightened and had the staff organized into a fire-fighting brigade, but the fire never got that close. It's doubtful that the blaze was a real menace, but we certainly weren't going to confess to her that we'd been responsible for starting the conflagration.

I'll never forget what happened the next day. Early in the morning, three miles from camp, we found tracks of a fairly large herd of buffaloes that had recently crossed the road. We followed the tracks into a streambed, covered on both sides for about one hundred yards with reeds and long grass, and came upon the herd.

We spotted a large bull, which quickly disappeared. On several occasions, cows ran by close to us.

Graham repeated what he'd told me earlier: "If you see reeds breaking down, going either left or right, or away from you, then things are fine. But if they break down coming toward you, then you definitely have a problem."

My hands tingled; my mind seemed exceptionally alert. The quail I'd hunted my entire life couldn't hurt me, but these buffaloes could! In this state of heightened alertness, I watched as, several times, dark ghostlike shapes appeared and disappeared in the long grass. I almost came out of my skin when a covey of francolin exploded in front of me just as a cow ran by.

We found the tracks of two large bulls that had separated from the herd and followed them. We believed the bulls were just ahead of us. Graham scaled a tree covered with leopard claw marks but couldn't see a thing. Another group of cows sped past, but no bulls were among them. And then we saw two bulls on the side of a nearby hill moving toward the stream we'd left behind. Luckily, the Land Cruiser idled nearby; we rode toward where they'd headed and stopped near a thicket, but we had lost them.

Hussein signaled that these bulls were nearby and hadn't made it into the long grass. Accompanied by the game scout, he circled a thicket to look for tracks. All of a sudden, the two bulls appeared out of nowhere—thirty yards in front of us—running from right to left. In that instant, the time had come for me to become a hunter of dangerous game.

I shot the closest one in the shoulder with the .375, but the buffalo continued to run. I fired again. Joey followed my shot with one from the .470. The bull fell in a heap as though poleaxed, apparently hit in either the brain or spine. (Later we determined this was not the case, but I've never been sure exactly what caused its sudden demise. Maybe the bull had been dying from my initial shot, which entered the heart and severed the great vessels, and was falling when Joey fired.)

By that time, the other buffalo, running directly away from us, was eighty yards away. "Shoot him as well," Graham said.

Bad advice. It was highly unlikely that I would have stopped him at that range and angle. My bullet hit the bull in the rear and penetrated into the lower part of the chest cavity. He stumbled but kept running as though only bitten by a tsetse fly.

We scrambled into the Land Cruiser and drove it to position ourselves between the bull and the long grass where he was headed. We stopped on the slope of a hill and spotted the buffalo on the other side of a thicket, just coming into view, black and glistening, about seventy-five yards from us.

The buffalo looked in our direction. I am certain he identified us as the cause of his anal discomfort and made up his mind to avenge the insult. He charged! The hatred evident in his eyes as he drew near made it clear that he'd intended to separate us into component parts. All of us fired. Sixteen hundred pounds of concentrated fury closed the gap rapidly between us. One bullet from my .375, one from Graham's .416, and two from Joey's .470 hit him. He kept coming, seemingly unaffected.

Luckily, he ran out of steam. He stumbled and fell—six feet from us! A final shot in the spine ended his life. Only then did I realize how badly this escapade could have turned out. I breathed a sigh of relief and eased my trembling self to the ground. As many hunters before me, I had witnessed the trademark of Black Death, continuing to charge after absorbing many times more than enough lead to kill.

After my breathing returned to normal, I realized that I hadn't noticed any vultures before we began shooting. Now, within fifteen minutes after the fact, the trees were filled with birds, just waiting for lunch.

Graham wanted to get a picture of the two buffaloes together. A "buffalo double" is a somewhat rare event. To accomplish this, one whole buffalo had to be transported several hundred yards. The Land Cruiser came equipped with a power winch, but loading the buffalo aboard still required some hard and serious effort. After the picture taking, we hauled the partially dressed buffaloes to camp.

It took three or four hours for the adrenaline rush to subside and for me to calm down and return to normal. When

I did, I asked myself, Why does an old man like yourself try to get killed?

Back in camp, activity swung into high gear. A considerable number of the local citizens helped cut up the meat and hang it to dry. The biltong from two buffaloes would provide them with a source of meat for several weeks. The skinning shed later became overrun with mongooses and, that night, with hyenas, all looking for a handout. Meanwhile, the cook had commandeered the choice cuts of meat for our table. I found the buffalo tail soup delicious, and the buffalo steaks, while chewy, had an excellent flavor.

Both bulls were old, each boss thick and gnarled. The widest measured sixteen inches, the other fourteen inches. They had a tip-to-tip horn width of thirty-five and thirty-eight inches, respectively, which, while nothing to shout about, suited me just fine. The adventure, or misadventure as in the case of the second buffalo, not the tape measure, makes the memories. I'll say this of the experience: Except for covey rises over pointer bird dogs, this incredibly intense buffalo hunt ranked at the time as my most memorable hunting adventure.

I spent the next two days collecting butterflies and videotaping animals. The butterfly collecting was reasonably fruitful; I obtained about twenty species.

We never saw elephants but did find scattered evidence of their feeding in the form of broken or uprooted acacia trees. Bird life was everywhere: doves, sand grouse, quail, francolin, and guinea fowl, all seemingly begging to be hunted. (If I return to Africa, the opportunity to bird hunt will be high on my list of things to do.) In addition to game birds, we saw a variety of hawks, eagles, a marabou stork, a Cory bustard, a ground hornbill, and a number of gaudy-colored small birds, including kingfishers, bee-eaters, finches, and rollers. Although I enjoy bird watching at home, our native species are generally far more plain and drab than those found in Africa.

Joey remained at the camp to hunt with two of his clients from Florida, so I made the return trip alone. In Dar es Salaam

I visited the physician who had been scheduled to meet me on arrival. A delightful individual, he brought me up-to-date regarding the political situation in Tanzania. The government is trying to overcome the serious problems resulting, in large measure, from the twenty-year experiment with state-sponsored socialism. Development of the safari industry is playing a very important role in an effort to attract foreign money.

I experienced a long wait at both the Arusha and Dar es Salaam airports on my trip home, but the journey proved uneventful, if somewhat long and taxing. I was tired but content to be back in North Carolina. The trip gave me a chance to reflect on the events of my first safari. I decided Cape buffalo hunting is definitely an adventure for me to do again . . . and again . . . and again!

Cape Buffalo

I went to Fortress Ikoma
On Africa's Mara Plain
To visit the Garden of Eden.
I'll never be the same!

I saw tommy, topi, zebra,
Wildebeest far as the sky.
Early one morn in the long grass,
I looked death in the eye.

Black, big and belligerent, his eyes
Seared through my soul.
Only a step or two further; this story
Would never be told.

He vanished into the long grass
And left me alone in peace.
But those eyes will ever haunt me.
My dreams will never cease.

Yes, I'll remember the Serengeti
Until I draw my last breath.
'Cause early one morn in the long grass,
I saw the eyes of death.

Timbavati Titan

Chapter III

With most memorable experiences in life, serendipity plays a major role. This safari to hunt African elephant is a case in point. After my successful initial foray to Tanzania to hunt Cape buffalo, I suggested to Joey that we try for a rerun. I left it in Joey's capable hands to plan where to go next. That's when serendipity came into play.

As a professional hunter, Joey had met Anton Wienand, the owner of a game ranch in KwaZulu-Natal, South Africa. Anton, whose father had been an ivory hunter, had lived most of his life in Zambia, farming and hunting elephants, both as a guide and for the ivory. In 1986, when the political situation in Zambia deteriorated, he moved to South Africa. After meeting Anton, Joey took several groups of clients to hunt plains game on Anton's ranch.

Anton told Joey that a good friend, who was part-owner of the Timbavati Game Reserve, which adjoins Kruger Park, in South Africa, had informed him that, for the first time in several years, limited trophy hunting would be allowed on this reserve. The description of the hunting sounded so good that I placed a bid to hunt buffalo, lion, and elephant. Actually, I wanted to hunt buffalo, Joey intended to pursue lion, and the elephant came as a bonus. Although outbid for the entire package, subsequent negotiations garnered us a twelve-day elephant hunt. A very positive aspect was that the trophy fees, which are paid in full prior to the hunt, are used to support an active antipoaching

Joey and the author—tired but happy.

program that enables the elephants and other game to live generally unmolested.

Anton, who hadn't hunted elephant since 1982, still suffered from a severe case of "elephant fever." Elephant fever is incurable, leaving the victim with an overwhelming and constant desire to hunt elephants. Not until the negotiations were completed, and I regained appropriate cerebral function, did I question whether this jaunt made any sense at all. In fact, with the exception of Cape buffalo, I had decided that big-game hunting wasn't for me. However, like it or not, I'd committed myself to hunt a bull elephant in South Africa.

Travel plans went without a hitch, a result I attributed to my being a veteran international traveler. Actually, this was only my second trip! With a great deal of trepidation, I decided to risk taking my cherished .500-465 Holland & Holland double rifle, having managed to obtain gun insurance endorsed by Safari Club International.

I had approximately twenty rounds of handloaded ammunition. By mistake I had ordered one hundred rounds of A-Square monolithic solids—about twice as much as I needed. I also decided to take my 12-gauge Beretta double shotgun because another and potentially desirable feature of this twelve-day safari was the possibility of hunting upland game birds on Anton's ranch.

I fired the Holland & Holland on two occasions during the month leading up to the trip, ten rounds each time, with good results, and I thought that was probably enough. Eighteen days before departure, however, because I had extra ammunition, I decided to shoot again. It was a good thing I did! At thirty yards, both the right and left barrels grouped at least two feet to the left of the point of aim. I examined the gun carefully and found that the front block, which held the two barrels together, had become loosened, most likely a result of my previous firing. I found myself on the horns of a dilemma: My well-being now depended on an inaccurate and unsafe rifle.

Fortunately, I knew just the person to call for help. I sent the gun via UPS to Dietrich Apel (a friend and superb gunsmith, owner of New England Custom Gun Service). He dropped what he was doing and resoldered the block. He regulated the rifle, using approximately thirty rounds of ammunition. In fact, it was more accurate than before—a two-inch group at fifty yards. We had averted a major disaster. I can only conclude that the Good Lord was looking after me since trying to kill a five-ton animal with a defective rifle would have been begging for serious trouble.

Nothing eventful occurred on the August trip to Johannesburg, a flight of eighteen hours from Miami with a single stop in Cape Town. Upon arrival, a former South African soldier drove me to a spacious lodge surrounded by a high wall. The owner, Trevor Shaw, told me that crime in Johannesburg was rampant (carjacking, mugging, and so on). Thankfully, the stay was uneventful. Joey, armed with a .470 Krieghoff double rifle, joined me from Tanzania that night.

Some sort of celebration was going on near the compound. Loud and disharmonious music, along with shouting and singing, made sleep impossible. On several occasions the crowd sounded as though they were just outside the wall. I prayed that the structure was adequate to keep them out. (It was.) The next day, glad to exit Johannesburg, we flew in a chartered airplane to the Timbavati Game Reserve.

Timbavati, a three-hundred-sixty-thousand-acre private reserve, is owned by approximately forty-five individuals who banded together to maintain their own game-management program, including a game warden and antipoaching staff. The game reserve, contiguous with the western boundary of Kruger Park, has no fences. The animals move freely between the park and the reserve.

We flew over well-maintained farmland, then through the highveld and across the escarpment into the lowveld where the game reserves are located. The lowveld was covered with bush; the trees were primarily mopane and acacia. From the air I saw little evidence of farming. It was late winter in South Africa, and the bush was as open and dry as it gets. Temperatures ranged from forty-five to fifty degrees at night to seventy-five or eighty degrees during the day.

Anton, his wife Erica, and a Zulu tracker-skinner named Simon met us at the airstrip. Anton shook my hand; actually his crunching grip almost broke it. His hand was huge . . . as was the rest of him. This six-foot, four-inch, two-hundred-fifty-pound, thick-boned man gave the impression he might not need a gun to hunt elephant. Actually, he was quiet and reserved with a competent manner that engendered confidence.

Simon worked on the game ranch for Anton. He was slightly built with wide-set eyes that seemed to take in everything instinctively. He was also very athletic. Joey informed me that Simon possessed remarkable skills. His natural tracking talents had been finely honed through experience and long, hard work.

I was surprised to learn that instead of a tent, our living quarters consisted of a fine lodge about two miles from Kings Camp, a palatial retreat designed for game viewing and photographic safaris. Our accommodations, which offered every civilized amenity, perched on the bank of a dry river and featured a spectacular view of numerous animal species walking up and down the riverbed. An electric fence ringed the area, chiefly to keep elephants from devastating the trees and shrubs near the house.

I met the game warden and members of his staff, who told us that the three previous elephant hunters had been successful. He assigned Franz, another reputedly excellent tracker with a thorough knowledge of the area, to be our guide.

Since we'd arrived on Sunday and the hunting wouldn't begin until the next day, we rode in Anton's Toyota Land Cruiser (the preferred vehicle of the African bush) to get a feel for the terrain. Numerous man-made water holes enabled the animals to survive the dry season. The rolling land, much of it red clay, had much denser vegetation than the Serengeti, but visibility was reasonably good. It resembled parts of Piedmont North Carolina covered in scrub trees. There the similarity stopped. A giraffe standing in the road made it abundantly clear we were not in North Carolina. Several herds of impala, as well as three large kudu bulls, crossed the road in front of us.

We rode along the road separating Timbavati from Kruger Park and saw spoor made by elephants crossing from one preserve to the other. Not far from our lodge we came across several lionesses and their young, lounging about sunning themselves, gorged from feasting on a recently killed zebra.

That evening I saw photographs of magnificent white lions on the wall of the dining area in our lodge. A light went on in my head. The pictures reminded me of a book I'd bought ten years before, *The White Lions of Timbavati,*[1] but I hadn't made the connection with Timbavati until now. Apparently the white lions have disappeared.

I'm sure that before the start of any elephant hunt, a major topic of discussion between the professional hunter and his client is the correct placement of the bullet. I felt up-to-date on the subject, having studied most of the classic books on African

[1]McBride, Chris. *The White Lions of Timbavati.* New York & London: Paddington Press, Ltd., 1977.

The elephant and the author shortly after the excitement was over. The double rifle is the author's .500-465 Holland & Holland.

elephant hunting as well as the detailed anthology *Hunting the African Elephant.*[2]

Discussing the frontal brain shot, Anton outlined what was, at least to me, a new technique. From the front, aim at the middle of the head at an imaginary rod passing through the ear apertures. This approach automatically corrects for distance from the elephant and position of the head. The side brain shot, halfway between the eye and the ear, was the same as I had read about.

Elephants should always be shot at close range, less than fifty yards. The professional hunter guiding clients must be able to stop a charging elephant at close quarters. Anton's choice of a "stopper" was a bolt-action rifle chambered for a .458 Lott cartridge.

Anton told me that his father had always shot at the heart. A missed brain shot frequently results in the elephant escaping, but

[2]Rikhoff, Jim. (editor) *Hunting the African Elephant.* Clinton, NJ: Amwell Press, 1985.

a bullet penetrating the chest cavity invariably results in a dead elephant. In the heyday of ivory hunting with modern weapons (1890–1950) and for elephant control work, professionals used head shots because, if successful, the animal dropped immediately without disturbing the herd, allowing the hunter to kill more than one elephant. A shot in the heart is always fatal but will not kill instantly. The animal will run and disturb the other elephants, making additional kills unlikely.

An elephant's heart is located in the upper part of the lower third of the chest behind the crease made by the front leg. Different from most big game, the front legs of an elephant are anterior to the chest cavity. The standard shoulder shot, commonly used for other species, may not be effective unless the shoulder bones are broken. The bullet may not even penetrate the chest cavity and may only slightly wound the tusker.

That night I went over in my mind everything Anton had said. I decided, if possible, that I would shoot for the heart and hope for the best. That way, even if we had to track for many miles, we'd eventually get the elephant.

Day One

Anton planned an early start, and, accordingly, we left to pick up Franz at the game warden's compound about 5:30 A.M. There was no moon in the heavens, but the stars were glorious. Orion and the Dog Star dominated the eastern sky, and, unlike in North Carolina, they shine in the northeast rather than the southeast. I also identified the Southern Cross (not visible in the United States) before going to bed. These constellations made me realize just how far I was from home.

The sun had risen by the time we picked up Franz, and then we drove to several water holes to search for tracks. We came across the carcass of a freshly killed Cape buffalo bull on the roadside between Kruger and Timbavati. Four large male lions who had devoured one haunch and the belly were still very much in evidence, guarding their food. We drove to within fifty yards of the kill. The lions, apparently satiated from feasting, paid little attention to us.[3]

About 9 A.M. we found tracks made by a large bull elephant; Anton decided the time had come to walk. He said that the circumference of the track coincided closely with the size of the bull but didn't necessarily indicate the weight of the ivory, age being a more important factor.

"The older the bull, the rounder the track," he said. "Professional ivory hunters used this characteristic, not size, to determine which tracks to follow."

I could see the tracks in the road but had no idea where the elephant went once we were in the bush. My status as a novice hunter contrasted starkly with the skills of Simon and Franz, who tracked the elephant effortlessly—as fast as I could walk. As we followed the spoor, piles of dung became fresher, or at least "warmer" by the "feel test," which they applied judiciously. This indicated that we were getting closer. Another sign we were nearing the bull was that the bark from broken tree limbs became progressively less desiccated.

About noon, Simon pointed toward a fairly dense mopane thicket, indicating that the elephant rested right in front of us. We moved thirty-five to forty yards closer, but even with field glasses I

[3]Three days later when we stopped near the kill, only one lion remained, but we saw a jackal and the nearby trees were full of vultures. The lion immediately took considerable umbrage at our presence. Quite agitated, he began growling and slowly walking in our direction. Joey grabbed the .470 just in case. Anton seemed calm—too calm to suit me. After a few minutes, the lion made a mock charge toward us, stopping about fifty feet from the Land Cruiser. He crouched down, malevolently staring, and began to move his tail slowly from side to side, a sure sign of a determined charge. That was enough for Anton. He put the "pedal to the metal," and we left posthaste. The difference in the lion's attitude between our two visits was remarkable, most likely related to the fullness of his stomach. The remaining lion was undoubtedly in a foul mood from having to chase away interlopers wanting to steal what was left of the feast. I guess he placed us in that category, making it advisable for us to flee the scene. Two days later the lion had gone. By that time, vultures and other scavengers had finished as well. Only the bones and a set of horns remained as mute testimony to these events.

couldn't see anything but bush and trees. Then, sixty yards from where I stood, a large dark object moved ponderously. The elephant was facing us, but only the rhythmic movement of his ears made him visible. I'd failed to see him earlier because I'd been looking too low . . . between his legs!

As we were downwind, the elephant was not aware that we were near. We moved slowly to his left. Anton quickly noted that the ivory was short and thick, estimating the weight at about forty pounds. Not trophy size. (A fairly accurate weight of an elephant's tusk can be calculated from estimating the visible length in feet and the circumference in inches where the tusk protrudes from the jaw. For example, three feet times eighteen inches equals fifty-four pounds, the weight of the tusk.) Anyway, the elephant sensed our presence and took a step in our direction. We slowly backed up and got away without mishap.

Seeing something that big so close without intervening fences struck me speechless. The word "awesome," overused in current sports reporting, best describes my impression of what happened. Although not really frightened, I felt overwhelmed. I wondered where I got the notion to hunt elephants!

We arrived back at the Land Cruiser unscathed, had lunch, and then went in search of other tracks. About 2:30 P.M. we found tracks where four bulls had crossed the road earlier that day. We followed, and found them feeding less than a mile from the road. They were young, with tusks in the twenty-five-pound range. One apparently winded us, moved his head proudly and defiantly from side to side, and gave every indication of wanting to become better acquainted. We quickly departed!

We found more fresh tracks about 4 P.M. and, after a mile walk, came within one hundred fifty yards of three fairly large bulls feeding in a thick stand of mopane. Franz and Simon became airborne to get a better view: Climbing trees doesn't adequately describe the speed that launched them from ground level to the top of a thirty-foot tree in a few seconds!

They signaled. One of the bulls only had a single tusk; the second's tusks were small. The third, Franz indicated, with a broad smile, was

Number One. We moved closer. From the vantage point of a large termite mound, Anton estimated that this bull had symmetrical ivory weighing between fifty-five and sixty pounds each.

Anton agonized over whether we should get close enough to take a shot. He finally decided that since this was just the first day we should hold out for something even heavier. Franz was obviously disappointed at the decision, expressing doubt that we'd find a bull with larger ivory.

The wind shifted slightly, and the elephants became aware of us. They unhurriedly walked away, but I got an excellent view of the bull in question and, in my unschooled opinion, the gleaming ivory looked big and beautiful. (Correctly estimating ivory weight when the tusks are viewed from behind an elephant is difficult at best. The tusks always appear too long.) This bull actually stood a foot shorter than the one-tusk bull, whose single tusk had been estimated at only forty pounds.

Back in camp, alone in my room, the events of the day seemed electrifying to me. I'd come within "shaking hands" distance of eight large bull elephants, one with tusks of trophy size, and had witnessed an absolutely astounding display of tracking.

Day Two

I was jarred awake several times during the night by the sound of branches being broken by elephants feeding nearby. After a cup of hot coffee, we left the lodge at dawn (about 6 A.M.). Just two miles from camp we saw a herd of about fifty cow and calf elephants, slowly ambling along. We located just one bull among them. His tusks were approximately forty pounds each. Anton pointed out the obvious: trying to get close enough to shoot a bull surrounded by cows invites disaster. Unless the ivory is exceptional and worth the risk, hunting bulls in a herd of cows should be avoided. We moved on.

Five miles farther on we came upon some twenty Cape buffaloes. Several of these bulls carried forty-two to forty-five-inch horns, considerably wider than the horns on the bulls I'd killed the

The author, Anton, and Joey with the magnificent tusker.

previous year. These Cape buffalo, as arrogant as their Tanzanian cousins, swaggered seventy yards from the road, staring at us with their typical "you-owe-me-money" look.

At 9 A.M. we found fresh tracks made by three bull elephants. We followed them for several hours; then Simon and Franz determined they'd been spooked and were running. Continued tracking, Anton said, would be futile. It was not clear how they had become agitated since we had been downwind. We returned to the vehicle and continued searching for tracks.

The road traversed a markedly variable terrain: hills, valleys, open meadows, and forests. As we rode, we saw a plethora of different game animals. Shortly after we spotted a large pile of dung, a huge white rhinoceros ambled by just thirty yards away, apparently unaware of our presence.

Farther on, the trackers had Anton stop the vehicle. They pointed out where a small female leopard had carried what apparently was an antelope down the road. The leopard tracks and drag marks from the antelope's hoofs became clear to me only when pointed out. How the trackers spotted them from a moving vehicle is beyond my comprehension. We looked in nearby trees to see if the leopard had left her kill but found nothing. "She may have young nearby," said Anton. "If so, we could find ourselves in an unscheduled boxing match. Let's go."

Around 1 P.M. we found a large elephant track (about twenty-one inches long) and followed it for three hours. We were getting close when the bull crossed into a sanctuary area, and we were unable to follow.

That evening the Timbavati game warden and a young English lady who was studying elephant behavior joined us for supper. We spent a delightful evening discussing the various aspects of elephant conservation. Her primary interest was to develop strategies to breed and raise elephants successfully on a small game ranch of five to ten thousand acres. She indicated that young females were quite amenable to this degree of confinement but that males, when they matured, would not stay at home. How then to breed the females in the absence of a resident male? Two possibilities were being considered: artificial insemination or transporting a "stud" male from one ranch to another. Trying to be polite, I didn't comment. After conjuring up a mental picture of either approach, I concluded, "You've got to be kidding!"

Another interesting topic of discussion revolved around the presence of man-eating lions in Kruger Park. Not infrequently, refugees fleeing across the border from Mozambique are intercepted and eaten by lions. A recent incident resulted in the death of four such trespassers. Feasting on human flesh may make the lions confirmed man-eaters, so the park rangers are compelled to destroy them. My guess is that the presence of lions has a significant impact on the desire to immigrate illegally. (Perhaps this approach should be tried elsewhere?)

Day Three

The next morning dawned misty, one half inch of rain having fallen during the night. The rain had washed out older tracks, making the job of estimating the age of new tracks much easier. Several miles from the camp we spotted an agitated kudu bull, and

Franz pointed out tracks indicating where several kudus had been chased by lions earlier that morning. We found no evidence of a kill, however.

We headed to the southern end of the Timbavati reserve, where two large elephant bulls had been spotted previously, and hunted in the area methodically. Concentrated tree destruction pointed to the handiwork of elephants. One large tree near a reservoir had mud on a limb eleven feet above the ground where elephants had scratched their backs. We found fresh elephant tracks, all made by cows. The reservoir contained several hippos resting in shallow water.

Leaving the area, we drove the Timbavati-Kruger road and saw three large bulls in the Kruger reserve. A mile farther on we found tracks indicating that a bull had crossed the road from Kruger into Timbavati. After following this track for an hour, we came upon the bull in an open area about one hundred yards away. He was huge but tuskless. Bull African elephants are seldom if ever born tuskless, but they frequently break off one or both tusks when fighting. Although not usually considered trophy quality, these elephants are often aggressive and dangerous and are fully capable of taking care of themselves. We quickly left.

At 2 P.M. we struck the track of a large bull, followed it, and determined he had been joined by three other bulls. At 4 P.M. we spied them, about five hundred yards off, feeding in a ravine and moving fairly rapidly. They were too far away to determine the size of the ivory, and, as it was getting late in the day, we decided not to try to close the gap.

Day Four

We drove back to the area where we had found the bulls the day before, crossed their tracks about 10 A.M., and began to follow on foot. Two hours later we came within one hundred yards of them. I didn't see anything, but the trackers did. The bulls were feeding in very thick mopane.

Franz ran up a tree (that's the word, ran) but could see only one of the bulls, which had a single tusk. Just then the wind shifted. The bulls scented us and walked away. We all had a good look at them. Two of the four bulls had tusks in the twenty-five-pound range, but one had symmetrical ivory weighing fifty-five or sixty pounds.

Most likely we had seen three of these bulls on the first day. "It's your decision," Anton said. "Do you want to try to kill this bull, or hunt for one with heavier ivory?"

I thought for a few seconds. I looked at him, and then at Joey. "Let's go for this one," I said.

My answer disappointed Anton, but there were three reasons for my choice. Franz was certain that this was the best trophy bull we would find, and we had already disturbed these elephants enough for them to move out of the area, leaving us empty-handed. Finally, I couldn't handle many more days with this level of excitement.

We notified the game warden of our decision by radio. He joined us, arriving in less than thirty minutes. We followed the bulls for an hour, at last closing to within sixty yards. The wind shifted, and the one-tusk bull became aware of our presence. He remained silent but seemed agitated. Then the four bulls moved off rapidly. We couldn't follow because they went downwind.

"I think I know where they're headed," the game warden said.

It turned out that he did. We rushed to the Land Cruiser, drove three miles, then walked beside a dry riverbed for about ten minutes. Simon and Franz spied the bulls directly in front of us in fairly open woods. Luckily we were downwind and able to move undetected within fifty yards of them.

Somehow, the old one-tusk bull again became aware of us. He began shaking his head and ears vigorously and testing the wind with his trunk. Though clearly agitated, he made no sound. As if on cue, the bull I intended to shoot stepped forward into the open, perhaps to determine for himself what was going on.

My position in our hierarchy suddenly changed radically. Always I'd been in the rear of the group, but now I was thrust forward. Anton said softly, "Take a shot whenever you're ready."

I checked the rifle, made certain the safety was off, and took a deep breath. I stood about thirty-five yards from this trophy bull, aware that the one-tusk elephant was fifteen yards farther away and to my right. I didn't see the other two bulls. My elephant, apparently sensing that something was amiss, moved his head from side to side, his ears outstretched, his tusks reflecting the glare from the afternoon sun.

I waited for what seemed an hour but was probably more like ten seconds. Time stood still. Then, this majestic bull turned slowly to his right and began to walk off. I had a clear view of the left heart region and quickly fired the Holland twice. I was unaware of the noise or recoil from the discharge of both barrels of the rifle.

As I shot, the bull finished turning and began to run to our right. I heard two other shots: Joey and Anton had both fired. My elephant continued to run full tilt for sixty to seventy yards, then collapsed and fell right side down. Just as the bull fell, Joey fired again, attempting to disable him by breaking a hip. This bullet barely grazed the skin. The other bulls cleared out, probably stopping in Mozambique. (Anton later informed me that one of the smaller bulls had run toward us, and he'd fired over its head to turn it.)

I reloaded, approached the bull, which still moved agonally, and fired into the brain from the top of his head. He had a generalized muscular spasm and died.

We learned later that my first shot penetrated the top of the heart and tore the great vessels. (A bullet in that part of the heart usually fells the elephant within a few seconds; if hit lower he may run for several miles.) Anton said he actually saw the dust made by my bullet when it hit the chest. "I knew he was done for," he said. Both my second and Joey's first bullet penetrated into the lungs.

It took a few moments for reality to set in. I'd actually killed an elephant. The hunt had ended. Relief, pride, and grief—these and other emotions washed over me in waves.

A dead elephant, although enormous, is not an uplifting sight. But all of us, especially Franz and Simon, were elated at our success. We examined the bull and the magnificent ivory and engaged in the usual picture taking. The tail was severed as ritual demands. (In the days of ivory hunting, possession of the tail established ownership of the elephant.)

A happy, wet urchin proudly displays a duck retrieved from a crocodile-infested lake.

Since night was coming on, we covered the head and neck with brush to discourage damage by hyenas and other scavengers. Only the soft skin around the mouth would be accessible to them. Lions were another story; we hoped that lions wouldn't find the carcass. With the tail in hand, we headed back to the lodge.

That night, in reliving the event, something seemed to be amiss. According to my extensive reading, elephants always fall on the side they are shot. However, this elephant fell right side down, but I shot the left side. I guess elephants don't always conform to the wisdom found in books.

Day Five

We left the lodge at 6:30 A.M. and drove back to the elephant, where we were met by a crew of approximately twenty-five men outfitted with sharp knives. After they had taken the skin off in two sections and removed the feet, the skinners dismembered the carcass rapidly and efficiently. Some twenty-eight-hundred pounds of meat ended up in a flatbed trailer to be distributed to the local villagers. The skinners recovered an A-Square 480-grain monolithic solid bullet from the neck. Interestingly, it had no deformities despite having penetrated the skull. The head with the trunk removed was taken to the game warden's compound to be buried. This procedure allows the ivory to be slipped out easily in a week or two, avoiding possible damage.

Simon spent the rest of the day skinning the two ears, each the size of a dining room table, while Anton and Joey worked on the feet. Anton prepared one of the feet without cutting the skin further, which required that the bones be removed from the top, one at a time. This process required about four hours. They split the skin on the other three feet to facilitate bone removal, which greatly simplified the effort. In the final tanning process, this turned out to be the superior method. The feet are remarkable. An elephant actually walks on tiptoes, supported by a thick cushion of fibrous, fatty tissue.

Day Six

We returned to the carcass about eight the next morning and found two to three hundred gorged vultures, a pair of hyenas, a few bones, and plenty of dung. I was, again, amazed by the thoroughness of the African sanitation system.

Returning to the lodge, we spotted a young bull elephant on the road. He seemed almost in mourning, as his trunk touched the road over and over again. Anton surmised that the bull scented some of the blood from the elephant meat. We watched this spectacle for about twenty minutes, at which point the elephant slowly trudged off. I felt guilty, for I had more than likely deprived him of a friend.

That afternoon we drove to the game warden's compound, where skulls, horns, and several sets of small tusks were on display. He told us that recently he had killed a young bull elephant that, although unprovoked, had attacked several villagers and, in the process, had destroyed a wagon. Luckily, no one was injured. They found that the root of one of the tusks contained a large abscess, which undoubtedly caused the bad temper. An infected tusk must produce a world-class toothache! I watched them place the head from my elephant in a fairly deep hole and cover it with soil. The ivory would be "drawn out" in a couple of weeks.

On the way back to the lodge we rode by a group of baobab trees, the first I'd seen. These trees are unique. The largest, with a diameter of at least fifteen feet, resembled an enormous keg. It took many centuries for this slow-growing tree to reach its current size. The limbs, devoid of leaves, gave the appearance of being roots, hence the common name "upside down tree." Dr. Livingstone aptly characterized the baobab as "that giant upturned carrot."[4] It provides both food and shelter for the number of fauna that frequent it. The baobab is truly an African marvel.

Days Seven to Twelve

The next day we drove to Anton's Zuka game ranch in KwaZulu-Natal. This six-hour trip was considerably longer than usual since Anton chose a circuitous route to circumvent one of the "homelands." Apparently, the local citizens were angry about a new government policy and, to show their displeasure, had dug up several sections of the highway and made them impassable. I never discovered the reasons for their grievance, but the method chosen to show displeasure was certainly an "attention getter." At any rate, we arrived without experiencing any problems other than the length of the journey.

The Zuka preserve consists of several thousand acres, which includes flat grassland and tree-covered hills. It was quite spectacular. The entire ranch was enclosed by a high-voltage fence and contained a wide variety of game animals. Anton had recently transplanted a small baobab tree near the gate. Talk about optimism: A sixty-year-

[4]Roodt, Veronica. *Trees and Shrubs of the Okavango Delta* (Shell Oil field guide series). Gaborone: Shell Oil Botswana (Pty) Ltd., 1998.

old man planting a tree that takes several hundred years to mature gives new meaning to the term.

For the next five days I hunted birds (primarily francolin, doves, and guineas), collected butterflies, and viewed the remarkable variety of game animals the ranch contained. Especially impressive were the record-size nyalas and a number of very large white rhinoceroses. A small herd of buffaloes frequently grazed on the open grassland.

Once Simon understood that I really wanted to shoot birds, he employed his exceptional skills to the maximum. (He was a big-game tracker and thought bird hunting was a waste of time.) I had several productive afternoons dove hunting after I determined their flight patterns. Simon became very adept at finding the downed doves, but I noticed that he was quite reluctant to search areas where the ground cover (broomstraw) was shoulder high. He indicated that this was a favorite haunt of the black mambas that inhabited the ranch. I concurred with his concern and immediately changed the location of my stand!

Two species of guinea (helmet and crested) were abundant. After spotting a flock, I circled them and waited. Simon flushed the guineas so that at least some of them flew in my direction, a tactic that gave us several successful guinea drives.

We hunted francolin from a moving vehicle. Riding on the front of the hood, Simon either saw or heard the francolin running in the brush—a very impressive feat! After he identified the general location, I usually walked and flushed the francolin, similar to hunting bobwhite quail singles. I did experience one situation quite different from quail hunting in the South. I was walking through a small field of thick brush and suddenly found myself about twenty yards from a very large female white rhinoceros and her young calf. The wind blew toward me; they were facing in the other direction. Luckily the behemoth remained unaware of my presence while I beat a hasty retreat back to the vehicle. I was later informed that "Gertie" was usually very docile. I am damn glad that she lived up to her reputation on this occasion. Birdshot from a 12-gauge shotgun is not the ideal weapon to deal with an irate rhinoceros!

Although I enjoyed the bird hunting experience and Simon's company, something was clearly wrong. I finally identified the problem: no pointer bird dogs. I am a bird hunter, not necessarily a bird shooter. I soon concluded that bird hunting ain't bird hunting unless my pointers play the primary role.

The ranch teemed with a variety of butterflies and Simon became quite adept at netting them, a new experience for him. We obtained about twenty species.

One section of the ranch was studded with a large outcropping of rock containing several caves. A large male leopard had been spotted near one of the caves, and Simon pointed out the pugmarks in the sand on a nearby trail. Hoping to photograph "Mr. Spots," we hung the front part of an impala carcass on the limb of a nearby tree, but no luck! The leopard did not "hit" this bait.

One afternoon we drove to a nearby lake owned by the local Zulus. The purpose of this outing was to hunt both ducks and spurwing geese. Several blinds had been constructed near the lakeshore. Toward evening a few stray ducks flew overhead; I killed several. A small Zulu lad, about ten years old, who had accompanied me to the blind, ran to the water's edge, jumped in, and rapidly retrieved two ducks. As he returned to shore, I noticed, to my horror, a number of crocodiles swimming nearby in the lake. Another duck had been only winged and swam off. The young urchin started back to the water to complete his retrieving tasks, but I managed to stop him. He seemed upset, but calmed down when I gave him some money and both of the ducks. I don't know how many children are lost performing retrieving duties, but I had no interest in being responsible for a possible disaster. Accordingly, I stopped shooting and enjoyed the blood-red African sunset.

The peaceful interlude at the Zuka Ranch put the icing on the cake for the safari. During our dinner discussions I learned a great deal about the current political atmosphere in South Africa from Anton. The issues related to tribalism were vividly illustrated by a recent situation regarding Simon. It seems that Simon had killed a man during an altercation over a trivial incident. To Simon's surprise, the authorities arrested him. From Simon's point of view, since the man was not a Zulu, killing him was of no consequence and certainly was not unlawful. (If he is representative of the prevailing attitude, it would seem essentially impossible for members of different tribes to function in a peaceful society.) After some discussion with the police, the fight was judged to be the other man's fault and Simon was released. However, his perspective regarding members of other tribes remained unchanged.

On the trip home I took a commuter flight to Johannesburg, obtained the luggage, including the cased double rifle, and proceeded to Customs. (It was necessary to obtain permission to export the rifle from South Africa.) Everything was in order; the serial numbers on the rifle matched those on the permit. However, I ran into trouble at the South African Airlines check-in counter. The agent insisted that the cased rifle had to be shipped separately, not hidden in the duffel bag. (An undisguised gun case provides an open, and frequently used, invitation to steal the weapon.) I was extremely unhappy.

Suddenly, I had a somewhat devious thought. I had never tried this approach before, but I opened my wallet and showed the agent a twenty-dollar bill. He smiled, placed the gun case in the duffel bag himself, and put my luggage on the conveyor belt. He tore a small ticket from a pad and wrote something on it. I turned to go to the waiting area; he followed and we exchanged papers. He got the twenty-dollar bill; I got the ticket. After pocketing the money, he indicated that this ticket allowed me to enter the room reserved for first-class ticket passengers. This lounge was very plush, making the four-hour wait quite pleasant. This interaction was so positive that if a similar situation arises, I will try this devious approach again. (I must remember to always have a supply of twenty-dollar bills.)

I boarded the airplane, took my aisle seat, and opened a book. At Cape Town, the only stop on the flight to Miami, the aisle was suddenly filled with minions of the law. I had a momentary concern that I was about to be arrested for bribery, but actually the man next to me was the object of their attention. I never found out the reason, but after a somewhat heated interchange he was escorted off the plane handcuffed. I breathed easier when I realized that jail time was not in my future. Other than this disquieting event, the trip home was uneventful. All my luggage arrived undisturbed.

Unfortunately, I may have killed the last trophy bull elephant legally taken from Timbavati. I understand that, due to pressure from the "Greens," trophy hunting for elephants may cease. This misguided policy, based on antihunting fervor, is not predicated on a shortage of bull elephants in the region. If anything, there are too many. What will be the result? The loss of trophy fees will eliminate the antipoaching units. Good-bye elephants!

It took me until the time I left South Africa to come down off my "high" from the elephant hunt. That experience left an indelible impression on me. I feel it is the most exciting big-game hunting possible. As opposed to Cape buffalo, which I know I will hunt again, I may not follow the "ivory trail" in the future. I'm probably ordained to kill only one elephant. I continue to relive my elephant-hunting experience to this day.

Aftermath: Tick Attack

The day after I arrived home from the South African adventure I noticed five dime-size red areas on my arms and back; I also felt "washed-out." Since I had just completed a twenty-four-hour airplane trip, I ascribed my malaise to jet lag. A day or so later, when these red areas crusted over, a light went on in my head. I had pulled several very small ticks from my arms the day before I left to return home.

I asked two of my physician colleagues, Dan Sexton and Ralph Corey, who specialize in infectious disease, to examine the lesions. After hearing my story, they became as excited as though I had brought each one of them a Krugerrand. They made a presumptive diagnosis of African tick bite fever (rarely seen in the United States). I took oral doxycycline. The skin lesions began to heal over the course of the next two days and disappeared within a week. I was well.

However, neither physician would be satisfied until their diagnosis was definitely established. I donated several blood samples, both immediately and several weeks later. These samples, sent to a laboratory in France, established the fact that indeed I had been attacked by *Rickettsia africae.*

African tick bite fever, a relatively common disease in southern Africa, usually does not produce a significant illness. In contrast, the American version, Rocky Mountain spotted fever, is much more virulent. At any rate, my story—along with pictures of the lesions on my arms—now are permanently on display in the scientific literature.[5]

Loxodonta africana

I've been burned by the African sun,
But the scars aren't on my skin.
My soul was seared by the iron of fear;
I won't be the same again.

Five tons of muscle, skin, and brawn,
Taller than trees was he.
At thirty yards his ivory teeth
Sent a chill of death through me.

A shaft of wood,
A tube of steel with a small lead ball inside,
Stood between me and certain death.
The Fates had to decide.

My shoulder moved as the bullet left.
Its path flew true as a lance.
The earth did tremble as colossus fell.
I awoke, as if from a trance.

[5]Sexton, Daniel J., G. Ralph Corey, Joseph C. Greenfield Jr., Claude S. Burton, D. Raoult. "Imported African Tick-Bite Fever: A Case Report." *American Journal of Tropical Medicine and Hygiene:* 60(5) 865–867, 1999.

Timbavati Titan

Emotions of triumph, joy, remorse
Coursed through my body in waves.
My thoughts raced back a million years
To a time when men lived in caves.

Yes, I've been burned by the African sun,
But the scars aren't on my skin.
The iron of fear has seared my soul
I won't be the same again.

Simon

A Zulu face with a white-toothed smile,
Eyes that shine like gems,
No matter how faint, no track on earth
Can ever hide from him.

Elephant to duiker and all between
He follows in a loping run.
One mile to ten it matters not,
'Til close enough for the gun.

Perhaps in another time and place,
He'd not so impressive be.
But out there in the African bush,
He's one in a million to see.

An Ivory Tale

Chapter IV

As this is written, I am looking at two very impressive African elephant tusks permanently displayed over my fireplace. This saga details the year-long trials and tribulations of getting the tusks home, which caused me a world of trouble and near nervous exhaustion.

Prior to my trip to hunt elephant in Timbavati, South Africa, in August 1997, I researched the necessary steps to import trophies from Africa. I obtained the appropriate Convention on International Trade of Endangered Species (CITES) permit to import a personal, sport-hunted trophy of *Loxodonta africana*. It was issued 5 March 1997.

The day I left Timbavati I saw the head of my elephant, with the tusks intact, placed into a pit and covered with dirt. (This technique allows the tusks to be slipped from the skull a week or so later, avoiding the possibility of damage. The usual technique is chopping them out with a hand ax.) I looked forward to the arrival of these trophies in the United States with great anticipation.

In November, Joey conveyed to me the first inkling that something might be amiss. My taxidermist's importer in Miami had informed Joey that the tusks had arrived but the South African CITES export permit was not with them. Joey concluded, erroneously, that this paperwork had been torn off the crate during the shipping process. The shipping bill contained a reference to permit #L4544, supposedly the South African CITES export permit. The United States Fish and

Wildlife Service and the United States Customs Service impounded the tusks until the CITES export permit could be located. The ivory was sent to a local warehouse.

Joey immediately contacted Anton Wienand, the South African professional hunter with whom we hunted, who assured Joey that the permit was available. Anton would send either a copy or the original immediately. At this point I wasn't worried, but I should have been.

After searching for the permit, Anton concluded that his son, Ryan, who had actually obtained the permit and shipped the tusks, might have it. Since his son was traveling in America and was planning to visit Joey in early February 1998, Anton felt the situation should easily be resolved at that time. Unfortunately, Ryan did not have the permit with him, but he was certain he knew where it was in South Africa.

Upon returning home, Ryan informed us that, although a copy was available, the original had been "misplaced." He applied to have the South African permit reissued, but an unfortunate glitch occurred. By that time, 5 March 1998, my CITES permit had expired: The local South African authorities informed him that to have the permit reissued I had to obtain an extension of my CITES permit.

I called the United States Fish and Wildlife Service in Washington (the first of many calls), explained the situation, and was informed that the reissue would not be a problem. "Please send a check for twenty-five dollars," I was told. I complied. Approximately two months later I called back and was notified that the CITES permit had been reissued and sent to me. It must have been lost in the mail. I was told to send them another twenty-five dollars to re-reissue the permit. I complied. (By the way, all the money was eventually returned.)

Approximately six weeks later (by now the middle of June), I again contacted the Fish and Wildlife Service in Washington. After explaining the situation, I was transferred to a very knowledgeable agent who apologized for the errors. She indicated that my CITES permit did not need to be reissued since the tusks had arrived during the time that it was still valid. In other words, I had wasted four months. This agent, who was very helpful, contacted the CITES authorities in South Africa. They had no record that a CITES export permit had ever been issued to Ryan Wienand. I was not happy, to say the least.

To add to my consternation, that same day I received a notice from the local warehouse in Miami. To wit, this notice stated: Since the tusks had been stored there for six months and since they had received no payment, the ivory would be confiscated and sold.

Well, I was clearly in over my head. I needed help. First I contacted the office of Senator Lauch Faircloth, whom I had known for several years, and explained the situation to his assistant, Mary Bear. I also asked Harry Dennis, an attorney in Miami, for help. (I had hunted quail on several occasions with him.) Harry, an officer in Safari Club International, was keenly aware of the issues regarding the importation of CITES-regulated trophies.

The first order of business was to retrieve the tusks from the auctioneer at the warehouse. Mary Bear contacted the Customs agency in Miami. They were very helpful. (Luckily I had met one of the agents through my quail-hunting activities in Florida.) The tusks were transferred to the Fish and Wildlife Service storage facility. The agent handling the case assured us that the tusks would remain under his control until the issue was finally resolved. I breathed a brief sigh of relief.

Harry contacted Anton, explained to him the gravity of the situation, and prevailed upon him to try to find the missing permit. He was successful. Unfortunately, permit #L4544 only allowed the tusks to be moved from one province in South Africa to another, not to export them to a different country. So there we were . . . a valid CITES permit had never been obtained.

Anton went to the authorities in South Africa, paid a significant fine, and obtained a valid CITES permit to export the tusks. This permit was immediately transferred to the Fish and Wildlife Service agent in Miami, along with documentation from the Timbavati game warden proving the tusks had been obtained legally. At that juncture, it was my impression that the problem would immediately come to a happy resolution. I was wrong.

In October 1998, I received a Notice of Seizure. The Fish and Wildlife Service had taken the position that the tusks had arrived

Joey and the author. The tusks, finally at home after a year-long struggle. Durham, North Carolina, 1999.

without the appropriate CITES export permit. Issuing of a permit after the fact did not correct the illegal importation. The agent indicated to Harry that, although they were seizing the tusks, they would not prosecute me for illegally importing the ivory into the United States (which would probably result in incarceration and/or significant fines).

I had three options, which I discussed at length with Harry. The first was to forget the whole damn thing. No way. The second was to refuse to sign the Notice of Seizure and let the courts in Miami adjudicate the issue. The fact was, however, I had broken the law. In Harry's opinion, we would lose in court. The third was to sign a Fish and Wildlife Abandonment Form, thereby officially relinquishing all rights to the tusks. This third option, however, did allow us to file a petition for remission. We selected the third option. Harry sent this petition for remission to the United States Department of Interior, Office of the Solicitor General, in Atlanta, Georgia. Whether this infrequently used approach would be successful was doubtful, but it was the only reasonable option. Let us pray!

In November, Harry submitted a detailed petition along with a number of supporting documents. In January 1999, Harry contacted the Office of the Solicitor General regarding the issue. He was told that the petition and documents had been received and that the office would make a determination in the near future. As an aside, Harry was advised that they did not need to hear from any more senators. (Besides Lauch Faircloth, I had asked help from Jesse Helms.)

On 5 February, Harry again called and spoke with the attorney handling the case, who indicated that the final decision had just been made. He was unwilling to convey the results over the telephone but would fax the document. Harry went to his fax machine. The material started to appear. I'm not sure how fast his fax machine prints, but he received a detailed five-page response, which he read as it was being printed. Harry told me that the suspense was nearly unbearable. Not until the last paragraph did he have any idea as to the judgment. The final paragraph stated, "It is therefore ordered that the petition for remission of Joseph C. Greenfield dated 30 November 1998 shall be granted."

Let the celebration begin! And we did. A year-long nightmare was over. Harry, who had expended a great deal of effort on my behalf, told me that the successful outcome of this case ranked near the top in personal satisfaction.

That's about all, except that it took us several more weeks to finally take possession of the tusks. (The United States Fish and Wildlife Service agent seemed somewhat less than happy that their ruling had been overturned.)

Lessons learned:

1) When hunting an endangered species, get all the correct permits. Make certain that the outfitter not only is knowledgeable regarding the necessity to obtain a CITES permit but also is compulsive about completing the job himself.

2) If in trouble, get a damn good lawyer. I did!

3) A little help from senators—and multiple prayer vigils—can't hurt either!

Buffaloes, Lions, and Snakes in the Rungwa, Oh, My!

Chapter V

I couldn't forget my first encounter with Africa's "Black Death" in the Serengeti. During the elephant hunt in Timbavati, South Africa, I saw a number of impressive Cape buffalo—arrogant, mean, vengeful. I wanted to hunt them again. Joey had hunted buffalo and lion in Rungwa, Tanzania, the preceding summer with Miombo Safaris. He reported that both buffalo and lion hunting were excellent and the skills of the trackers unbelievable.

I felt that I owed Joey a big favor. Without him I would not have had any African adventures. Joey's longtime dream was to kill a lion and I wanted to hunt Cape buffalo, so a Rungwa safari should be ideal for both of us. When we were hunting Cape buffalo and elephant, I always took the first shot and Joey backed me up if needed. I told Joey that we would reverse these roles when the opportunity to shoot a lion arose. He was elated!

After meeting Alex Walker, a Kenyan professional hunter (PH) for Miombo Safaris, I signed up for a July trip to Rungwa. Although quite young, at least by my standards, Alex had been a professional hunter for twelve years. Raised in Tanzania, Kenya, and Sudan, he has had a wide variety of experiences hunting dangerous game.

Richard Stack, a physician colleague at Duke, agreed to share the safari with me. Richard asked Bud Malstrom, a martial arts instructor, to accompany him as an observer. We finalized the plans for the safari. Alex would guide Richard and Bud. Gordon Church, an accomplished PH from Kenya and a close friend of Alex's, would guide Joey and

Pius carrying a butterfly net—obviously not his favorite occupation.

me. Joey had recently passed the examination for a Tanzanian PH's license and would act as an apprentice on this trip.

I agonized as to whether I should risk taking my .465 Holland & Holland double rifle to Tanzania. I had taken the rifle to South Africa with no problems, but I finally concluded not to risk it being damaged or stolen in Tanzania. This turned out to be a very poor decision.

To fulfill the role as a "genuine African hunter," I needed a double rifle. As luck would have it, the Colonial Gun Shop in Hillsborough, North Carolina, was offering a specially engraved Krieghoff Classic model .500 double rifle for sale. A divorce, requiring immediate cash, afforded me an opportunity to purchase the gun at such a bargain price that I couldn't turn it down. (Taking advantage of marital discord to obtain fine weapons for a small fraction of their value is a tried-and-true path for me. I had obtained a 12-gauge Purdey shotgun that I use to hunt quail under similar circumstances.) I had a Bushnell laser Holosight installed on the rifle. After I became accustomed to the weight and the recoil of the Krieghoff, I felt reasonably confident using it, although it was second-rate when compared to the Holland. As a backup rifle, I purchased a Sako .375 H & H with a plastic stock and a 2–6X variable Leupold scope. This light rifle was quite accurate, although the recoil was excessive.

Richard and I met Bud at the Atlanta airport. Bud, who turned out to be a delightful individual, impressed me as the type of person not to have as an enemy. We traveled (Richard first class, Bud and I steerage) on KLM to Dar es Salaam via Amsterdam. Flying from Raleigh-Durham to London and transferring to British Airways would have been much more convenient, but I learned that a number of hunters had experienced significant problems, including actual seizure of their weapons, trying to transport rifles through Gatwick Airport in London. Too bad. I guess the Saxon-Norman sporting blood is running a little thin!

For the trip I concealed a hard case containing my double rifle along with a 12-gauge Beretta shotgun in a duffel bag. A large aluminum gun case contained Richard's .470 Krieghoff and my .375. Although long, the trip was uneventful—that is, until we arrived. The gun case and Richard's other luggage were nowhere in sight.

We stayed at the Sheraton Hotel in Dar es Salaam for two days hoping the luggage would arrive, with no luck. It was still in Atlanta! Richard borrowed a .375 H&H Model 70 Winchester from Miombo Safaris. I had the .500 Krieghoff double rifle. On the third day, after checking out of the hotel and becoming nearly apoplectic at the charges, we flew via air charter to begin our adventure.

During our very expensive sojourn in Dar es Salaam, I met Gordon Church, a six-foot, five-inch, very impressive young man who exuded an air of confidence. I felt quite comfortable with him as our leader. I explained my plan regarding Joey shooting the lion to Gordon. His response: "It's OK with me—just don't tell anyone else." Since the license was issued to me, I was the only one legally allowed to shoot (except as a backup on wounded game).

Alex and Pius, our chief tracker, met us at the airstrip in Rungwa. Joey had informed me that Pius was first-rate. (Future events proved this assessment to be a marked understatement.) During the drive to camp, I saw a decrepit old lioness, a few warthogs, and a recent giraffe kill, but by no means the abundance of game that I had seen previously in both the Serengeti and Timbavati. We saw a number of francolins and guineas, and, luckily, I had brought my shotgun.

The area where we were to hunt was very hilly with a considerable outcropping of rock, much like the foothills of Appalachia. The bush was not thick, so there was reasonable visibility. I noted a considerable amount of standing water in a number of places. Alex indicated that the game was dispersed much more than usual this time of year because of the heavy rains.

After sighting-in the rifles, Gordon, Joey, Pius, and I, along with the Tanzanian game scout and two general factotums, boarded the Toyota Land Cruiser, ready for the hunt to begin. The first order of business was to hunt buffalo and, thereby, obtain lion bait. We drove along a road through hilly country and saw a variety of animals: zebras, impalas, giraffes, and warthogs to name a few, but no *mbogo* (Cape buffalo).

About 5:30 P.M. Pius spotted a solitary male buffalo feeding in fairly thick broomstraw approximately one hundred yards from the truck. Gordon indicated that he was a very old bull, horns somewhat

Hanging kongoni bait. Two lions were killed with this bait.

broomed, but of trophy size. After searching for several minutes with my binoculars, I finally saw a black object that I assumed was *mbogo.* The wind was blowing in our direction, and the bull appeared totally oblivious to our presence, so we made a brief stalk. For the last forty yards I moved crablike on my rear end while cradling the Krieghoff in my lap. When we were within approximately thirty-five yards, Pius quickly set up the three-legged shooting sticks, and I eased into a position to shoot.

The buffalo moved from behind a bush, giving me an unobstructed view of the "vital triangle" near the left shoulder.[1] At the report of the rifle, he rolled over as though hit by a pile driver. Joey also shot a few seconds later. The bull attempted to get up but was clearly dying. As we approached from the rear, he emitted a low characteristic bellow. Gordon had me shoot into the cervical spine, but this buffalo was dead. As we went through the usual picture taking and celebration, I couldn't get over the feeling that

[1]Robertson, Kevin. *The Perfect Shot.* Long Beach, CA: Safari Press, Inc., 1999.

killing this *mbogo* had really been too easy. At any rate, I had a very impressive trophy and we had a lot of lion bait.

The next day both parties moved to a fly camp about twenty miles south of the base camp. As we prepared to begin the morning's hunt, I noticed that Bud's feet were encased in a pair of soft leather boot-socks. Seeing my incredulous stare, Bud quickly informed me, "These are the correct footgear for a Ninjutsu warrior." I smiled inwardly and said nothing. That evening Bud walked with a very pronounced limp. Ninjutsu training undoubtedly conditioned him to walk on hot coals in those boots, but acacia tree thorns were another matter. I noticed that this Ninjutsu garb never reappeared during the safari.

We spent the day hanging the two halves of the buffalo for lion bait. It was impressive to see how meticulous Gordon was to pick the right place for the bait, usually the confluence of several game trails. We suspended the bait from a tree limb at a height so that hyenas could not reach it but a lion could, covered it with branches to hide it from vultures, and dragged the intestines and other parts through the area to attract the lions. Gordon advised me, just in the nick of time, that urinating near the bait was a no-no. The human scent might dissuade the lions from "cashing in" on a free meal.

While searching for an appropriate place to hang the bait, we saw numerous zebras, kongoni (hartebeests), wildebeests, giraffes, impalas, several elands, a herd of roan, and an impressive male sable antelope. The sable, standing about one hundred yards from the truck, was clearly agitated, rapidly twisting his head from side to side and violently shaking his tail. The cause of his strange behavior became obvious after observing him through the binoculars for a few seconds. He was literally covered with tsetse flies. Whether he spotted us or left to get away from his tormentors, he gracefully trotted off.

As we drove through a fairly thick mopane woods, I saw a small kudu male facing us about eighty yards from the truck. Guess what? Pius hadn't seen him. This was the only time I beat Pius "to the draw." In fact, even when he pointed out the location of game and I was using my binoculars, I frequently failed to see what Pius was pointing at. However, on this occasion I let him know, with tongue in cheek, that my eyesight was "number one."

A word about the tracker is in order. First, "tracker" describes only a small part of his duties. Besides following the tracks of a specific animal, wounded or unwounded, until the conclusion, the tracker plays a major role helping the PH plan the best way to approach the quarry. The tracker must follow the spoor until the game is spotted, then take advantage of the cover and wind direction in order to place the hunter in the appropriate position to shoot. When hunting dangerous game, especially if the animal is wounded, the tracker's role becomes paramount in preventing a life-threatening incident. Remember, the tracker is in the lead and armed with nothing more than his good looks. Nerves of steel and bravery are prerequisites, along with an absolute trust in the ability of the PH to deal effectively with dangerous game at close quarters.

These tasks may be the most exciting, but the tracker performs numerous other duties. He must be able to spot game at a reasonable distance, either walking or from a moving truck. While riding in the truck, he directs the driver along the appropriate paths to avoid stumps, rocks, holes, and other obstacles. He also must have an unerring sense of direction. (Good trackers are never lost.)

It is obvious that a very high level of ability and training is required for a tracker to be truly good. How do they train? Learning how to follow tracks, beginning about the same time they learn to walk, is essential. Tracking domestic animals around the village is the first job to be mastered, and shortly thereafter they start hunting. Most of the truly good trackers are also notorious poachers since they learn their hunting skills mostly through illegal hunting. Finally, experience with both dangerous and nondangerous game is a key factor.

It takes years to really hone their skills, and very few make the grade. Like any other profession, there are many people who profess to be competent, but very few who can really do the job. After watching them perform, I have become absolutely convinced that a topnotch tracker not only follows the trail but somehow is familiar enough with the animal's behavior to instinctively know where to find it.

Gordon, Joey, Alex, and typical heavily maned Rungwa lion.

Let's return to the activities at hand. Much to my consternation, the area was teeming with deadly poisonous snakes. We saw none on my prior safaris. The second day we spotted two cobras and a black mamba, and on the way back to camp, I used my shotgun to deal with a very large puff adder that was crossing the road.

The next day the lost rifles arrived. We decided to return to base camp, leaving Alex, Richard, and Bud to fend for themselves. The base camp was a damn sight more comfortable, so I didn't object to the plan. Especially nice was the quiet during sundowners and the evening meal. Listening to the African night sounds was far superior to Bud's extraordinarily crude jokes. The hyenas congregating near the skinning shed were especially vocal.

About this time, the staff dubbed me *Bwana Babu* (grandfather in Swahili). Joey informed me that this indicated a sign of respect. Old men are generally revered in their culture; however, I secretly suspected they accurately described my physical abilities. At any rate, I didn't complain. (This title has followed me on subsequent safaris.)

After checking the lion baits, we searched for buffalo tracks in the low grassy areas that still contained significant water. The buffalo were feeding in these areas, and we spied and followed a number of tracks. The walking was quite difficult, since elephants had used the area extensively and their hardened tracks made the ground markedly uneven. Like a good soldier, I followed Gordon, who has at least a six-foot stride and was able to jump easily from one dry spot to another. On several occasions my best effort resulted in wet feet. My discomfort was made especially difficult when I glanced back at Joey and the Tanzanian game scout, who were greatly amused by my clumsiness. To hell with them!

During this time, Gordon taught me different meanings for certain words in the King's English. To him, a four-hour forced march crossing multiple *chem-chems* (wet areas) is a brief amble. In spite of all our efforts, we didn't find a trophy bull buffalo in these areas.

Each noon we were generally served an elaborate lunch, either at the main camp or, usually, in the woods. After locating a shady and picturesque spot, we would spread a tarp on the ground and open a wooden chop-box containing a variety of foods; the chop-box also served as a makeshift table. Lunch consisted of freshly baked bread, meat or chicken, boiled eggs, tomatoes or other fresh vegetables, and several varieties of fruit, along with tins of sardines and corned beef. It was a distinct challenge not to eat too much. After lunch, an hour siesta was in order. The staff ate separately, building a fire and roasting meat, either fresh or dried, depending on our hunting success. While we slept, the trackers frequently scouted the area for signs of game.

Both guineas and francolins were evident in great numbers, and I killed a number of both on short trips from the truck. Pius excelled at retrieving wounded birds. However, I came to the same conclusion I made when previously bird hunting at the Zuka Ranch in KwaZulu-Natal: Hunting upland birds without my pointer bird dogs just "ain't my cup of tea." After a few days, the 12-gauge shotgun was assigned only the duties of "snake charmer" and will stay at home on subsequent safaris.

Pius saw a fresh track, not too far from where we killed the buffalo the first day. We followed it for about forty-five minutes and found ourselves quite close to a forty-inch buffalo with a hard boss, very similar to the one I had killed the first day. I didn't see him. Gordon indicated he was standing next to a dead, straight tree. Well, fine! The only problem was that I saw no dead trees. There was, however, a very straight tree, and I finally spotted the buffalo at its base. This was a lesson in Gordon's vocabulary, where "dead straight" means "very straight." Oh, well. Who was I to argue about the use of the mother tongue by a gentleman educated in England?

I decided not to try to kill this buffalo, which in retrospect was a stupid mistake. It did, however, teach me a good lesson: Always take what Africa offers, for there usually is no second chance. I did not want to get into the same situation that I had in both the Serengeti and Timbavati. When the animals on license are taken, the hunt's over. I wanted to keep on tracking and hunting buffalo.

For the next two days or so we continued to check the lion baits, which were becoming very ripe. Gordon decided that we needed additional bait. I killed a zebra and a kongoni, which we hung in different places.

Most of the time we continued to follow buffalo tracks, made by either small herds or solitary bulls. We made contact on several occasions but were either outsmarted or the quarry was not of trophy size. One entire morning we followed a very large, old bull that managed to stay just in front of us until he finally lay down for a noon nap. Just as we got into position to shoot, he slipped away. All I saw was his disappearing rear end.

The terrain containing the majority of the solitary bulls had significant outcrops of weathered rock. While crossing one of these ledges, we found tracks—about four inches long made by a three-toed animal—embedded in the rock. How many million years had elapsed since those tracks had been made?

The plethora of poisonous snakes continued in the form of two black mambas. The first I killed correctly by shooting its head off with a shotgun. I made an unfortunate judgment on the second. I couldn't visualize the head but thought I had aimed about two-thirds of the way up the body. Unfortunately, my shot blew a major section of his tail off, whereupon the enraged reptile slithered rapidly toward the truck, upsetting our entire contingent. Gordon

This mamba is contemplating whether to join the crowd in the Land Cruiser.

exclaimed, "Doctor, that was an atrocious shot." I agreed, but quickly corrected the error and killed the snake.

One morning, while we were following a solitary bull, Pius, who was in front, shouted and ran by me full tilt. Gordon jumped to my right. I quickly spied a spitting cobra, "hooded up," about fifteen feet away. The cobra decided to leave while we went the other way. It is amazing how fearless everyone seems to be around dangerous mammals, but snakes are a different matter!

Joey and Gordon spied a pair of oribi on the edge of a fairly large grassy field and had quite a discussion regarding the size of the horns on the male. (An oribi is about as big as a large collie dog.) The horns didn't look very impressive to me, but then I'm not an antelope trophy hunter. Joey really wanted that oribi, so I said, "Go ahead; show off your marksmanship." The game scout agreed. Joey aimed carefully with the .470 at a distance of about thirty yards. After the shot, the oribi seemed unimpressed and sashayed off into the long grass. Joey borrowed my .375, and he and Pius gave chase! To make a long story short, after three more shots, he finally connected and returned to the vehicle with his prize. Good-naturedly, he accepted my "slightly" sarcastic comment, "I hope you shoot more accurately if we're in real need!"

The chase was worth it. Roasted oribi is outstanding. That night I penned the following as a tribute (spoof) about Joey's oribi hunt.

Joey vs. Oribi

You can brag about the lion
And the mighty buffalo.
But the little Rungwa oribi,
He's the toughest guy I know.

Covered with a skin so rare
That holes heal immediately.
Five hundred grains from Joey's .470
Didn't phase the oribi.

He sauntered off to the long grass
To rest a spell did he.
It took three loads from the .375
To bring home that oribi.

Yes, brag about the lion
And the mighty buffalo
But the little oribi Joey shot—
He's the toughest guy I know.

Finally, it looked as though several lions had partially eaten kongoni bait. Gordon found long hairs on the tree, indicating that this pride contained at least one male. Excited at this lucky turn of events, we hung additional bait. The next morning, approximately three hundred yards from the bait, we saw several lionesses and one large male lion. They presented a reasonable shot, but Gordon elected to wait.

Gordon carefully chose a site about sixty yards from the bait and constructed a blind. Taking advantage of several small existing

The frontal view of the completed blind—constructed for hiding, not as protection from lions.

trees, as well as a few planted posts, Pius and comrades lashed poles horizontally to form a three-sided structure. They covered the walls with thick layers of broomstraw to a height of approximately six feet and carefully opened several holes for viewing and to shoot through. Finally, they cut a lane to allow an unobstructed view of the bait and the surrounding area. The completed blind was ready for occupancy by 2 P.M.

The entire structure looked flimsy as hell to me. I finally figured out that the sole purpose of the blind is to hide the hunter, not provide protection from the lions. Why was the backside left open? Most professional hunters prefer this configuration since lions approaching from behind the blind can be seen and dealt with more effectively with the rear open. At any rate, we had a place to spend the late afternoon awaiting a visitation from the *simba* clan.

Gordon's plan was to leave and return about 5 P.M. Just as we started to leave in the truck, however, we saw the pride again—two male lions and two lionesses. Gordon, Joey, and I slipped back into the blind, and the truck left. Well! There we were—no lunch and very little water to drink. It was extremely hot. Unfortunately, I had not taken an opportunity to relieve my slightly distended bladder. Four hours later, my bladder was more than slightly distended. I was in pain.

About 6 P.M. a beautiful lioness, lithe and graceful, suddenly appeared and looked up at the bait. She grabbed a hold and swung on the bait while pulling off several large chunks of meat. She ate for about fifteen minutes and then pulled off a piece of the rib and laid down about ten yards from the bait. As if on cue, a male appeared and looked at the bait but did not eat. He moved behind a tree. Another male, slightly larger, walked slowly into view. He stopped, presenting a good, clear shot. As per our agreement, Joey fired. In fact, in the excitement he pulled both triggers of his .470 Krieghoff double rifle, damn near breaking his shoulder. Immediately the lions all ran off.

I took the opportunity to put an end to my suffering. So far, the best part of the lion hunt for me was this blessed relief. By that time, the truck had arrived, and we drove in the direction the lion had taken. There he lay, approximately seventy-five yards from the bait, shot through the heart. After thoroughly pelting the lion with rocks, Gordon judged him to be dead. He was a very impressive lion with a full mane, approximately five years of age.

I was not prepared for what happened next. The entire staff, including Gordon, started whooping, hollering, dancing, and celebrating. By the time we loaded the lion on the back of the Land Cruiser, it was dark. We drove approximately twenty miles to camp, all the while being serenaded with a continuous chant. When we arrived at camp, a really serious celebration began and lasted for at least an hour, everyone dancing while showing off his own particular style of hip movement. (Bud's training in body control made him especially talented.) All the staff continued to congratulate me. In fact, I felt a little like a humbug, since Joey had administered the killing shot. But so what? We all had a very good time.

Alex, Richard, and Bud had returned to camp earlier that day. The next morning they got up early and went back to the same bait, and Richard shot the other male lion. These lions were apparently brothers and had stayed together, sharing the pride. On the way back to camp, Richard also killed a large Cape buffalo.

A jubilant Pius holds up freshly caught supper.

That night, while consuming our evening libation, a very elated Richard outlined his plan for displaying the lion. He wanted a full body mount with the lion fighting a hyena. Either too much drink or the "devil" made me suggest another plan. "Richard, a hyena is not a suitable foe for a lion. You need to have him fighting a Cape buffalo." I will be damned if he didn't agree. (The chief taxidermist at Animal Artistry took on the job. This impressive mount was displayed at a recent Safari Club International convention.) Joey concluded that I had a mean streak in me for conning Richard into spending so much money. No doubt he's right. On the other hand, Richard seems quite happy with the result.

With Joey's lion chasing now finally finished, we could concentrate solely on buffalo. For several days we rode in the Toyota from dawn to dusk looking for buffalo spoor, but to no avail.

The Toyota Land Cruiser is a rugged vehicle but continued use on rocky woods roads invariably causes mechanical problems. The sole duty of one of the staff is to keep the truck running. (Remember, there is no store around the corner that sells spare parts.) The ingenuity displayed by these "woods mechanics" is remarkable. By far the most common material employed to fix nearly everything is rubber cut from an old inner tube. There does not seem to be a problem that cannot be repaired with inner tube rubber.

A case in point occurred one day when a steering rod in our Land Cruiser was knocked loose by a strategically placed rock. The truck could not be driven. I figured we were out of business and would be walking for several days. Not so! Thanks to several applications of inner tube rubber, we were back riding in a few minutes. In fact, I'm not certain any additional repairs took place during the entire safari. If inner tubes are ever totally replaced by tubeless tires so that this rubber is unavailable, truck repair will be severely crippled. In fact, vehicle transportation on an African safari will come to a screeching halt.

On several occasions we had seen a troop of baboons and smelled their awful odor. (If baboons are even distantly related to man, our ancestors were in desperate need of deodorant.) I had little interest in baboon hunting, but Joey, with a twinkle in his eye, informed me that he really would like to have a baboon mounted. We spotted an old male, and after I shot, Joey retrieved his prize. I immediately forgot the incident, but about eighteen months later when I went to the bathroom in the lodge at Joey's hunting preserve in Florida, there sat the damn baboon, holding a role of toilet paper. Clearly, what is considered humor varies considerably. Joey did say that a number of his clients, especially the ladies, seemed to take umbrage at having the baboon staring while they were engaged in bathroom activities.

The next day we crossed the tracks of a fairly large herd of buffaloes and decided to follow. It was about 8:30 A.M. when Gordon remarked, "Doc, this might be a long one." His comment turned out to be prophetic.

We came upon the herd about one hour later and saw several large bulls, but we could not get into position to shoot. We continued to follow, and about noon the buffalo herd (nearly one hundred) lay down for their noon siesta. We did the same, about sixty yards from them. Approximately one hour later, the wind shifted, and the herd became aware of our presence and ran off.

We followed for approximately one mile and came upon an excellent bull with a wide horn spread. The bull was standing beside a bush facing me about seventy yards away. The lower part of his chest was partially covered from view, but the red dot from the laser sight seemed to be in the right place. The rifle was quite steady on the sticks. Following my shot, Joey fired almost immediately. We distinctly heard both shots hit home. The buffalo appeared unhurt and ran off. We hurried to where he had been standing and found a small amount of frothy blood, which was judged to have come from a lung. Gordon smiled. "We should have him in short order."

We quickly took up the wounded buffalo's tracks. *Mbogo* fell behind the running herd (usually a sign of a severely wounded buffalo). One cow remained with him. We saw them briefly, but the cow was in front of the bull, so we couldn't get a shot. We followed the tracks and blood, expecting to come upon the bull any moment. At that point, our level of apprehension was high. When found, would he run away or charge? Somehow, though, the bull continued to travel. About 6:30 P.M. we gave up. Three hours of tracking and expecting a mad, wounded buffalo to come at us at any second had kept my attention sharply focused.

Unfortunately, I had drunk little water that day. It was hot and I became quite dehydrated, so much so that I could hardly talk. Gordon indicated that I could drink some of the water in a "spring" which drained into a *chem-chem,* but this oasis contained copious amounts of buffalo dung and a large variety of crawling, wriggling critters. I declined. (I had treated the game scout for diarrhea the day before.) When we arrived back at the truck, an orange soda and a few quarts of water straightened things out. I had no serious aftereffects.

We spent the next day trying to find this buffalo but were unsuccessful. That was really too bad. I'm sure he died. I guess the best way to avoid severely wounding Cape buffalo is not to shoot at them. Could I have made a more accurate shot? Undoubtedly, a low-power telescopic sight would have allowed a clearer view of the buffalo's chest.

A killing shot on a buffalo facing the hunter is very tricky. The bullet must penetrate the center of the chest. A few inches

The entire group and a display of the skulls collected during the safari. First row: Gordon, the author, Joey, Richard, and Bud. Second row: The trackers and camp staff (wearing the red fezzes).

off to either side may allow a rib to deflect the path of the bullet, causing only peripheral damage to a lung or forcing the bullet on a trajectory where it doesn't even enter the chest cavity. Imagine a rib capable of turning a 570-grain bullet. Cape buffalo truly are tough hombres!

When I reflected on the experiences of this safari, a number of adventures outside hunting proper added to its excitement and interest. Poisonous snakes were the order of the day on this safari. In addition to the ones we had to deal with, Richard and Bud had a mamba try to join them in their Land Cruiser. Let's hope I filled my lifetime quota of these pariahs on this safari.

Another enjoyable experience was my interactions with Pius. He not only was an extremely accomplished tracker but he also had a wealth of hunting experience. Tireless and energetic to the extreme, Pius was never still and always wore a smile. Each day after lunch, while everyone else napped, Pius became involved in some venture. Fish were abundant in many of the streams, and Pius proved to be an adept fisherman. He invariably caught supper with a fishing line he kept in the truck. Our outings for butterflies resulted in me collecting about ten new species, which was quite a plus. Pius became extremely good at spotting butterflies and, although not wildly enthusiastic, he even tried his hand at netting them.

Probably the most vivid memory occurred early one morning. We saw a large male leopard walking slowly across a mist-covered green field near the bait. It was an absolutely gorgeous sight. After a minute or so, he became aware of us, turned, and gazed at us intensely, as though delivering a message to a sworn enemy. Suddenly his mood changed, and, as if by magic, he disappeared.

When we flew back to Dar es Salaam, the turmoil resulting from the destruction of the American Embassy while we were in the bush was quite evident. Members of the U.S. military patrolled the streets. At the airport, we saw an airplane used by the secretary of the Department of State being prepared for departure. We were informed that our flight might be significantly delayed because of the security situation. I had a bright idea. Why not try to hitch a ride with Madam Secretary? However, knowing how incompatible our political leanings were, I concluded that even if we were allowed on board, the long trip would be intolerable. (At the time, I was certain that these events would spur our government to action regarding terrorism, which proved to be a major misjudgment on my part.) At any rate, we left on time and had a very pleasant flight home.

To sum things up, Joey killed an impressive lion (and chased down an oribi). I got a majestic buffalo, but more important, I experienced some of the most exciting buffalo hunting imaginable. I left knowing that I am really hooked on hunting Cape buffalo.

A Rungwa Leopard's Message to Man

I first met you, a long-legged ape,
On the broad East African plain.
Weak and slow without tusk or claw,
So easily you were slain.

I watched you learn to hunt in a troop,
And throw a sharpened spear.
You killed for food, but not for lust.
From you I first knew fear.

I followed on your northern trek
To a frozen Pleistocene plain.
With fire in hand, none could best
The hunter you soon became.

Now only a few years have passed,
As time is reckoned by me.
You've changed from a mighty hunter
To a despoiler of all you see.

The virgin forests you brutally raped.
With plough you ravaged the plains.
The swift flowing rivers are fouled with muck.
For me no home remains.

You spread across the earth like a blight,
Destroying all in your path.
For coats, for rugs, or just to kill,
My kin did suffer your wrath.

We few now left on this earth
Cannot change our plight.
Face to face I can still best you,
But that's not how you fight.

I've held my own for a million years.
The future I cannot win.
Die I will, but not kneel down
And be a pet of men.

I'll live my life as I always have:
Free to my last breath.
I know full well when I meet you—
My reward for defiance: death.

Selous, Lions and Buffaloes

Chapter VI

A truly descriptive title for this safari would contain a combination of "The best laid schemes o' mice and men gang aft a-gley"[1] and *All's Well That Ends Well.*[2] Clearly, everything that could go wrong did! In spite of these misadventures, the overall experience was outstanding. To set the stage for this safari, a number of different issues need to be described and woven together.

The most memorable event of the Rungwa safari for me was the immolation of the *mbogo* even though the major focus of the safari was to hunt lion. While we waited in the blind for lions to appear, two events that have a major bearing on this safari stand out clearly.

A beautiful lioness, lithe and graceful, approached the kongoni (hartebeest) bait first. With the late afternoon sun shining on her coat, she was a thing of beauty as she rose up on her hind legs and pulled a piece of flesh off the bait. The male appeared next. Although larger, his extensive mane detracted from his athletic appearance, at least to me. (As usual, I'm at odds with the rest of humanity with this opinion.)

The second memorable aspect of the wait in the blind was more prosaic. We had seen the lions nearby and had to creep into the

[1] Burns, Robert. "To a Mouse" in *Poems I Remember*. Compiled by John Kieran. New York: Garden City Publishing Co., Inc., 1942.

[2] Shakespeare, William. *All's Well That Ends Well,* in *The Works of William Shakespeare*. New York: Oxford University Press, 1938.

blind early in the afternoon, about 2 P.M. Unfortunately, Gordon Church failed to advise me to enter the blind "empty." By late afternoon I was convinced that if the lions didn't get me, I would die anyway from a ruptured bladder. Correcting this problem was not possible. The odor of human urine might dissuade the lions from paying a visit.

When the male finally met his demise, the blessed relief seemed heaven-sent. This experience greatly strengthened my dislike of hunting from a blind.

After the tumult and shouting was over, I mentioned to Joey how much more impressed I was with the appearance of the lioness. I wondered aloud why the hairy male is always judged the more desirable trophy. This remark unwittingly planted a seed in Joey's mind that I would be quite content with a male lion having a "short" mane.

One of the best components of any safari, at least for me, is detailed planning for the event. (I guess I'm obsessive-compulsive.) The first decision I needed to make was where did I want to go. I had read about the large number of Cape buffalo in the Selous game reserve. Although their horns might not score high enough for the record book, their aggressive behavior provides a lot of excitement. I don't give a damn about the record book anyway. The quality of the hunt is my primary focus. Another issue, but very important to me, was to have sufficient contact with bull elephant to enable me to decide whether to hunt them again.

When I met Alex Walker during his trip to the annual Safari Club International Convention, I conveyed my wishes to him. He indicated that large bull elephants are rare in Tanzania, but a reasonable number inhabit the southern part of the Selous. He suggested that I plan a ten-day buffalo hunt in Mahenge. Everything sounded fine; I made the decision to go.

Joey had booked several other clients with Miombo Safaris. This was his second year as a fully licensed Tanzanian professional hunter (PH). Joey's experiences in both South Africa and Tanzania, coupled with a lifetime of hunting in Florida and keen woodsmanship, have made him an outstanding big-game guide. When we sorted out the dates based on his schedule, the best time seemed to be 10–22 October, a week after our annual pilgrimage to Wyoming to hunt sage grouse. These dates placed us in Tanzania during the latter part of the dry season. The long grass would be reasonably dead and much of it burned; consequently, the animals would be easier to spot.

Getting to and from Africa cannot be arranged on a daily basis unless one is very wealthy (which I'm not). The reservations required that I be there for twelve days. I would spend the first two days either in Dar es Salaam (my second favorite city in the world, the first being any other city) or in camp as an observer. I quickly chose the latter option; everything seemed to be in order for a combined buffalo hunt and elephant-observation safari.

The next issue I needed to resolve was which weapons I should take. The rifles I had used in Rungwa weren't ideal. The .500 Krieghoff was too heavy for me to use comfortably. The safety on the .375 Sako had released accidentally on several occasions, and the loaded magazine kept falling out. I sold both rifles—at a profit, I might add.

After considerable discussion with myself, I decided to carry my .465 Holland & Holland double rifle. It fits me perfectly and is a joy to shoot. To hell with worrying about the value. If it's stolen, I'll cry then. (The gun is insured.) A similar situation confronted Joey. His decision influenced me. A grateful client recently willed Joey a beautiful .470 Rigby double rifle. Joey had to decide if he should hunt with a gun worth more than his house. His answer? Yes!

Dietrich Apel of the New England Custom Gun Service had resoldered the barrels of the Holland on a hurry-up basis just prior to the Timbavati elephant hunt. Although well regulated, both barrels shot significantly to the left, reducing its effectiveness even at close range. My eyes no longer accommodate well enough for me to use iron sights accurately, so I need a different sighting system. I had previously used a Bushnell laser Holosight on the .500 Krieghoff double rifle. Even though I worried that this addition would ruin the looks of the Holland, I felt I had no choice but to go that route. Mr. Apel, using a German claw mount, installed a similar device

The group resting on the first day of the hunt. Front row: Alex, Pius, and "Little Mama." Back row: Makanyanga, the author, and Singi.

on the Holland and returned it to me for inspection. Because of significant drop in the stock, I had to use a leather cheek pad to be effective. The rifle became a monstrosity instead of a work of art. This plan just wouldn't do.

We finally settled on a Swarovski 1.25–4X variable power professional hunter scope. I could shoot with both eyes open on low power, and the open circle reticle with small cross hairs was ideal. The scope on the claw mount was low enough so that the obnoxious pad could be thrown in the trash can. Also, these optics would perform much better than the Holosight in poor light.

My next problem was to straighten and re-regulate the barrels. At the SCI convention, Joey and Alex had both heard horror stories regarding the damage done to vintage double rifles by A-Square monolithic solid bullets. I called the Holland & Holland store in New York to confirm this rumor. The salesman said that under

Singi, the author, and Makanyanga with a record-book hartebeest (shot for lion bait).

no circumstances should this bullet be used in their double rifles. Although I had already shot about one hundred rounds through my rifle and had killed an elephant, I ruled out further use of monolithic solids.

Thus began a prolonged and difficult search for suitable ammunition. I had read a recent advertisement from Kynamco Ltd. listing .465 ammunition loaded to the same specifications as the original Kynoch cartridges; I felt that the problem had been solved. Unfortunately, these cartridges did not work out. Mr. Apel obtained enough of this ammunition to regulate the rifle, but he informed me that it was nearly impossible to eject spent cartridges since it required considerable pressure to open the breech after firing. A representative at the factory told him that the chambers of my rifle must be pitted; otherwise, their ammunition would eject properly. This was not true. The chambers of the Holland & Holland were smooth. All the other brass—Bell, A-Square, and original Kynoch—had functioned perfectly. Later, I found out from Alex that he had a similar problem with Kynamco ammunition in his Westley Richards .470 double rifle; he was treated to the same lame excuse.

After briefly trying .465 cartridges loaded in Germany and finding that the bullets keyholed, Mr. Apel commissioned Lee LaBas of Carson City, Nevada, to make the ammunition. He chose standard Woodleigh softs and solids and obtained new A-Square and Westley Richards brass. Loaded to the original Kynoch specifications, this ammunition turned out to be ideal. Mr. Apel straightened and re-regulated the barrels and returned the rifle to me two weeks before the hunt. (There was not enough time even to re-black the barrels.) At eighty yards, I was able to consistently place bullets from both barrels in a four-inch circle. The Holland was ready to go!

The next issue was the choice of a backup rifle. (I really am too compulsive.) Through the Colonial Gun Shop in Hillsborough, North Carolina, I obtained a new safari-grade .458 Winchester Model 70 bolt-action rifle with a synthetic stock. Joey poked a lot of fun at me for my choice because I'm quite enamored of the beauty of a double shotgun stocked with a fine piece of walnut. I replied, "A bolt-action rifle, while a superior serviceable weapon, ain't pretty. In this regard, quite similar to a mule, very little is gained by trying to make them more attractive."

I had the barrel cut off to twenty-two inches and an easily removable muzzle brake and thick butt pad installed to suppress recoil. The rifle was rebored to accept a .458 Lott cartridge. (Anton Wienand had carried a .458 Lott bolt-action rifle as a "stopper" on my elephant hunt in Timbavati.) I had a Swarovski scope (the same as on the double rifle) installed using an EAW swivel-type quick detachable mount. Since the rifle shoots regular .458 as well as the .458 Lott ammunition, I initially sighted it in with the readily available .458 ammunition. I bought three new boxes of .458 Lott A-Square cartridges, two solids and one soft. Although it kicked noticeably, the rifle was quite accurate. I had made an excellent choice for a backup rifle.

During the sighting-in process, one seemingly minor problem occurred, which later turned out to be a major issue. One of the .458 Lott cartridges misfired. I took the cartridge to the gunsmith at the Colonial Gun Shop, and he felt that oil may have gotten into the primer of that cartridge. Since the Winchester rifle had functioned properly otherwise, I didn't worry about it—but I should have!

Africa is replete with game birds—quail and several varieties of francolin and guineas. I had taken a shotgun on the previous two safaris, but try as I might, I just didn't enjoy hunting birds. Without my pointer bird dogs, bird hunting ain't bird hunting. The shotgun stayed at home.

Although I thought we had finalized our plans, a problem arose right before we were to leave. Joey called about two weeks before the departure date to tell me the Mahenge option had fallen through and that Alex wanted us to go back to Rungwa. This plan didn't suit me at all as the only elephants I had seen in Rungwa had been running away at top speed. (Apparently there had been significant poaching in that area.) On his prior trip to the Selous, however, Joey had seen a number of elephant, and he told me that buffalo were plentiful in Block LA-1. As he expressed it, "A blind man could find a buffalo." I decided on this location. In addition, the duration of the hunt was increased to twelve days.

Since lions were numerous, Miombo Safaris had several left on their quota. Alex arranged to have a lion license issued to me. I had not planned to hunt lion again, but I looked forward to this unplanned opportunity. Most of the male lions in the Selous do not have extensive manes. From my standpoint, an old male with a sparse mane would be a very "proper" trophy.

Based on my prior experience with luggage in Dar es Salaam, I devised a fail-safe plan. I carried the .465 Holland & Holland double rifle (enclosed in an Americase) in a two-tiered duffel bag. Joey packed the Winchester and twenty rounds of .458 Lott ammunition. My duffel bag contained ammunition for both rifles. In addition, I had carry-on luggage with all the essentials, including one change of clothing (washing is done daily on safari) and other accouterments necessary to survive.

I had been in the Dar es Salaam airport twice. The first time, my luggage had been pilfered and a number of items stolen. On the second trip, a colleague's baggage didn't arrive for four days. We made the stupid mistake of staying in Dar es Salaam waiting for the luggage, truncating our safari and reinforcing my dislike of the town. At any rate, everything was packed and I was ready to go.

I met Joey in Atlanta. We flew on KLM to Amsterdam and from there to Dar es Salaam. We arrived and proceeded to baggage claim, where, guess what? My luggage was nowhere in sight. Joey's luggage, however, had arrived intact. My plan worked; I had a rifle.

We flew to camp the next morning to start the adventure. I would use the Winchester until the other luggage arrived—if ever. Joey had brought twenty rounds of A-Square .458 Lott ammunition, and the majordomo of Miombo Safaris, Scott Cole, was able to find an additional twenty rounds.

A complication arose when I discovered that the video camera I had used on all my prior trips didn't work. Either the camera was broken or the batteries, which I had thoroughly tested two weeks before departure, were defunct. Thinking there was no real problem since I had a new battery in my luggage, I searched my case to discover that, well, actually . . . my overly compulsive self had forgotten to pack it! None were available in Dar es Salaam; thus, I was unable to document the safari on video.

We arrived in camp via air charter by noon. Alex was on another safari and would join us two days later. Our head tracker, Makanyanga, had been working for Alex during the previous eight years. Alex, who was devoted to Makanyanga, described him as the best tracker in Africa. Makanyanga had guided many of the best-known professional hunters, beginning in 1964 with Kevin Torrens, followed by Brian Herne, Danny McCallam, and Robin Hurt. He had hunted exclusively with Alex since 1991. I soon learned that his reputation was well deserved. Makanyanga is a member of the Wakamba tribe in Kenya, the legendary elephant hunters. Fifty-plus years old, he has seen it all and then some. Makanyanga has had as much experience with dangerous game as anyone alive. His partner, Singi, is a member of the same tribe. They made a first-class pair!

The author, glad to be alive, poses with his dysfunctional .458 rifle. In spite of four misfires, the author got his buffalo.

Pius and the "King of the Selous"—a very proper trophy.

The camp was topnotch and had been built recently. It was situated on a riverbed that contained several large pools of water, one being right in front of the dining tent. A beautiful African fish eagle occupied a nearby tree where a number of gaudy-colored weaver birds were nesting. I saw no mosquitoes.

After I moved in, I fired my only rifle several times to be certain that it had remained sighted-in after the trip. Everything functioned well. The Tanzanian game scout assigned to us turned out to be a short, young woman. She carried a .458 Winchester Model 70 rifle . . . "Little Mama" with big gun!

As in Rungwa, the camp staff designated me by the descriptive Swahili name *Bwana Babu* (grandfather), probably reasonable if unflattering. Joey had been dubbed *Bwana Marlboro*. His western hat mimicked the Marlboro man. Alex was identified as *Bwana Tembo* (elephant). From this name one might conjecture that he was wise, strong, and powerful. Actually, what the staff really meant was that he pushed down a lot of trees with his Land Cruiser!

We saw little evidence of buffalo tracks on our first foray, but other game was all over the place. Apparently, it was the season for impala to produce young. There seemed to be a baby impala behind every blade of grass. That night, we began the usual evening ritual around an acacia-wood campfire: two glasses of "cheap white wine," a Churchill-size Romeo and Juliet cigar, followed by a delicious meal. Lions roaring nearby *serenadwwwwwwed* us.

A heavy cloud cover and occasional rain kept the weather cool for the first three or four days of the hunt. The rest of the time, it was as hot as hell. Even the *mbuga* (low-lying grassy plain) was dry; there would be no wading through swamps on this trip. The ground was uneven due to hardened elephant tracks, making walking very difficult. Much of the underbrush had been burned.

It was soon evident that Makanyanga had another talent. I'm not sure whether he or Joey is the most accomplished pyromaniac, but both excel. Everywhere we went, we were followed by burning brush!

Hunting lion was a major component of this safari, so it was mandatory that we hang sufficient bait. The camp also needed meat. Since I had the license, I assumed the task of provider. Makanyanga saw a large wildebeest facing us about two hundred yards off. He put the sticks[3] down.

Hit in the chest, the wildebeest ran off. I watched Makanyanga and Singi follow a faint blood trail for a mile or so—impressive tracking, to say the least. When we caught up with the wildebeest, it could go no farther. I finished it off with two more rounds. We had our lion bait.

---

[3]The word sticks is a term describing three sticks held together with inner-tube rubber. This tripod is used to support the rifle while firing. Actually, it's a wonderful invention and one that facilitates very good accuracy when used properly: Hold the sticks in the left hand, have the rifle rest in the V, and place one finger around the barrel. This approach fixes the rifle to the tripod. An experienced tracker will position the sticks so that, when the hunter places the rifle in the V and looks through the scope, the animal to be shot is centered.

The next day, we spotted a very nice impala with a wide set of horns about one hundred fifty yards off. I squeezed the trigger. *Click . . . click . . .* and again . . . *click.* My response was blasphemous. The impala took an immediate dislike to my cursing and left.

We collected the new, misfired A-Square cartridges. The primer seemed depressed somewhat and not flush with the surface of the cartridge. The primer was dented, but apparently not sufficiently to ignite the powder. To prove that the cartridges were the problem, I borrowed the bolt from Little Mama's .458, put it in my rifle, and squeezed the trigger. *Click.* Then I tried one of her .458 cartridges, which fired perfectly. I said a few "choice" words about A-Square. But I had other .458 Lott ammunition that Scott had given me. The primer on these cartridges was flush with its case, and I concluded after firing several rounds that they would function just fine. The problem was defective ammunition, and I still had twenty rounds of good ammunition. Problem solved?

We needed additional lion bait. During the next two days I killed a kongoni (hartebeest) and another wildebeest—one shot each, I might add—as well as a zebra that required four shells. The ammunition worked perfectly. Although we did not specifically seek trophy-quality animals, the horns from both the kongoni and wildebeest would qualify for the SCI record book.

On the third day Alex arrived with Pius, the superb Tanzanian tracker who had been with us at Rungwa. Pius remembered me: *Bwana Babu kwenda kipepeo* (grandfather goes for butterflies). Alex hunted with us for three days, during which time we discovered that lions had chewed on one of the baits. We built a blind and waited one afternoon and early the next morning, but to no avail.

We often walked in a wide, dry riverbed when searching for lion tracks. In several places elephants had dug for water using their feet and trunks. Interestingly, they dig a hole, drink the water, and frequently fill the hole with sand. One afternoon as we approached the river, we spied a young bull elephant excavating. We parked the truck on the bank and crept to within thirty-five yards of the bull. He was completely unaware of our presence and continued his water-digging exercises. Alex, who is a superb photographer, took several pictures of this tranquil scene.

The author (a pitifully poor dancer) and staff celebrating simba's *demise.*

Makanyanga became bored, I guess, with elephant viewing and decided to intervene. He threw a large stone and hit the bull on the head. The elephant whirled around to find the cause of this disturbance, fanned out his ears, and brought his trunk up. He surveyed the bank but, luckily, did not spot us. We quickly retreated to the truck. I looked somewhat reproachfully at Makanyanga, who shrugged his shoulders in a "what the hell" manner. I'm certain Makanyanga thought that provoking the elephant was great fun. But I didn't appreciate his warped sense of humor.

Due to a scheduling mix-up, two hunters from Denmark arrived early at the other nearby camp. Alex had to leave to guide these clients, and he took Singi with him. He felt that Makanyanga, Pius, Joey, and I would do just fine alone. Actually, this turn of events was OK with me. Makanyanga and Pius could find game, and I knew Joey was an outstanding PH and a superb rifleman. Armed with a .470 Rigby double rifle, he would provide more than adequate backup and keep me out of trouble.

At that point, we had found only a few fresh *mbogo* tracks and no herds. For several days we followed the tracks of a number of

Makanyanga, Bwana Babu, and the very large Selous lion. The shot was

taken from the bush across the dried riverbed on Makanyanga's right.

old bulls but didn't get within shooting range of a trophy bull. About the sixth day, we trailed two old buffalo. After a couple of hours, we found them grazing in a fairly open field, as awesome and impressive as I had remembered. The larger bull carried wide, symmetrical horns with a solid boss. The other, smaller bull was young and not of trophy quality. With a certain amount of help, I slid on my butt and then crawled to within eighty yards. We weren't going to get any closer. Although this was a long distance, I felt fairly confident of a good initial shot because my quarry stood broadside. (In hunting dangerous game, the first shot must count. If not, you're usually in for a mess!)

After Makanyanga planted the sticks, I stood up, took my time, and aimed at a spot near the shoulder overlying the heart. *Click.* I didn't lose my cool! I quickly ejected the misfired cartridge and squeezed the trigger again. *Click.* The third cartridge fired, but my aim was bad. (By that time I was, to say the least, somewhat distracted.) The bullet entered the buffalo's chest forward of the "vital triangle." Rather than running forward, he turned back in our direction—both he and his buddy—at full tilt. I quickly reloaded. They both stopped about thirty yards from us after getting our scent. The larger bull looked malevolently at us as if to say: "Were you responsible for that damn noise and the pain in my chest?"

I fired again. This time the rifle functioned properly. The bullet entered low in the center of the chest—a mortal wound. Joey also shot his Rigby. I fired again. *Click.* Again, I fired, and this cartridge did its job. Well, that's not too bad an average: six cartridges and only three misfires! The buffalo, hit in the heart and clearly dying, fell. His buddy left the environs. Well, not really. After running about one hundred yards, he turned around and ambled back toward us. He stopped about forty yards away and gave us the "once-over." Even though he was fully capable of creating a serious problem, we didn't want to engage in hostilities because of his young age.

I had two shells left. Whether either one of them would go off or not, I had no idea. Joey reloaded. There we were. *Mbogo* looked at us, we looked at him, and he continued to look at us. After about a minute (it seemed like at least an hour), God must have intervened. The buffalo snorted and retreated, staring back at us on a couple of occasions. Finally, he was gone. I breathed easier. We walked close to the dying bull to deliver the coup de grâce. I fired, and again I heard the click of a misfire; the next cartridge did go off. It was all over.

I'm not sure what would have happened had the other bull decided he wanted to become better acquainted. The first shell going "click" would not have been fun! I decided to relegate the Winchester to the trash heap and borrow another rifle. There might have been a problem with the A-Square ammunition, but on examining the misfires, we found the firing pin had only made a slight indentation in the primer. The rifle was not functioning properly.[4]

There was good news when we arrived back in camp. My luggage had arrived. I had my .465 Holland & Holland double rifle. I unpacked it, and everything seemed in order. Well, nearly everything. The overly expensive German claw mount wouldn't function. The spring that pushes the locking device forward was frozen. We installed the scope, hammered it closed, and hoped it would stay tight. Actually, it did fine. I just didn't have a quick detachable mount. Well, problems do occur. I shot the rifle several times—still on the money.

The next day, buffalo herds came back into our block en masse. We found the tracks of a large herd of at least fifty. The wind blew toward them, which was exactly the wrong direction. Makanyanga indicated that we would circle them. We traipsed around for about two hours, and I was starting to doubt his woodcraft, but I shouldn't have. All of a sudden, we found ourselves behind a bush and within sixty yards of the herd. I could see two fairly nice bulls milling in and

[4]On returning to North Carolina, I had both the Winchester rifle and the A-Square ammunition checked out to determine the cause for the misfires. I owe A-Square an apology for all my nasty thoughts—their ammunition was not defective. The problem stemmed entirely from an error in reboring the rifle to accept the .458 Lott cartridges. Over-boring caused the ammunition to intermittently seat too far forward in the chamber.

out of the herd. Makanyanga planted the sticks, and I stood with the rifle positioned, ready to shoot, for at least thirty minutes. My right hand began to cramp, but the bulls never moved clear of the herd, and the possibility of wounding a cow precluded my shooting.

Finally, a nice bull moved out on the left side of the herd about one hundred yards from us. Makanyanga spotted him and repositioned the sticks. That's a long shot for a buffalo, especially with a double rifle. We waited, but the herd began to walk off. Joey and Makanyanga both signaled, "Give it a try." The bull had his head down facing to my left. At the report of the rifle, he dropped like a stone. The rest of the herd exited posthaste.

A buffalo that falls as if "poleaxed" from a bullet in the chest usually has a spinal injury, but the spinal cord may only be grazed by the bullet rather than severed, causing temporary paralysis. If this is the case, the buffalo may recover and decamp. We quickly ran to where the buffalo lay. Joey arrived first and fired an insurance shot into the brisket, but the buffalo was quite dead.

Instead of the usual celebratory gestures, both Joey and Makanyanga seemed quite restrained, in fact, disgusted. The reason for their attitude soon became obvious. The bull was quite young and the boss soft. I had killed the wrong buffalo! They couldn't blame me. I did exactly as I was instructed. Apparently, during the time I got ready to shoot, the old bull had walked into the herd and was replaced by the younger one. Since my quarry had his head down obscuring the horns, the switch went undetected by any of us.

After I realized the problem, I asked Joey for a rag. He gave me a blank stare. "I need to wipe the milk off my trophy's lips," I said in a rather derogatory tone. Joey didn't seem to appreciate my humor. We did actually need lion bait, but much more importantly, this episode allowed me to assume a "holier-than-thou" attitude with both Joey and Makanyanga. I decided to let them sort out which of them was to blame, knowing full well that neither would take responsibility. In spite of the mix-up, this episode gave me a lot of confidence in my double rifle.

The buffalo-hunting part of the safari was certainly on track, but so far we had had no luck with lion. A pride of lions had

Pius, the author, and Makanyanga with the buffalo shot at dusk.

been roaring nightly close to camp, but other than one episode our baits had been left untouched. We had seen numerous large tracks, indicating that a male lion had walked close to the baits, but had left them alone. They were either too wary or too full of young impala to be tempted. It seemed that baiting for lions was an exercise in futility.

Makanyanga devised another plan. During dinner that evening he appeared and outlined this new approach to Joey. Joey's Swahili, as Makanyanga expressed it, is *baya sana* (very bad), but he can communicate. I can't. After a considerably animated discussion, they concocted a simple scheme. To recapitulate: Since there were numerous lions near the camp, we would sashay around early in the morning before daylight to see if we could get close to them. We would hunt lions the way they're supposed to be hunted, without using bait. When Joey spelled out the idea to me, my response was an incredulous, "We're going to do what?"

To add to the difficulties of this plan, I have a very significant blind spot. I can get around reasonably well using both eyes, even in bad light, but looking through a scope is worthless. It takes good light for me to be able to see well enough to shoot. Joey knew about this problem but said, "Well, we won't get to the lions until you can see to shoot." (Really! How in the hell could he be sure?) To add to my consternation, I knew that lions have exceptional night vision. They could see us; we couldn't see them!

It wasn't clear to me exactly what Makanyanga and Joey had been drinking, but, apparently, I was dealing with two lunatics. I had to decide whether to join them or to hide in camp. After mulling over the plan in my mind and remembering that my insurance premiums had recently been paid, I decided to be one of the "boys" and go along with this hare-brained scheme. Bwana Babu shoots a lion, gets killed, or both!

Anyway, about 5:30 A.M., away we went, two double rifles, the shooting sticks, and four intrepid hunters—one with significant reservations regarding the sanity of his adventure. Makanyanga indicated that a male lion had moved off to the long grass about 5 A.M. He was not sure if there was anything left but lionesses. We went anyway.

The night was nearly dark with only a quarter moon. But there was enough light so that I could see Joey's back, although it faded in and out, depending on whether he was in my blind spot. Pius brought up the rear, his primary function being to stop me from running back to camp. Makanyanga had already told us that the lions would be on the far side of the dry riverbed. Well, fine. I wasn't at all convinced they had read that part of the script. Even if correct, my guess: it would take about two to three seconds to right that error and for them to get on our side. Anyway, we began our trek.

We crept slowly, for perhaps five hundred yards, to the edge of the riverbed, where we were hidden by fairly thick brush. It was light enough now so that I could actually see through the scope. My heart rate slowed, at least somewhat, but I was a long way from being calm.

All of a sudden, a large lioness walked out of the bushes and across an open glade on the other side of the riverbed and lay down (exactly as called for in the plan outlined last night). She was about sixty-five yards off. We waited. After three to four minutes, the first rays of the rising sun shone on the head and body of a very large male lion lying about ninety yards away, just past the lioness. He gazed in our direction as if contemplating whether it was worth the effort to dine on the monkeylike creatures looking at him.

Joey whispered, "Can you kill him?"

"Of course!" I replied, pretending to be calm. "Why do you ask?"

In fact, I was much less self-assured as I thought to myself: *I don't know, but you better damn well pray that I do!* (Following a wounded lion is a blueprint for disaster.)

Makanyanga planted the sticks. After the report of the rifle and the subsequent thud as the bullet went home, the lion jumped straight up in the air about five feet. He roared and fell down. He got up just as the bullet from the second barrel hit his chest. Joey exclaimed, "He's toast." (What he actually said is unprintable but conveyed the distinct impression that the lion was seriously impaired.) The lion continued to roll over. I reloaded. Joey shot; I shot again. The lion became still. The lioness had apparently exited.

Makanyanga gave his usual high-pitched warbling victory yell. I heard the truck in camp start up. In a few minutes, the rest of the contingent arrived, and we drove to where the lion lay. When he was judged dead, all hell broke loose. I'm not sure why, but killing a lion elicits the damnedest celebration imaginable. It is not staged. The entire crew, especially Pius, began hollering, singing, and dancing. As for me, I looked toward heaven and thanked my Maker for pulling me through this one!

This lion, although much bigger than the one Joey had killed in Rungwa, had a shorter and less extensive mane. Estimated to be about eight years old and covered with scars, he was a magnificent creature. I had a "proper" trophy. Joey's eyes were shining like a rat caught in a barrel. This was his fifth or sixth lion killed as a professional hunter, but I am sure it meant more to him than any of the others, including the lion he had killed in Rungwa. I remembered the story by Robert Ruark, extolling in great detail the attributes of Cape buffalo and ending the paragraph with "and I killed him."[5] I felt exactly the same way about my lion. This experience was clearly the high point of the hunt or, in fact, any hunt. I had killed a large male lion, having blundered around in the dark with the entire pride nearby.

I probably owed Joey and Makanyanga an apology for doubting their plan but, true to form, I didn't admit anything. (I always heed a maxim ascribed to John Wayne: "Never admit a mistake. It's a sign of weakness.")

In reliving the experience, Joey had a confession to make. "I didn't tell you but we had a major worry about the late-night stalk: There was the real possibility of inadvertently getting too close to elephants in the riverbed."

I thanked Joey for keeping this concern a secret. Undoubtedly, the possibility of being trampled by elephants or being ingested by lions would have precluded my participating in what turned out to be a very exciting event.

The celebration became even more intense. It took the entire contingent to load the lion into the truck. On the way back to camp I found out what our game scout did well. Little Mama, could she lead a chant! I have no idea as to the meaning of the words, but she stole the show.

When we arrived at camp, I was toted around in a chair with a garland of toilet paper around my neck. The dancing involved

[5]Ruark, Robert C. *Robert Ruark's Africa.* Edited by Michael McIntosh. Traverse City, MI: Countrysport Press, 1991.

everyone, even me. After about an hour, the entire crew was exhausted. Finally, we ate lunch.

Later in the afternoon, I went to the skinning shed and got frightened out of my wits by looking at the size of the lion's paws and teeth. The first bullet had entered the front of the chest, gone through the heart, and exited the chest into the leg, finally lodging in the paw. The double rifle had performed flawlessly. Now I could pretend I was a real African big-game hunter: elephant, buffalo, and now lion, all with a Holland & Holland .465 double rifle. Not bad for Bwana Babu!

It was still hot at 4:30 P.M., but we decided to look for another buffalo. (I had one more left on my license.) Also, we had a number of baits to chop down, making access for the hyenas and vultures easier. We drove into a fairly thick extensive area of long grass but saw nothing. Then Makanyanga spotted a couple of oxpeckers (a small bird that frequents buffalo and eats ticks and other vermin from their hides). As events turned out, the oxpeckers didn't do these buffalo any favors. We stalked toward the herd.

I have a significant problem when hunting in long grass. It's too damn tall. Joey is over six feet and can see above the grass. I'm considerably shorter, and when the sticks are planted, I'm usually looking into an impenetrable wall of grass. Makanyanga and Joey spotted three old bulls, but I couldn't see them. Makanyanga planted the sticks.

"Shoot," Joey said.

"OK," I replied. "At what?"

After some discussion (in which Joey advised me to buy elevator shoes), the buffalo decided that they had enough and left. We followed, but the same sequence occurred again. Now, for reasons unclear to me, the buffalo left their safe haven in the long grass and went into a more open area. (When I say "open," I mean the grass was only about four feet high. I could just see over the top.) Poor light was beginning to be a problem, but I could still see through the scope. We hustled toward them as quietly as possible.

Suddenly, a big, arrogant old bull was facing me about forty yards off, his eyes radiating the message: "I see you. I don't like you. Why don't you leave?" At the report of my rifle, *mbogo* turned and ran, apparently uninjured.

Joey said, "I think you've missed."

He didn't hear the bullet hit, but he did see dirt fly up at the buffalo's feet. He felt that I might have shot low into a termite mound. I disagreed. "I'm certain I hit the mean bastard."

The sun had set and darkness was closing in rapidly. Only shadows were discernible to me. We probably should have left well enough alone and waited until morning, but we didn't. Makanyanga and Joey took up the trail. *Here we go again, tempting fate!* I thought. After tracking for only about sixty yards, a low mournful bellow broke the silence approximately forty yards in front of us. Makanyanga looked back at me and smiled. The world suddenly became all peaches and cream.

The buffalo had run about one hundred yards and turned, facing the back trail, ready to charge anything that followed. Luckily, the bullet had entered the top part of his heart. He had run out of steam and collapsed. As we approached, he raised his head and gamely tried to get up, but he was done for. A bullet in the brain left no doubt. The "old boy" had positioned himself perfectly to seek retribution for the injury. He just didn't last long enough, thank God!

We took a few pictures. Then darkness settled in. I sat down and breathed a sigh of relief. What a day! What a hunt! What a life! Bwana Babu could not be more content.

That night, shortly after 1A.M., I was awakened by the nearly continual vocal outpourings of three lionesses. Apparently looking for their deceased "Lord and Master," they had camped on the other side of the dry riverbed, about eighty yards from my tent. Both Joey and Alex had informed me that, as long as I remained in the tent at night, I was safe from predators. Well fine! Had these lionesses read the appropriate instruction manuals? I quickly loaded the Holland and sat on the bed, listening to the ladies roaring. I assumed that as long as I could hear them, I would be all right.

After about an hour, all became suddenly quiet. A loud noise made by a creature in the nearby bathroom broke the silence,

The author, Pius, and a warthog killed by a "Texas heart shot." The .500-465 Holland & Holland double rifle is hanging on the prized shooting sticks.

which, to say the least, got my undivided attention. I pointed my rifle in that general direction and turned on the flashlight. The light outlined a large bat, the cause of the ruckus, trying to extricate itself from the mosquito netting. I breathed again.

The ladies restarted their serenade from approximately the same location. After about an hour, they wandered off, their roaring fading in the distance. I breathed a sigh of relief and lapsed into a restful sleep.

That's about it. During the next three days, we saw numerous herds of buffaloes. To supplement the camp larder, I shot an impala with the double rifle at a distance of two hundred twenty-five yards, which was more luck than good marksmanship.

I really wanted a warthog; however, we rarely spotted them throughout the safari. On our last morning, Pius saw a male warthog facing directly away from us rooting in the dirt. He keeled over at the report of the double rifle—a perfect "Texas heart shot." His long tusks were clearly of record-book quality. While I got my warthog, I had one minor disappointment to this safari: I only collected a couple butterflies that I didn't already have.

In contrast to Rungwa, we didn't see any snakes. I didn't miss them. I hope I filled my lifetime quota last year. On the other hand, I did see a lot of elephants. But I was unable to make up my mind whether I wanted to try to hunt them again.

My best trophy of the trip was the set of sticks that Makanyanga made to support the rifle for every shot. Makanyanga gave them to me just as I left to catch the charter plane to Dar es Salaam. I'm as proud of them as anything I own. For the trip home, I strapped them to my duffel bag. I was concerned that they might be broken in transit, but, luckily, they arrived intact. Also, the Customs agent didn't object to importation of fresh-cut "forest products." Of all the African trophies I have accumulated to date, these sticks mean the most to me. I will keep them forever.

The trip home through Amsterdam was uneventful. Joey and I said good-bye in Atlanta. Reflecting on the experience, it is amazing how many things went astray. But, in spite of the problems, wonderful, unforgettable memories were the hallmark of this safari.

Frankly, I hope the Lord will smile on me in a similar fashion in the future.

Addendum

Bucky Flowers of Skins and Scales Taxidermy in Naples, Florida, measured the lion skull. For some inexplicable reason, I submitted these data to the *Safari Club International Record Book of Trophy Animals*.[6] I will be damned if the "old man" didn't rank forty-fourth. Maybe, just maybe, I may yet become a real trophy hunter.

[6]Safari Club International *Record Book of Trophy Animals*. Edition 10, Vol. 1 (Africa Field Edition), Tuscon: Walsworth Publishing Co., 2002.

Selous Lion, A "Proper" Trophy?

400 pounds of muscle and brawn,
He's King of the Selous.
But for all his strength and grace,
He's not "good" enough for you.

Paws as big as dinner plates
And teeth that are razor keen,
But you declare him second rate.
You've got a lot of spleen!

Only the mighty *tembo*
Can best him in a fight.
But you don't praise his majesty,
'Cause his neck hair just ain't right.

So he's not a "proper" trophy
'Cause his mane is short and sparse.
Consider this, my arrogant friend—
Kindly, kiss my arse!

The Sunshine State, Buffaloes

Chapter VII

My hunt for Asian water buffalo in South Florida came about because of a poorly draining canal. Let me explain. About twenty-one years ago, Joey moved J&R Outfitters, a quail hunting business, to a four-thousand-acre tract of land near Indiantown, Florida. This new location contained a considerable amount of reasonably well-drained, low-lying land that provided excellent quail habitat. Over the ensuing four to five years, a combination of unusually heavy rains and poorly functioning drainage canals (choked by floating tussock) caused about fifteen hundred acres to remain wet year-round. Most of the seed-bearing plants died and the remaining high ground became covered with dense palmetto clumps. The quail disappeared, making this portion of the ranch essentially useless for upland bird hunting.

Quail hunting is seasonal, with the preserve quail season lasting approximately six months. Hunting at J&R ceased during the off-times. To expand his business, Joey took advantage of this downtime and began guiding clients to hunt big game in Africa. I had joined him on several occasions and had excellent hunts in both South Africa and Tanzania. Although we hunted elephant and lion, our primary focus was Cape buffalo. Joey began to examine the feasibility of providing similar hunting experiences in Florida.

In May of 1998, a fairly large herd of exotic Asian water buffalo became available for purchase. The swampy area of the ranch was an ideal habitat, so Joey acquired the herd, planning to provide outstanding "close-to-home" buffalo hunting. The herd of approximately one hundred animals contained a number of bulls with heavy trophy-class horns. The predominant color was black, but a few were dark buckskin.

These buffalo readily adapted to the area. I saw them occasionally during the early part of the quail season. I had not seen Asian buffalo before, but they looked quite similar to the African Cape buffalo. The primary distinguishing feature for the water buffalo is the absence of horn structure on the center of the skull in the male; in other words, they do not have a boss. When they become aware of an intruder, they either run or assume a typical nose-forward stance, gazing with an icy stare. The impression they give is quite clear: They aren't particularly happy to be in a stranger's presence, and their stance shouts, "I don't like you; if you come any closer, watch out!"

Several of Joey's clients had hunted these buffaloes successfully and reported the experience as outstanding. I decided to give it a try. We completed arrangements and set a date for the hunt. I arrived at the ranch with my Holland & Holland .465 double rifle and a dozen or so cartridges loaded with 480-grain solid Woodleigh bullets. Backup, if needed, would come from Joey and his .470 Rigby double rifle.

Joey, "Weasel" (Johannes Lubbe, a professional hunter and close friend of Joey's visiting from South Africa), and I drove to the swampy area about 4 P.M. We immediately saw a number of fresh tracks. I noticed that the tracks of these buffaloes were considerably larger than those made by their African cousins.

We spotted a group of five, including a very wide-bodied buckskin-colored male with an excellent set of horns, standing in a field densely covered by myrtle and palmetto. The visibility was marginal. The wind direction was variable but was generally blowing in our direction. We stalked to within sixty yards. At that point, the buffalo became aware of our presence and moved forward a step or two as if to investigate what was going on. It was impossible to get a clear shot at the big bull because of the intervening cows.

Very old buffalo cow with an impressive set of long, curled horns.

I got in position to shoot and waited several minutes. The male slowly walked around a myrtle bush toward a small clearing. As often happens, the wind apparently shifted just as he came into view. A second before I fired, the bull wheeled around and ran off rapidly. The rest followed. Although not certain, I thought I had likely missed, shooting in front of him. We quickly ran to where the buffalo had stood but found no blood. We lost the trail after tracking for a mile or so. It was getting late, so we decided to start anew the following day.

Early the next morning, just as the sun came up, we resumed the search. A heavy ground fog covered the surface of the land, and Lady Luck smiled. There stood the same buffalo group in the same myrtle-and palmetto-covered terrain, about six or seven hundred yards from where we had made the initial contact. As we watched, a blood-red sun rose, coloring the thick fog. The buffaloes, partially covered in this red mist, seemed almost ghostlike as they stared toward us. We quickly detoured to approach downwind, but when we reached the spot where they had been, the buffaloes were gone.

We tracked them for about an hour and a half as they traveled in a wide circle. We got pretty close on several occasions, but each time they either saw us or smelled us. We didn't see them, but we did hear branches breaking as they ran off through the thick undergrowth. The buffaloes followed a path along the edge of one of the large drainage canals toward a more open area. As we came to this field, we spied them approximately two hundred fifty yards from the edge of the woods.

The wind was blowing directly from them to us, and they didn't appear aware of our presence. "Let's get closer," said Joey.

We moved carefully forward under the cover provided by a large myrtle bush until we could go no farther without being spotted. We waited, and waited, and waited. After what seemed like an hour (but was probably only twenty minutes) Lady Luck smiled again.

The buffaloes slowly grazed toward us to within about one hundred yards but suddenly stopped, heads up, looking in our direction. They seemed to have either spotted or smelled us. We thought that they were unlikely to come any closer. Although it was a long shot for the double rifle, Joey whispered, "Give it a try." The last thing I wanted was to wound this magnificent animal, but I overrode my concern and took his advice.

The large trophy bull, the closest to us, was separated from the others by twenty to thirty feet. He was facing from my right to left and presented an excellent shoulder shot overlying the heart-lung area. At the report of the rifle, he jumped vertically two to three feet, ran about thirty feet, and fell. The remaining herd exited rapidly. The other male turned around after running about one hundred fifty yards and briefly gave us the impression that he might try to defend his fallen friend. Luckily, he thought better of it and left.

We approached the downed buffalo cautiously from the rear. The bull, clearly dying, emitted a low bellow. To be doubly sure, I gave him an insurance shot between the shoulders. He gave up the ghost. He was a gorgeous animal, probably tipping the scales at eighteen hundred pounds or so, with wide symmetrical horns.

We went through the usual congratulatory exercises, picture taking, and reliving the morning.

Shortly after lunch, Joey and I decided to "plunder around" in the swampy area in the back part of the ranch. Much of this land was covered with water from the recent rains. Accordingly, we loaded our paraphernalia in a swamp buggy and set out.

For the uninitiated, a swamp buggy is a homemade vehicle designed to navigate low-lying and swampy areas. It is constructed using the running gear of a small truck with the gearbox altered so the buggy can be run quite slowly. An aluminum deck containing the passenger seats is welded above the motor approximately ten feet off the ground. This contraption is capable of easily traversing boggy areas with its very large tires.

We saw a number of buffaloes in small groups congregating in the semidry sections. While negotiating a particularly thick palmetto-covered area, we spied a buffalo with a narrow but very long set of horns that curled directly upward. Joey exclaimed, "I thought she was dead!" He had not seen this old buffalo cow for a number of months and assumed that she had died.

When Joey purchased the original buffalo herd, it contained about 15 percent mature cows. He had initially planned to use these cows to breed and raise their offspring to be hunted, but he quickly determined that the presence of cows made the mature bulls continually fight, resulting in serious injury and death in a couple of instances. He rounded up the majority of the cows and arranged to have the breeding program housed in a remote facility. The few cows that he had not been able to corral were hunted and killed, so he had assumed that this "old lady" had been long gone. "We need to get rid of her," Joey exclaimed. "She is likely to be quite wild and difficult to approach, but let's give it a try."

For no particularly good reason, we had brought both double rifles, so we quickly dismounted from the buggy and stalked toward the old cow. We got close to where we had spotted her and peered through the palmettos. She was gone. However, the ground was reasonably soft and we were able to follow her tracks with little difficulty.

After about thirty minutes, we saw her again. We circled to get the wind in a favorable direction and stalked to within about forty yards. Just as we were about to shoot, a sow and several piglets became aware of our presence and ran off, creating quite a commotion. As expected, the cow took the hint and left. After uttering a few choice words about the "pesky" pigs, we continued to follow the buffalo's tracks. She circled toward where we had left the swamp buggy, essentially returning to the same area where we had first seen her. This time the stalk was undisturbed and successful. We shot almost simultaneously, putting an end to the affair.

We had some difficulty dragging her out of the dense swamp with the swamp buggy. We finally arrived on high ground and took a few pictures. Her horns were much longer than any of the males and make a nice display in Joey's hunting lodge. (The much-appreciated meat from both buffaloes was donated to a local substance abuse rehabilitation center.)

Summing up the day's experience: I never thought that the palmetto country in South Florida could be a backdrop for a truly great buffalo hunt, but I was wrong. (One of the best parts of the experience was not having to endure the twenty-four-hour flight to Africa.) I'm eagerly looking forward to a repeat performance.

I'm really glad that canal stopped up!

Selous Again, Hill Country Buffaloes

Chapter VIII

The pattern of my trips to Africa is well established. After each safari I make a halfhearted decision that these excursions are over. This notion is based on two precepts: 1) I have experienced everything the Dark Continent has to offer. 2) As one of my daughters recently pointed out, I'm spending her inheritance. The first of these is obviously wrong. One could spend two lifetimes in Africa and not even scratch the surface. I dealt with the "guilt trip" regarding the money as follows:

Your Inheritance

Five years ago, a money hoard
You'd get when I "checked out."
But Africa called! It's all gone!
So just sit down and pout.

I bequeath to you this elephant foot,
To remind you every day
I spent your money having fun,
In a land so far away.

At any rate, Africa called again, and I was ready to plan an adventure for the year 2000. The "die was cast" for this trip when Joey told me that this year would be Makanyanga's last as a tracker.

Whether this was true or not, I didn't want to miss the opportunity to hunt with this talented tracker again. All that was left was to decide on the location and dates.

Miombo Safaris offers a significant reduction in the daily rate for Cape buffalo hunts in the Selous. (Two birds with one stone: hunt buffalo and spend less of the inheritance.) The final plan was a ten-day Cape buffalo hunt in the block adjacent to where we had hunted the preceding year. Joey would lead the expedition as the professional hunter (PH); Makanyanga and Singi would function as trackers. The dates were set, 17–30 August.

Joey was by now a seasoned African PH, having developed all the qualities that the job requires. He and Makanyanga had hunted together enough to trust each other implicitly, an absolute requirement for success. My confidence in them was such that I had no qualms regarding the safety and success of the hunt.

Now I could begin the usual extensive planning for the safari. (Next to the actual trip, I enjoy spending the preceding six months getting ready to go. Truthfully, I'm too compulsive.) The first issue to be settled was my armament. This decision should have posed no problem. The .465 Holland & Holland double rifle had performed flawlessly on the previous safari. All that remained was to have it re-blued and the frozen claw mount fixed. I sent the rifle to Dietrich Apel (New England Custom Gun Service), who made the repairs and returned the rifle in early December. The claw mount worked perfectly; however, I fired the rifle to be certain that the scope was still correctly aligned.

At eighty yards, the bullet from the right barrel struck the target approximately three inches to the right of the point of aim. I adjusted the scope, but it made little difference. Further adjustment resulted in the bullet striking even farther to the right, and the hole in the target appeared to be eccentric. Since I was using the same ammunition that had functioned perfectly before, I was certain that the fault lay elsewhere.

I immediately sent the gun back to Mr. Apel, hoping that a loose scope mount had caused the problem. He confirmed my worst fears: The bullets were keyholing. The rifling, which had been damaged by the monolithic solids I'd shot previously, no longer functioned properly. My spirits improved somewhat when I realized that the defect in the rifling had not appeared during my previous trip. If it had to fail, now was the best time, not when trying to kill a lion or a Cape buffalo.

What should I do? Retire the rifle and hang it under the elephant tusks, or try to fix the problem? It occurred to me that it might be possible to have the rifle rebored to a .470 caliber. I discussed the situation with Mr. Apel, who agreed and found a gunsmith willing to take the job. The reboring was successful, and both barrels produced good groups. However, regulation of the barrels could not be done in time for this trip. That meant that the "reclaimed" .470 Holland & Holland would have to wait for a future hunt.

Anticipating the worst, I had borrowed a .470 Krieghoff Classic double rifle from Joey. He had carried this rifle on our first three safaris but was currently using a .470 Rigby double rifle given to him by a grateful client. I had the Holosight on the Krieghoff replaced by a Swarovski 1.25–4X variable power professional hunter scope. The rifle was reasonably accurate. Using Federal ammunition with Woodleigh soft and solid bullets, the barrels grouped about four inches apart at eighty yards. I had an acceptable primary rifle. For a backup rifle, I purchased a Model 70 Winchester in .375 caliber Holland & Holland. A similar Swarovski scope was installed using an EAW swivel-type quick detachable mount.

I checked on the various travel options. Although my baggage failed to arrive with me on the previous two trips, the best plan still seemed to be to fly on KLM airlines from Atlanta to Dar es Salaam via Amsterdam. What could I do to increase the odds that the luggage would arrive with me? After some discussion with a Delta airline agent, I obtained a first-class ticket from Raleigh-Durham to Atlanta on an early flight (a five-hour delay at the Atlanta airport). Traveling first-class should result in better care of the luggage, and the long delay should give the airlines plenty of time to get the bags to KLM. I also discussed the situation with the KLM representative, who advised me to affix duct tape marked with the flight numbers on my luggage. Nothing else could be done but pray. I used both of these options.

Two of Joey's clients booked a ten-day hunt just prior to my arrival, so Joey would precede me by two weeks and meet me in the bush. He carried the Model 70 Winchester .375 backup rifle with him. This procedure, coupled with the fact that my carry-on bag contained enough paraphernalia to start hunting even if my luggage did not arrive, assured me that the safari would start on time.

The trip was quite pleasant, in spite of being somewhat longer because of the time taken by the delay at the Atlanta airport. I obtained a box of Romeo and Juliet Cuban cigars at the Amsterdam airport. I had brought along a box of Romeo and Juliet Churchill-size Dominican cigars just in case the Cuban cigars were unavailable. (Talk about being a compulsive planner!)

I arrived at the Dar es Salaam airport and was met by Scott Coles, a Miombo Safari representative. My baggage was nowhere to be seen. It seemed as though the third strike had been thrown. Scott asked the baggage handler to check the plane again. After about a ten-minute delay, more luggage was located in the cargo space, mine included. I breathed a sigh of relief. Everything was in order.

After the usual restful, but ridiculously expensive, night at the Sheraton Hotel, I flew to the Selous early the next morning. I shared this charter airplane with three Spanish hunters who were dropped off at a camp about sixty miles from our destination. The pilot flew the last sixty miles close to the ground, so I got a good view of the terrain and spotted a number of animals, including several elephant.

We arrived in good shape. I was met by Joey, Makanyanga, Singi, and Joseph, the Tanzanian game scout. Joseph proved to be an excellent woodsman and became a valued member of our group (as opposed to Little Mama, the game scout on the previous safari). Both Makanyanga and Singi seemed truly delighted to see Bwana Babu again. In addition to Makanyanga and Singi, there were several members of the camp staff who had been on my previous safari to the Selous. Abu, the camp director, also remembered me. Everything was in order to begin the new adventure. There was one problem of note. The stock on Joey's double rifle had been broken in transit. He had wrapped the

Makanyanga laboriously shaping the Wakamba bow with a machete.

stock with duct tape and it remained functional—another entry in the long list of uses for duct tape!

The base camp, located on the banks of the Ruaha River, was spectacular, especially at sunset. A resident fish eagle demonstrated his fishing skills daily. The river contained a large concentration of hippo, whose continuous grunting effectively drowned out most of the other African sounds. I've read that the hippo can be very aggressive and dangerous, but these seemed quite willing to leave us alone.

Although adjacent to our previous hunting block, the current location, R-3, contained very little *mbuga* (flat land). The terrain was very rough and hilly. The annual burning program had progressed reasonably well. With Makanyanga and Joey in charge, it couldn't be any different. Since we were hunting much earlier than last year, a lot of the land remained unburned.

Joey informed me that the previous group had hunted primarily in the block used during my prior safari. He and Makanyanga had saved the hilly country, which contained a number of trophy-size bulls, for my hunt.

The weather throughout the safari was nearly ideal. Although hot, most days had enough cloud cover to block out the sun's oppressive heat. I did manage to acquire an impressive "redneck" tan. A shower of rain fell during the night on several occasions.

Abu was surrounded by an excellent and well-trained staff who did everything they could to make this safari very pleasurable. Obviously, one of the key players is the cook. One can easily spot the cook among the staff because he's the only fat one. Our cook, especially fat and especially gifted, provided outstanding cuisine.

I observed the usual evening ritual: taking a hot shower, then sitting near a bright red fire listening to Africa's night sounds while enjoying a glass of white wine and a good cigar. The Cuban cigars were a big disappointment. They were improperly rolled, making adequate drawing close to impossible. Sixty percent had to be discarded, a just reward for my dealing with a communist dictator.

The white wine seemed excellent to me. (I can't tell the difference between good and bad—my favorite is "screw top.") However, the "pomp and circumstance" of removing the cork from a bottle of excellent vintage is a time-honored ritual on safari. As I went through the motion of wine tasting to indicate acceptance of the bottle, the "devil" got into me. I sampled the offered glass and immediately spit it out as though I had just tasted vinegar. Surprised and horrified, Abu ran to the bank of the river and emptied the bottle before I could stop him. I fulfilled a lifelong desire to express my disdain for the wine-tasting ceremony, but I really felt like an ass, which I had been, for upsetting our wine steward. We finally made Abu understand that everything was fine. After things settled down and I had a couple of glasses of the vintage, I sampled the cook's excellent table fare. Abu eyed me with suspicion for several days. He eliminated the bottle-opening ceremony for the rest of the trip.

Abu got revenge. Toward the end of the safari he asked me in a rather nonchalant manner, "Is it really necessary for me to take my tuberculosis medication?" I nearly became apoplectic. After regaining my composure, I answered emphatically that it certainly was necessary. Remembering that Abu had served all our meals, I chalked up another danger, exposure to tuberculosis, to be encountered on an African safari.

I noticed our nightly fire seemed especially hot and bright. The wood being burned was a variety of teak, which was fairly abundant in the forest near camp. When asked why this valuable wood wasn't being sold, Abu replied that regulations forbid harvesting and selling timber from a hunting concession. There is no telling how many dollars worth of this precious wood went up in smoke. Apparently, government rules are the same silly nonsense the world over.

The next morning, after sighting-in the rifles, our contingent got into the Toyota Land Cruiser and "away we went." One thing was immediately apparent: Ours was a "geriatric safari." Makanyanga and Singi are in their late fifties, and Bwana Babu is considerably older than that. We frequently referred to Joey, age forty-three, as

Makanyanga giving the author a Wakamba elephant hunter's bow, arrow, and quiver.

mtoto (baby). At any rate, we proved that "old folks" could still hunt effectively.

The underbrush was broken down and the grass grazed down to the roots for a couple of miles from the riverbank. It took me a while to figure out that the hippos were responsible. Hippos leave the river at twilight, feed at night, and return to the river at daylight, where they spend the day. Depending on the number of hippos and the amount of available food, they may need to travel as much as ten miles from the river each night to fill up. Paths made by hippo were everywhere. These trails are unique in that the feet on each side form separate tracks; a trail made by a hippo path has two depressed tracks separated by a raised area three to four inches wide. Hippos are territorial and can be very aggressive when disturbed in the water. However, the majority of problems with man occur as they are returning to the river early in the morning. Getting between a hippo and its river domain is very likely to result in a bad interaction. I understand that hippo kill more people than do any other animal in Africa.

As we drove along the woods road, we viewed the usual menagerie of African animals: giraffes, zebras, impalas, wildebeests, hartebeests, even sables and elands. The warthog population had made a major comeback and was very much in evidence.

Shortly after we got into the hills, we saw three lionesses. One of them had a recent, but well-healed, scar on her back near the tail, but the wound did not appear to interfere with her movement. The lions rested approximately forty yards from the truck, as lithe and graceful as always. They are beautiful animals. After spotting us, they slowly walked off.

About a mile farther on, we crossed the tracks where two buffalo bulls had walked several hours before sunrise. The time had come to go to work. As is his custom before "taking up" a trail, Makanyanga opened his snuff container and partook liberally of the contents. "Snuff helps me see," he indicated in Swahili. Maybe for him . . . the only response I get from snuff is a headache and a runny nose. This ritual carried out by both Makanyanga and Singi began a very impressive show.

The trail made by these buffalo as they fed crossed several hills and intervening valleys. They had stopped briefly at a water hole. (There was plenty of water remaining in the streams and low places; consequently, the buffalo had not yet migrated to the river.) Makanyanga showed me the tracks made by a herd of *punda* (zebras) being chased by lions earlier that morning. This commotion had all but obliterated the buffalo sign, but the trackers found it again after a careful search. We continued on. Makanyanga used the rifle support sticks to point out the buffalo's trail to me. Singi did the same with a machete. Joseph took an active role and on several occasions helped keep us on the right path. After about three hours and several miles, Makanyanga showed me a puddle of urine that had not completely soaked into the ground. We were getting quite close.

About ten minutes later, we spotted two dark shapes in a wooded valley about a hundred yards ahead. We retraced our steps and approached from a different direction to keep the wind from blowing our scent toward the buffalo. After about ten minutes of walking and crawling, we arrived approximately sixty yards from our quarry. Both buffalo were lying down and quietly resting, totally oblivious of us. The larger one was facing in our direction, his body at a forty-five-degree angle.

I had briefly seen the buffalo but had not been able to judge the size of his horns. On the other hand, I'd made up my mind that, unless he was young enough to have "milk on his lips," I would take a shot. I felt the unbelievable tracking I had witnessed must have a climactic ending. Joey got a good look at the horns and indicated with his fingers that *mbogo* had a wide boss and what I interpreted as only a thirty-inch spread. Well, what the hell! So his horns were narrow. So what? Makanyanga planted the sticks, and I stepped into position to shoot. When I finally got a good look at the bull, I realized that I had clearly misinterpreted Joey's sign language. He was an old bull with a hard boss, and the horn width was at least thirty-eight-plus inches.

The bull was lying down, but his shoulder was distinctly visible, allowing me to aim at the "vital triangle." He jumped up at the report of the rifle, ran a few steps, and fell. I shot again, followed by Joey. The bull struggled to his feet, but fell again, this time into a shallow ravine. *Mbogo* was unable to rise. He emitted a soft bellow and died. The other bull hastily ran off. Makanyanga gave his usual high-pitched victory warble.

Singi went back to get the truck while we took the usual pictures. On examining the buffalo, we found a number of fresh but well-healed scars made by lions on his buttocks and left side. Perhaps the scarred lioness we saw earlier had made these wounds. If so, score that encounter *mbogo* one, *simba* zero. Since I wanted only a skull mount, dressing the animal proceeded rapidly, and we had the buffalo loaded on the truck within a very few minutes. (I noticed that Makanyanga cut a fairly large piece of skin from the back. At the time, I thought little about his action.)

Killing a buffalo on the first day presented a major problem, for I had only two buffaloes on the license. If I killed another, we would immediately be degraded to a game-viewing safari. This being the case, with eight more days to hunt, we weighed the options. I decided that unless the biggest *mbogo* in Africa jumped out at us, we would hunt, but not shoot, for at least the next six days. We didn't convey this information to Makanyanga. If we had, his response probably would have been, "Well, why don't we stay in camp for six days and then go hunting?" Makanyanga expects his stalks to culminate in a dead buffalo!

For the next two days, we decided to hunt farther back in the hills where little burning had taken place. I soon discovered that Joseph was another adept pyromaniac, almost as talented as Makanyanga. Wherever we drove, we were followed by a conflagration!

At least two interesting episodes resulted from their desire to burn all the grass in sight. While traversing some long grass that was easily set ablaze, we discovered that a large fallen tree had blocked the road. This meant we had to make a quick detour and cross a gully with the fire right behind and gaining on us. The heat from the blaze became intense, and I began to have my doubts as to whether we would make it. We did, and I seemed to be the only member of the group concerned. After we got out of harm's way,

The author with the first Cape buffalo, tracked for three hours by

Makanyanga and Singi.

Makanyanga and Singi went back, gathered some wood, and started a fire around the obstructing tree. Two days later when we drove along the same road, we found that the tree, reduced to a few gray ashes, no longer blocked the road.

The second fire-related incident occurred while we were following four old bulls through some rather thick long grass. Tracking was very difficult, and Makanyanga muttered that he was having a hard time. Joey misinterpreted the whispered Swahili. Joey, concluding that Makanyanga had given up, asked Joseph to "light things up." When Joseph complied, Makanyanga became agitated. For damn sure he hadn't lost the track! In any case, we had to abandon our search and skip out quickly before we became toast.

On the third or fourth day, we followed a small herd of buffaloes for several hours and found them resting at the top of a wooded hill. They soon discovered us and moved off fairly rapidly. We climbed to the top of the hill and saw the bulk of the herd running away. We had walked halfway down the hill, when suddenly about ten buffaloes, several impressive bulls among them, ambled into the open on the next hill, about eighty yards from us. They fed, totally unaware of our presence. One *mbogo* with a wide boss, down-sweeping horns, and a spread of forty-plus inches would have been an outstanding trophy—clearly the best I had seen in the Selous. Makanyanga was unhappy with Bwana Babu's decision to let this *mbogo* escape. We sat, took some pictures, and watched the buffalo until they ambled off. Makanyanga smiled, shrugged his shoulders, and seemed to forgive me.

The next morning, we drove Joseph to a nearby railroad train station where a voting booth had been set up. I didn't learn the particulars of this national election, but Joseph seemed to be thoroughly indoctrinated into the benefits of a democratic process. I hope the Tanzanians learn that, in spite of major drawbacks, an enlightened democracy is head and shoulders above any other mechanism of government.

After voting was concluded, we decided to visit our previous year's campsite and hunt in the nearby *mbuga* and long grass. I was especially keen about this plan since a number of elephants frequented this region. The old campsite had completely grown up with vegetation and was almost unrecognizable. (The Tanzanian government has a mandatory rule: When a campsite is abandoned, all evidence of the previous use must be destroyed.) I counted eleven hippos in the pool close to where my tent had been pitched.

We did see elephants—in fact, a number of elephants. One bull appeared to be of trophy size. (Tanzanian rules require that a shootable bull must have at least one tusk weighing twenty kilograms or be one-and-a-half-meters long.) The ivory on this old bull, a typical small-bodied Selous elephant, was long but narrow. He was asleep under an acacia tree. We drove reasonably close and took a few pictures.

The area was teeming with buffalo. We followed one fairly large herd into the long grass. To locate the buffalo, Singi decided to climb a nearby sapling about four inches in diameter. Up he went. However, as he got a few feet off the ground, the tree bent. The farther Singi climbed, the more the tree leaned over. When he reached the top, he was only four feet off the ground, about where he started. Needless to say, he could not observe the buffalo from this perch. The expression in his eyes when he realized what had happened was priceless. I laughed so hard I nearly made myself sick.

We continued our stalk, walking slowly in the long grass. All of a sudden, a few feet away, we heard a grunt on our right, a grunt on our left, and a grunt in front of us. We had walked right into the middle of the herd! I could see nothing but grass. This situation is guaranteed to raise the anxiety level to the maximum. The buffaloes suddenly became aware of our presence and noisily ran off in several directions, which luckily didn't include directly over us.

Later on we found the same herd, approximately one hundred fifty strong, peacefully grazing in an open area. Suddenly they became motionless, the closest gazing at us with the usual malevolent stare, but we didn't spot a trophy-size bull. We carefully exited, quite happy to withdraw and leave them in peace.

We did take several other animals during the next few days. I shot a large-bodied warthog with excellent tusks, a bigger animal than the one I had killed the previous year, but his tusks were not as long. Joseph asked me to shoot an impala for camp meat and I complied. Joey indicated that he wanted a wildebeest skin rug, and we secured a reasonable bull for him.

I caught two butterflies to add to my collection. I captured one of these while it was flying, making an especially good action with the net. (No one but me seemed impressed with my dazzling performance. There really is no respect for real talent.)

On my previous safari, Makanyanga had indicated that my khaki clothes were really too white and might scare the game. I didn't tell him, but when I left the United States my clothes were dark khaki. Two to three washings with lye soap bleached them to a much lighter color. I wore dark green, which didn't bleach so readily, for the current safari. However, I did wear a light-colored khaki cap. Singi also had a similar-colored cap. I noticed that when we were making a final approach to the game, he always took his cap off to be sure the light color didn't attract attention. I hated to tell Singi, but this action created a significant problem. Singi is as bald as a billiard ball, and his scalp reflects sunlight nearly as effectively as a mirror. So, what he was doing was trading his white headgear for a shiny dome. I'm not sure which was the least obvious.

With three more days to go, we returned to hunting in the hills. I noticed Makanyanga doing something that at the time seemed bizarre. He found some fresh buffalo dung at a water hole. He retrieved a black object wrapped in plastic sheeting from the truck and proceeded to gather up the dung and cover the object completely, resealing the plastic cover. What the hell was he doing?

The next day, we saw a fairly large herd of buffaloes on the road. While we were trying to size up the bulls, the wind shifted and they hustled off. We elected not to follow. An hour or so later, we saw that a large herd had crossed the road within the previous few minutes, so we took up their trail. We walked for no more than a half-mile, and there they were! Approximately seventy-five buffalo milled around in a fairly open area on the side of the hill. We crept to within about eighty yards when Joey and Makanyanga spotted a very impressive trophy bull. A large area on his shoulder was covered by white mud, so it was quite easy for me to locate the right *mbogo*. I rested the rifle on the sticks, positioning myself to take an unobstructed sideways shot at the "vital triangle" near the shoulder.

At the report of the rifle, the bull jumped vertically, signifying a hit either in the heart or the lungs. The herd did not run off, but continued to mill around. The buffalo remained on his feet. With its head down, he appeared quite "sick." He turned and faced away from us. The previous shot had been with a soft bullet. This time I shot with a solid. He lurched forward but still stayed on his feet. The herd walked off, he with them. It was impossible to shoot again because of the interposed buffalo.

We ran to where he had stood and found a considerable amount of frothy blood. The bullet had undoubtedly penetrated at least one lung; Makanyanga was quite certain that *mbogo* would remain nearby. The herd moved into the thick long grass. Our search proved fruitless, so with night coming on we prudently gave up the chase.

Very early the next morning we arrived back at the area, expecting to find the bull close-by. The herd had left during the night, and our initial search revealed nothing. Makanyanga and Joseph suggested that we burn some of the low-lying long grass, suspecting that the bull was in the vicinity but hidden in the grass. They proceeded to set fire to the area as we traversed the place back and forth. No luck. After a couple of hours, I was becoming despondent. Severely wounding and losing any animal, but especially a Cape buffalo, is a very demoralizing occurrence.

We continued searching along the side of a hill. On the other side of the hill an elephant began trumpeting and generally raising hell. I'm not sure what had made *tembo* mad. Perhaps he didn't like the smoke from the fire. At any rate, he continued to serenade us. By this time I was beginning to get dehydrated. Joey and I stopped for a drink of water while Makanyanga, Singi, and Joseph walked on ahead around the hill. After a few minutes they came running back toward us at top speed. Joey and I grabbed our rifles, expecting to be forced to deal with an irate pachyderm, but this was not the case. Makanyanga signaled to bring the sticks, and we ran toward the trackers. As we rounded the hill, we saw two buffaloes. One was the wounded bull, and the other was a cow. I completely

Singi, the author, and Makanyanga with the second Cape buffalo. This mbogo*, severely wounded the previous day, was still standing when found.*

forgot about the nearby elephant, and I guess he forgot about us. We heard no more from him.

Still standing, the wounded bull was partially obscured by the smoke. We were able to crawl undetected to within about fifty yards. After two quick shots, *mbogo* fell and lay still. The cow ran off. Our daylong anxious search ended successfully, and my spirits went from moderate depression to a high level of elation. How could anyone ask for a better hunt? This old *mbogo* had a very impressive boss and a beautiful, wide set of horns that swept backward. He was an outstanding trophy.

We returned to camp, and although I was delighted with every aspect of this safari, I found myself already going through my standard withdrawal. This would undoubtedly be my last buffalo hunt.

The next morning I was in for a real surprise! As I packed to leave, Makanyanga appeared and gave me a Wakamba elephant hunter's bow, two arrows, and a quiver made from buffalo hide. (Both Makanyanga and Singi are members of the Wakamba tribe, Kenyan elephant hunters from time immemorial.)

I was completely flabbergasted, and, I must admit, I became very "teary eyed." Joey said that Makanyanga had never before given anyone anything. Joey had been trying to get a pair of sandals made from an old rubber tire from him for a couple of years, but to no avail. Why had he chosen Bwana Babu?

At the beginning of the safari, about two weeks before I arrived, Makanyanga told Joey that he was going to make something for Bwana Babu. He had Joey stop the truck while he and Singi cut down a *miombo* tree approximately six inches in diameter. For the next three weeks, he spent each night shaping the bow and drying it over a fire. Makanyanga found the carcass of a giraffe killed by lions, retrieved the tendons, and used them to weave the bowstring. He carved the arrows from the same tree and fletched them with bird feathers. He forged the arrow points using a charcoal fire to heat a piece of iron, and lashed these metal arrowheads, about six inches long, to the wood with the giraffe tendon. Makanyanga constructed the quiver out of the piece of buffalo hide cut from my initial buffalo and sewed it together with buffalo sinew. (The quiver was the black object that I had seen him cover with buffalo dung two to three days before. I'm not sure what the dung did. I'm assuming it has some role in curing rawhide.) I am now the proud owner of equipment used by Wakamba elephant hunters to kill elephant. The only thing missing is the poison!

The standard approach used by the Wakamba elephant hunters, and Makanyanga in his earlier days, was to stalk an elephant until they were within a few feet and shoot a poisoned arrow into the underbelly. They would track the elephant until it died, which might take many hours. The meat and ivory would be harvested for food and barter.

Preparing to board the airplane for the return flight to Dar es Salaam, the author is holding tightly to the newly acquired bow.

Talk about guts and woodcraft! We're impressed by the danger involved when using a high-powered rifle to kill an elephant. In reasonably practiced hands, a suitable rifle can stop an elephant in its tracks. On the other hand, the Wakamba hunter has no such armament. If located by the wounded elephant (that has at least several hours to live before the poison does its work), the Wakamba man would be reduced to unrecognizable component parts.

For the trip home I packed the arrows and quiver with the rest of my luggage. Scott found a six-inch piece of PVC pipe for the bow, which we sealed carefully at each end. When I arrived at the Atlanta airport, the bow was nowhere in sight. I was completely despondent. I was told that I would need to report the loss at the Raleigh-Durham airport. At the lost baggage claim office, while I was filling out the paperwork regarding the lost bow, the agent spotted the container on the luggage carousel. Apparently it had been placed on the plane without going through Customs. I didn't ask questions, but grabbed the bow and left the airport.

In retrospect, this was by far the best buffalo hunt of them all. How could it be better? The only thing that marred the event was the realization that Makanyanga, Singi, and I have hunted together for the last time.

Or have we?

Mbogo's Trail

Two hours after sunrise
On a sunlit African morn,
They found where old *mbogo*
Had walked and fed 'fore dawn.

Makanyanga and Singi,
The pride of the Wakamba clan,
They've tracked *mbogo* for two score years—
As true as any man.

They "took up" the trail *mbogo* made
On hard and rocky ground.
Through long grass and by riverbed
We followed—not making a sound.

He crossed where a herd of *punda*
Had run from *simba* that day.
Mbogo's sign was all but gone,
But on his trail they did stay.

He walked fast, he ambled slow.
But his tracks were read like a book.
For three long hours they followed
Every turn and twist he took.

Most trackers I've seen would quickly lose
So twisted and faint a trail.
But Makanyanga and Singi—
I knew they wouldn't fail.

Then, just ahead a large black shape
Loomed silently close to a tree.
A few seconds later, *mbogo* fell:
Final victory for Mak and Singi.

I'll scarce remember *mbogo*'s death,
Or the shot that brought his end.
But I'll never forget that tortured trail
Unraveled by these Wakamba men.

Botswana Elephants, The Meeting

Chapter IX

Although it clearly was the most memorable event of my career hunting dangerous game, I felt markedly ambivalent about my successful elephant hunt in Timbavati, South Africa, in 1997. My emotions ran the gamut between elation and sadness. At the time, I'd made up my mind that killing one elephant was enough of an emotional drain for one lifetime. However, during each of my subsequent trips to Tanzania, I specifically sought out elephants and became more than a little excited by each encounter. I had yet to decide if I wanted to hunt elephant again.

This issue came to a head in the spring of 2000 when Alex Walker called Joey to ask if I would be interested in hunting elephant in Botswana. Alex had been contacted by Mike Murphy, a professional hunter with Johan Calitz Safaris. He indicated that they had opened a new area near the Moremi Game Reserve that would be available in May 2001. Alex told Joey that, if I was interested, he was certain that Makanyanga would come as our tracker. One added and, in fact, important, positive feature was that the cost was markedly less than hunting elephant in Tanzania.

The success rate on bull elephant the previous year for Johan Calitz Safaris in Botswana had been extremely high. The average tusk weight was greater than fifty pounds. I weighed all of the positive and negative features. With a certain degree of reluctance, I told Alex to go ahead and make the arrangements.

The author, Makanyanga, and Joey standing near the marker designating Chobe National Park, which borders the hunting area.

I'm still not sure why I had a change of heart. I felt as if an irresistible force was drawing me on. *Loxodonta africana* and Bwana Babu must meet again. Once the decision was made, I had no regrets and eagerly looked forward to the experience. As with any safari, half of the fun is in the detailed planning.

The government quota allowed us to kill two elephants. Richard Stack, who had hunted with me in Rungwa and wanted to continue his quest for the "Big Five," agreed to go. This meant the safari would not be finished if we found a trophy bull in the first few days. As events turned out, this was a lucky happenstance. Although theoretically he could function only as an observer, Joey eagerly agreed to join the expedition.

The first order of business was to decide on the arms. My Holland & Holland double rifle was still out of commission. I had the .465 rebored to a .470, but the bent barrels caused it to shoot markedly to the left. Dietrich Apel had retired, but Mark Cromwell (New England Custom Gun Service) assured me that he would fix the problem. Fix it he did! (Mark told me that the temperature at the rifle range was nearly zero degrees. The rifle had to be fired so many times that his shoulder was black and blue for several weeks. That's my definition of a dedicated gunsmith.)

I was becoming concerned when I received the rifle only four weeks before the safari began. I needn't have worried. It was quite accurate and reasonably well regulated with Federal ammunition (500-grain Woodleigh solids) at eighty yards. (Although the velocity is about the same and the bullet weight only twenty grains more, the recoil is noticeably more with a .470 than with a .465. I have no idea why.) For a backup rifle, if needed, Joey brought his .470 Krieghoff double rifle.

Richard purchased a vintage .465 Holland & Holland Royal double rifle and used the ammunition that had been handloaded for my first hunt in the Selous. He had obtained ammunition from Kynamco Ltd., but a similar problem occurred as I had experienced. After firing, the empty shells could not be readily ejected. Richard brought his .470 Krieghoff as a backup. With four double rifles and ammunition, we were ready to go!

The elephant permit situation in Botswana is such that a CITES import certificate is not required. Since the outfitter obtains an export certificate, there is no reason to worry about getting the tusks through Customs. After my previous experience getting ivory home, I was delighted.

I had been immunized against most of the diseases Africa has to offer, so I did not have to have any further shots. I began taking an antimalarial, Lariam, a week before departure. As usual, I began to have vivid dreams at this juncture. In my recurrent dream, we found an old bull with one very large tusk, the other broken off about halfway, guarded by an aggressive young bull (askari). I killed the old bull but was chased away by the askari for the rest of the day. On one occasion, we nearly got into serious trouble. The dreams were so vivid that I began to wonder if they foretold the future.

The daily weather reports for Maun, Botswana, indicated that the temperatures ranged from fifty to eighty-eight degrees with only occasional showers. I outfitted my wardrobe accordingly. While I completed packing (including the butterfly net), I developed an intense feeling that I was being drawn to a rendezvous.

A large bull elephant taking a noon siesta near the Moremi Game Reserve. Note the tree damage.

Richard and I met Joey in Atlanta, and we flew together via South African Airways to Johannesburg (eighteen hours). Praise be! All the luggage arrived. After I secured a supply of Castro's best cigars, we spent the night in a newly finished hotel across the street from the airport. The next morning, quite refreshed, we flew via Air Botswana to Maun, the only hitch being an overzealous agent who charged us for one hundred kilos of excess baggage, actually more than the total weight of our baggage. It was either pay, or don't fly. Other than this annoying inconvenience, everything went as clockwork.

After clearing Customs, we were met by Danny Leibenberg, one of the senior professional hunters for Johan Calitz Safaris. The original plan had been for us to fly via helicopter to the camp, but the helicopter was not available. We rode with Danny instead, which was a lucky break. We saved a lot of money and got to see the country. Danny, who was very knowledgeable, filled us in on a number of details regarding the upcoming hunt.

Our hunt was to be in an area east of the border between the Moremi Game Reserve and the Chobe National Park where a number of trophy bull elephants had been spotted recently. We were the second party to hunt this season, and the previous hunter had taken a fifty-six-pound bull. Johan Calitz Safaris had a quota of forty-nine elephants for the year, but only thirty-three buffalo and no lion. (Lion hunting was closed for the season, apparently due to overhunting by the local tribes.) Even when there was an open season, the company had only nine lions on its quota, along with fifteen leopards. The number of plains game available is also significantly restricted. This entire safari industry is built around elephant hunting.

The drive was approximately three hours. When nearing camp, we saw several bull elephants feeding near the road. We stopped to look, but they paid us no attention. This scene, highlighted by a deep blue sky and the ever-present call of African doves, made it abundantly clear that I was home again.

Alex and Makanyanga, who had driven from Kenya several days before, met us at the camp. Alex had suffered a severe case of malaria

Spoils from the successful robbing of a beehive.

An elated Richard Stack, his "first-day elephant," and the author.

requiring intensive-care hospitalization the preceding fall. He had recovered, but was not as robust as usual. Makanyanga had lost some weight but appeared as spry as ever, if not more so. (I could kick myself for not mastering enough Swahili so that I could actually communicate with him.) Alex told us that he and Makanyanga had seen two large elephants with impressive ivory the day before. Makanyanga assured Alex that I would kill the largest. We'll have to see what comes true, my dream or Makanyanga's prediction.

Approximately thirty members of the local tribe who had been hired to work in the camp greeted us by singing and dancing. In Botswana, the local inhabitants have a strong voice in deciding the recipient of the hunting concession, so the safari company actively courts their favor with jobs, clothing, and meat, to name a few perks.

I was surprised to note that about half of the camp staff members were women. On my previous safaris, the staff was exclusively male. Undoubtedly, enough problems arise during a safari without the additional issues relating to "he-ing and she-ing."

The camp manager and his wife, Chris and Monica Coetzer, showed us around. Everything was first-rate. My tent had hot water, electricity, and a flush toilet. (As opposed to Tanzania, where the campsite has to be torn down and reconstructed each year, Botswana allows the camp to be permanent, so it can be continually improved.)

Danny introduced us to his two trackers, Two Boys and Mabury, who had extensive experience hunting elephant in this region. Two Boys, of Bushman origin, was rated the best of the local trackers.

After unpacking, we got into Alex's Toyota Land Cruiser about 5 P.M. The actual hunting began the next day, but we checked out the rifles and rode around to view the game. The landscape is nearly flat and quite sandy, with much of it covered by brush approximately five feet high. The rest is fairly thick scrub forest, primarily mopane. A number of depressions (pans) still contained water. Wildlife in all varieties (mammalian, avian, and reptilian) from predator to prey was very much in evidence. There were no mosquitoes or tsetse flies to be tolerated, which was a major blessing. In fact, I had the impression that we had entered a hunter's paradise.

Just before sundown, Makanyanga signaled to stop. He pointed to a gray object about eighty yards off, almost obscured by a bush. Everyone, including the Bushman trackers, concluded it was an anthill . . . until it moved. A very impressive Cape buffalo bull walked around a bush and glared at us. Makanyanga can still see pretty damn well!

That night we began the evening ritual: a campfire, a sundowner (cheap white wine for me), and a good cigar followed by an outstanding meal—all the while being serenaded by the night sounds of Africa and gazing at the Southern Cross. The group discussed a wide variety of topics as the evening progressed, but the talk invariably came back to experiences while hunting.

Alex, who is usually quite reserved regarding his own exploits, related to us a recent encounter with a wounded Cape buffalo in Tanzania. Although the client's bullet had entered the chest cavity, *mbogo* left the environs as though unhurt. They followed the tracks and got within shooting distance on several occasions, but the crafty

The author and Makanyanga proudly display a spurwing goose acquired with the double rifle.

bull eluded them and ran off each time. Approximately four hours later, the bull went into a small (approximately fifty by seventy-five yards), thick reed bed.

Leaving the client and tracker on the outside, Alex entered the thicket, expecting the bull to run again and exit on the far side, allowing the client an open shot. *Mbogo* thought otherwise. When Alex first saw him, the bull was fifteen yards away and charging full tilt. Alex's shot entered the skull a hair's breadth below the brain. *Mbogo* didn't slow down. The next shot, taken as the bull lowered his head, entered the neck but missed the spine. Luckily, the impact of the bullet turned the bull enough so that instead of being hooked by the horns Alex was struck a glancing blow below his knee. Knocked head over heels and landing flat on the ground, Alex held onto the now-empty double rifle. Alex could not see the buffalo because his back was toward him, but he heard the sound of heavy breathing close-by. Alex's only recourse was to play dead and pray, hoping *mbogo*, by now on his last legs, would not attack before his strength gave out.

How long this impasse continued is conjectural, but for Alex it seemed like hours. The tracker finally spotted the bull, and the client shot and hit the heart. The buffalo fell, finally giving up the ghost about three feet from Alex's back. Severely bruised but intact, Alex felt the overwhelming need for a very stiff drink. That episode, coupled with a serious bout of malaria, made Alex's preceding hunting season a hazardous one. African professional hunters are clearly a special breed!

Before going to bed that night, Alex told us that he had not seen any elephants until midmorning, so an early start was not warranted. About 8:30 A.M. we climbed aboard the Land Cruiser. Alex did not have a Botswana professional hunter's license, so Danny and his trackers also accompanied us. We had no shortage of elephant hunting expertise with us.

Shortly after leaving camp, Makanyanga became very agitated, a response that only sighting a black mamba can elicit. Willing to share the environs with the serpent, we left it alone.

About two hours had elapsed when we spotted a large bull elephant feeding approximately six hundred yards from the road.

Small tusks, found near a pan, being carried by the trackers—reminiscent of earlier scenes from the quest for "white gold."

The long right tusk warranted a closer examination. (Richard and I had previously agreed that he would have the first choice.) We walked to within one hundred fifty yards; the bull remained completely unaware of our presence. Richard decided. He wanted this one!

Richard, Makanyanga, Alex, and Joey eased up into shooting range, with the elephant still feeding peacefully. Richard made an excellent shot into the lung. Joey also fired a backup shot. The bull, carrying very impressive ivory, ran approximately fifty yards before Alex anchored him with a shot to the spine. It was all over. A prodigious amount of blood poured from the trunk, making me revise the old saying "bleeding like a stuck pig" into "bleeding like a lung-shot elephant." An elated Richard could not believe his good luck. From my vantage point, I felt that it was so damn easy that it marred the experience.

We took several rolls of film while waiting for the arrival of the crew to deal with the aftermath. The large amount of blood attracted a number of butterflies, and I busied myself augmenting my collection.

The sky became overcast, and soon the rain fell. As I gazed at the dead tusker, I had the same ambivalent feelings that I had experienced before. My sadness was reinforced when I heard the camp manager's four-year-old daughter say, "An elephant died and God is crying."

There were no vultures in sight. I didn't realize it, but they don't fly in rainy weather, apparently due to a lack of updrafts which they depend on to soar. We remained at the elephant until the majority of the butchering was completed, then went back to camp and celebrated the event. That night, I had the same very vivid dream about the broken-tusk bull.

Danny decided to hunt an area that had contained a number of bull elephants the preceding year but had not been hunted so far this year. We drove along the cut line between the Moremi Game Reserve and the hunting area for about twenty miles before moving into a heavily forested area. The middle of the woods contained an open plain with a number of water holes. We hunted this section for the next four days, primarily from the truck, but on several occasions we followed recently made tracks on foot. We did not find a trophy bull. There were several separate herds of cows and calves containing young bulls, but the only large bull we saw had broken tusks. For nearly an hour, we watched one herd shaking camelthorn trees to feed on the pods. Trees damaged by feeding elephants were everywhere, but only a few areas appeared really devastated.

One day during lunch, we spotted a beehive. The trackers devised a ladder, smoked out the bees, and came away with a large tub full of honey. Each of them got stung several times, but it didn't seem to bother them particularly. At one pan we found the skull of an elephant that had died approximately a year before. The small tusks of approximately fifteen pounds each were still intact. The ivory was covered with mud and water so it had not deteriorated. We extracted the tusks and marked them to give to the government. The fact that these tusks had not been removed is clear evidence that, at least in this area, the poaching of elephants is not a problem.

One of the open grasslands where we hunted contained a number of small pans frequented by spurwing geese. Two Boys indicated that their larder was depleted and a spurwing goose would be a welcome addition. Joey quickly volunteered. We stopped the Land Cruiser approximately eighty yards from a small gaggle. Joey took careful aim with the Krieghoff double rifle. *Blam*. The geese flew off. A few miles farther on, he repeated this lackluster performance; in fact, a somewhat disgusted Joey emptied the second barrel at the departing geese, again to no avail. At the next water hole, I thought to myself, here is an opportunity to be a real hero. Without hesitation, I preempted Joey and grabbed the Holland. *Blam*. Two geese fell over, dead as a hammer, and were quickly retrieved by the elated Mabury and Two Boys. I nonchalantly indicated to them that if they needed any more geese, just let me know. So what if it was a lucky shot! Why not capitalize on the results? Joey was somewhat less than his normal ebullient self for the next hour or so. It took a monumental effort, but I refrained from making any smart-ass remarks.

We did see a variety of other game, including eland, roan, kudu, zebra, impala, giraffe, gemsbok, and ostrich. Also, a number of really impressive Cape buffalo stared at us—several with a horn spread in excess of forty inches—but they appeared not to be particularly concerned by our presence.

On the sixth day, Danny elected to try another area that was more open and closer to the camp. Late that evening we saw four large bulls; one seemed to have heavy ivory. We walked to within one hundred yards, and the experts all "allowed as how" the tusks would weigh between fifty and sixty pounds. This clearly wasn't the one-tusk elephant of my dreams, or the bull that Makanyanga had seen. Danny, whose judgment I had learned to really respect, made a very interesting comment. "When we find the right elephant, you will know it. There won't be any discussion regarding the tusk size or anything else. We'll just figure out how to approach the bull for a killing shot." This elephant did not elicit such a feeling, so we withdrew.

While driving back to camp, we saw a young bull elephant that seemed somewhat agitated. After screaming at us, he walked off toward the setting sun. I noted that he was close to the remains of

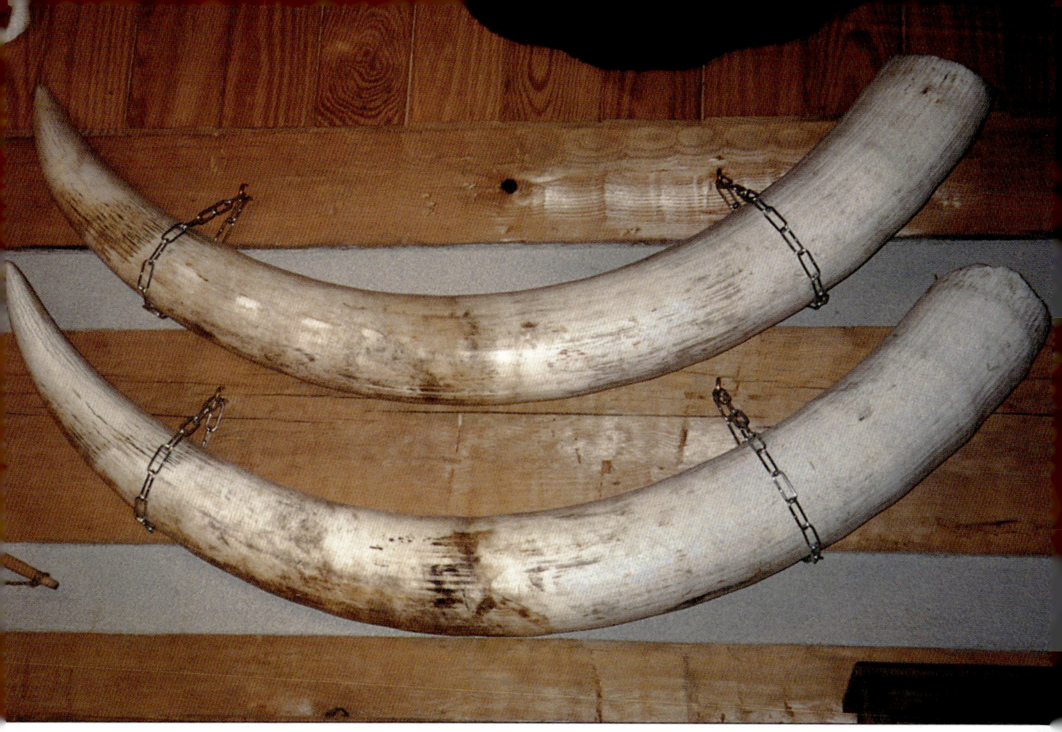

Short, heavy tusks from "The Meeting" in Botswana.

Richard's elephant. Perhaps he trumpeted to let us know that he disapproved of the fate that befell one of his compatriots.

A nearby hyena's chatter woke me the next morning. I had the distinct premonition that my quest would end today.

We hunted through some thick mopane into an open area and saw where two large bulls had crossed earlier that morning. We followed their tracks for about two miles in the truck when we saw both elephants feeding about eight hundred yards in front of us. The first bull had reasonable ivory. When the second turned in our direction, we could see the right tusk. My quest had been answered. The ivory was very thick with little taper and protruded better than three feet from the lip. No question about it, this *tembo* and I were scheduled to meet. I scrambled from the truck—avoiding a puff adder that had just been run over—and tried, unsuccessfully, to be calm.

The wind blowing toward us made the approach quite simple. The feeding elephants were moving slowly. Even with my short legs, we got within range in a very few minutes. The bull we were after was approximately fifty yards away facing to my left, the other perhaps one hundred fifty yards in front.

"The Meeting"

Makanyanga planted the shooting sticks. Just as I got ready to shoot, the bull became aware of our presence and whirled, looking directly at us with ears outstretched and trunk up. He did not like what he perceived and decided to leave, turning to his right and affording me an unobstructed heart shot. Following the report of my rifle, the bull lurched forward, quickly regained his footing, and ran. I fired the left barrel and Joey and Alex also shot. After running about one hundred yards, the elephant slowed, began to wobble, and fell. We quickly approached the fallen monarch. I ended the episode with a bullet to his brain. Makanyanga sounded his loud warble of victory and cut off the tail, using my pocketknife. (In the days of commercial ivory hunting, the severed tail proved ownership of a dead elephant.)

As before, pride, elation, and sorrow coursed through my being, but I knew my summons had been completed. As we waited for the crew, my emotions crystallized:

The Meeting

Two patriarchs will come together
On a broad Botswana plain.
Though lives were spent a world apart,
This meeting, the Gods ordained.

One, a feeble human,
To renew his life he came.
The other, a mighty colossus
Who sought no special gain.

Early one mist-filled morn
This destiny became fulfilled.
They walked toward one another.
And then—time stood still.

They met. In that instant of death,
Their essence became entwined.
Now they are one; woven together
In the fabric of eternal time.

Well, Bwana Babu now is part elephant and part man!

The ivory was very thick with only minimal taper, quite symmetrical, and estimated to weigh in excess of sixty pounds. Makanyanga and Alex both indicated that this was the bull they had seen before we arrived and the one Makanyanga had foretold that I would kill. Well, he was right. My dream was wrong. There was no broken-tusk bull, at least not this time.

I had kidded Makanyanga that I planned to use the bow and arrow that he had made me on the previous safari to kill this elephant. Makanyanga showed me where he always shot the poisoned arrow, into the belly just in front of the back leg. Poison delivered to that region is rapidly absorbed, and the elephant will live no more than four hours. It can take considerably longer for the elephant to die if shot in the muscle.

Danny told us the formula they use to estimate the ivory weight for the thick, short tusks of Botswana elephants: The circumference of the tusk at the lip is assumed to be eighteen inches. The length in inches exposed is added to twenty-six. That's the weight. (If the circumference is seventeen inches, subtract 10 percent; if nineteen inches, add 10 percent.) In my elephant's case, its thirty-seven inches would make each tusk weigh approximately sixty-three pounds. (This estimate was four pounds greater than the actual weight.) When the crew arrived, I left. I wanted to remember the elephant as he had been and not as a mass of meat.

Richard elected to go home the next day. I had not had enough and decided to ride into a block where they conducted photographic safaris. About halfway through the day, although I was having a good time catching butterflies and viewing the game, I knew that

Bwana Babu and a happy Makanyanga holding the tail. (Proof of ownership was not really necessary.)

A happy group: Alex, Makanyanga, and Joey posing with a magnificent Botswana tusker.

this safari was over. In retrospect, I should have traveled to the Okavango Delta since it's unlikely I will return. Danny even offered to guide me on a short hunt for sitatunga. However, I couldn't develop any enthusiasm for more hunting, preferring not to dilute my "meeting" with this elephant.

Accordingly, Joey and I changed our reservations. The next day we drove back to Maun, had a good steak dinner, and said good-bye to Danny, Makanyanga, and Alex. I didn't envy their tedious drive back to Kenya. (Alex estimated that the trip would take at least three days.) Our trip from Maun to Durham took much less time.

The flight from Johannesburg to Kennedy Airport in New York was nearly empty, so I stretched out on the four center aisle seats and slept through most of the entire trip. I arrived at the airport in fine shape, retrieved the luggage, and cleared Customs. After thanking Joey for accompanying me, I manhandled the heavy luggage onto a shuttle bus and rode to the appropriate terminal for the final leg of my trip to North Carolina. Then I ran into trouble!

After processing my ticket and not charging me the added cost for a change of reservations, the agent said that I would need to

Botswana elephant skull used as an end table—quite a conversation piece.

take the luggage containing the double rifle to be inspected by the airport personnel. She accompanied me to this area and promptly left. I was on my own. The two luggage handlers spoke a variant of English that, try as I might, I couldn't understand. I had no success communicating verbally, and they had no idea how to deal with the rifle.

Eyeing the rifle and me suspiciously, they called for help. Help arrived in the form of two additional citizens, but they also were not able to deal with the issue. The fact that the luggage did not contain ammunition didn't seem to matter. We were clearly at a stalemate. (I began to understand how a "stranger in a strange land" feels.)

Suddenly I had an inspiration. The rifle case contained a small document that had been issued when the rifle was initially checked on my outgoing trip. I showed this "official looking" paper to the assembled multitude (by then several guards had joined the group). The result was miraculous. Everyone smiled and began nodding in unison. They immediately passed the luggage, containing the rifle, through the checkpoint. It's amazing how a scrap of paper can be lifesaving. I boarded the airplane in the nick of time, arriving in Durham along with all of my luggage, including the rifle.

As promised, in due course the ivory, along with the elephant skull, arrived at my home without any problems. (The lower jaw remained in Botswana to determine the elephant's age.) The beautifully matched tusks now decorate the wall, and the skull functions as an impressive end table. Debbie Peak of Mochaba Developments in Maun arranged to have the ears and a portion of skin tanned in Zimbabwe. The ears were mounted and James Young, an excellent young artist, painted an elephant bull on them, one for me and one for Joey. These scenes are spectacular. The painting, along with the elephant skull and ivory, remind me daily of my outstanding adventure.

Well, I've killed two elephants, certainly not a record. However, since I used two calibers, .465 and .470, in the same rifle, my guess is that not many hunters have had a similar experience. I can truly say that elephant hunting is in a class by itself. Maybe Bwana Babu won't have a repeat performance. But maybe he will.

Kilombero, Long Grass and Buffaloes

Chapter X

I decided to forgo my annual hunting expedition to Africa in 2002 for very logical reasons. The events surrounding the attack on the World Trade Center had led me to have concerns about international travel. Following the precipitous fall in the stock market, the decision to stay at home became quite easy. By late December, however, Africa's "genetic pull" on me became overwhelming. I began to explore the possibilities for 2003.

Two situations coupled together made another trip feasible. First, Bill Richey, Joey's partner in the Indiantown Game Ranch, decided to embark on a month-long trip to hunt the "Big Four." He is a delightful individual, and the opportunity to share this safari with him for part of the time, significantly reducing the cost, was quite attractive.

Michel Mantheakis, co-owner of Miombo Safaris, visited Joey during my January trip to Florida to hunt quail. We worked out a nearly ideal situation for my upcoming hunt. I would share the camp in Kilombero North with Bill Richey for a twelve-day Cape buffalo hunt. (Joey would guide Bill Richey.) This area had recently been acquired by Miombo Safaris and was reported to be teeming with buffalo. My license would allow me to kill three bulls.

When Michel guaranteed that Alex Walker would be my professional hunter, I was ready to go. I not only wanted to hunt with Alex, for whom I have a tremendous amount of respect,

An irate hippopotamus surfaces a dozen feet from our boat. We left posthaste.

but I also wanted to obtain detailed background information on Makanyanga. I planned to write a synopsis of Makanyanga's career, so it was critical for me to obtain this information. Makanyanga would be hunting elephant in Lukwika and would be unavailable. Even with this drawback, the plans seemed to be ideal. I made a decision to sign on. Bwana Babu goes back home. I would be in Africa from 7–21 September, which gave me a lot of time to plan for the safari, a large part of the fun for me.

As always, the first issue is the appropriate armament. My Holland & Holland double rifle had been converted, both inside and out, to a .470. After firing a few rounds for practice and to check on scope alignment, I obtained a generous supply of Federal ammunition, both Woodleigh softs and solids. Everything was in order. The Holland was ready to go.

I needed a backup rifle. Several years ago I had purchased a customized pre-1964 Model 70 Winchester in .375 H & H caliber. This rifle was fitted with a Griffin and Howe quick detachable side mount. I tested the rifle a few times and found that the mount was unreliable: The scope did not return to zero. I had the side

The author and Philippe, the boat captain, start the day's activities.

mount removed and an EAW quick detachable mount installed and fitted with a Swarovski 1.25–4X variable power scope, similar to the one on the double rifle. The rifle was restocked with an original Winchester stock. I shot it a number of times and was quite pleased with the accuracy. Problem solved. Joey agreed to use this rifle as a backup. He carried it along with Federal ammunition (Trophy-Bonded Sledgehammer solids and Bear Claw softs) to Africa in July. I would have a functioning rifle in case I had problems with my luggage—my usual "fail-safe plan."

I went to the Duke Travel Clinic and brought my immunizations up-to-date. I found out that a new antimalarial drug, Malarone, was available. Although it had to be taken daily, the side effects were reported to be minimal, so I would avoid the Lariam-induced nightmares I had suffered. I decided to switch to the new drug, but I made a serious mistake in not testing the side effects of Malarone on myself prior to the trip.

About the first of August, I started an exercise schedule consisting of three-mile walks, three to four times a week. As events turned out, we made extensive use of "shank's mare" during the safari. This walking program proved to be extremely worthwhile.

My travel plans were made without a hitch. Perhaps the best part was that I got a cheap ticket. I would fly from Raleigh-Durham to Detroit to board a KLM flight to Amsterdam and then on to Dar es Salaam. I packed everything in a large two-compartment duffel bag and was ready to go. At the airport there was no problem with transporting the rifle and ammunition, but I was informed that the bag was overweight by approximately ten pounds. The additional charges would be $450! The agent, a very agreeable soul, suggested that I divide the contents into two bags, and, he said, "Everything will be just fine."

Well, I didn't have another large bag. However, I did have a small soft satchel. I quickly transferred ten pounds of ammunition and several other heavy items into it. The satchel couldn't be locked, but I used plastic ties to secure the buckles. I had some concern whether the ammunition would arrive undamaged. I now had two bags instead of one, but I didn't have to pay the overweight fine. As always, I had arranged for a significant layover to be certain that my bags were transferred to the overseas flight. Although long, the trip was quite uneventful, and I slept most of the way. I did purchase a box of Castro's overly expensive cigars in Amsterdam.

Upon arrival in Dar es Salaam, the small satchel with the ammunition arrived in fine shape. The large bag containing the double rifle didn't. It was still in Amsterdam. Well, what the hell! This was entirely in keeping with my previous experiences. In fact, for four trips, using the same airline schedule, my luggage arrived with me only once. Since Joey had brought the Winchester rifle and

I had my carry-on luggage containing the essential accoutrements, including a change of clothes, I didn't get too upset.

Joey and Scott Coles, a co-owner of Miombo Safaris, met me at the airport. Scott graciously suggested that we spend the night at his home, so I avoided buying a very significant stake in Hilton Hotel Enterprises. I also felt much safer not being alone. Bill Richey had been in Dar es Salaam for two days to become acclimated to the six-hour change in time.

We departed for Kilombero early the next morning via a small commuter plane, stopping in the Selous to pick up Alex, who had just finished a safari. I was in for a very agreeable surprise. Alex informed me that Makanyanga would join us as soon as he could get from Lukwika to Kilombero on the bus. This revelation made my day, although it was a very unfortunate event that had made the change of plan possible.

Makanyanga had been the tracker for a twenty-eight-day elephant hunt. On the third or fourth day, they successfully stalked a large bull. The client, an obnoxious German who claimed to be a seasoned elephant hunter, insisted on shooting the animal without backup from the professional hunter. The elephant, a sixty-five pounder, was shot in the belly and, although mortally wounded, escaped. Makanyanga tracked the animal for four days until it crossed the border into Mozambique where they couldn't follow. The "Safari from Hell" was over. The client, in typical fashion, blamed the professional hunter for the mess. Miombo Safaris lost a lot of money. Worst of all, the elephant undoubtedly died a lingering and painful death. As unfortunate as these events were, Makanyanga was "out of work" for three weeks and would join my buffalo hunt. Bwana Babu and Makanyanga would hunt together again!

The flight to Kilombero was uneventful, except for a brief discussion with a very obnoxious trial lawyer at one of the intervening stops. This worthy, who is on a self-proclaimed mission to kill one of every critter in Africa, launched off into a vociferous explanation about the dangers of tort reform. As best I could detect, the primary danger was to his already overstuffed pocketbook. Shakespeare's suggestion, "kill all the lawyers" seemed to be in order.[1] I had a major problem restraining myself from choking him and ending my safari prematurely.

Although a new airstrip was under construction close-by, the one we used required a three-hour drive to the camp. The road left much to be desired. Although heavily traveled, it was far bumpier than the usual woods roads. We drove through two fairly densely populated villages, one of which was on the edge of the hunting concession. Many of the structures were made from locally fired brick. (Small functioning kilns were ubiquitous.) Maize, sugar cane, cassava, and bananas were the primary crops. The roadside was dotted with a number of small stands used to sell vegetables and other items, including smoked fish.

Once we crossed into the hunting block, the road traversed fairly open and recently burned *miombo* forest. Then we descended to a wide flood plain covered with long grass that bordered the Mnyera River. The camp, located on the banks of the river, was quite comfortable. We met the camp staff, unpacked, and settled in. The camp manager exhibited a decided military posture. It turns out that he had been in the Tanzanian armed forces for several years, during which he participated in the ousting of Idi Amin in Uganda. It probably goes without saying, but the camp staff was well trained.

After lunch the whole contingent climbed into a Toyota Land Cruiser. After a brief stop to sight-in the rifles, we drove around for the rest of the day, getting an idea as to the best approach for the upcoming hunt.

The hunting block was divided into two parts by the river. The most logical approach would be that each party hunt on one side of the river. The only drawback to this plan was that there was no way to get a vehicle to the other side of the river, so transportation for one group would be entirely via "shank's mare." In addition, for at least the next few days, there would be only one functioning truck.

[1]Shakespeare, William. *Henry VI* in *The Works of William Shakespeare*. New York: Oxford University Press, 1938.

A large crocodile, one of many, sunning on the riverbank.

Since Bill Richey and Joey were primarily hunting lion and leopard and needed to cover a wide area to collect and place bait, they took the truck and the camp side of the river. Alex and I used the boat and hunted on the far side.

That evening we heard from Scott that my luggage had been found and would be in Dar es Salaam shortly. The plan was for Makanyanga and my luggage to arrive in about two days.

The next morning our party, consisting of Alex, Kijazi, Philippe, and myself boarded the boat. Kijazi, the Tanzanian game scout, had been a champion football player. Philippe, the boat driver, had a thorough knowledge of this river, having worked for a professional crocodile hunter for many years. He was also a reasonably accomplished tracker. The boat, a sixteen-foot aluminum johnboat, was quite stable and was outfitted with a more than adequate outboard motor.

Using a boat to search for productive hunting venues was a new African experience for me. At first I was concerned about becoming seasick (one of my significant weaknesses), but it did not happen. In fact, I thoroughly enjoyed this mode of travel. Cruising upriver for approximately fifteen miles, as far as the rapids, we saw a large number of water birds, including a plethora of fish eagles, a few crocodiles, and an occasional hippopotamus.

Our crew examined areas near the bank in several locations, then disembarked and walked to an open field that had been partially burned. Although much of the dense long grass had been burned, the stubble was approximately four feet high, quite brittle, and difficult to walk in. In addition, the ground was heavily covered with ash, which was easily stirred up by walking and which made breathing difficult. The grass in the unburned area was quite thick and damn near impassable. This type of flat terrain, which stretched for one to two miles from the river, gave way to low hills covered with *miombo* forest.

The primary strategy was to use binoculars to view a large area and to look for the birds that accompany the buffalo herds. These included oxpeckers and cattle egrets, especially the latter, since they are larger and white, thus making them easier to spot. After locating a herd, we first determined the direction they were moving. The objective was to get in front of them in an open area where shooting was possible, and then intercept the herd, if things went as planned.

The other approach was to find fresh tracks and follow them. Using both plans, our party hunted various locations along the river until it became quite hot around 1 P.M. Then everyone went back to the boat, had lunch, napped until about 3 P.M., and began a similar excursion until sundown. I did note that later in the day, as the temperature warmed up, the banks of the river became teeming with crocodiles.

I fared reasonably well, although I had to work very hard not to become dehydrated. The cloud cover was quite variable and at least for the first two days was sufficient to keep the temperature in the low eighties. Our crew saw several herds of buffaloes and made a number of approaches, but none of us came in contact with an old mature bull.

Cloud cover masks the direct rays of the sun and reduces the temperature significantly, if intermittently, but it can be a mixed blessing. Alternating sun and shade invariably sets up a swirling wind due to the irregular cooling. The wind direction may shift frequently, making close approaches to game difficult at best. On several occasions, the fickle wind proved to be our undoing. After long hours of tracking groups of old bulls through both tall grass and *miombo* forest, our entire quest was abruptly terminated by an unstable gust of wind.

As expected, two days later Makanyanga arrived with my luggage, including the double rifle. He'd had a "minor" mishap on the way from Lukwika. The bus he was on turned over completely. Luckily, Makanyanga was not seriously injured. In fact, he looked "fit as a fiddle" and was ready to hunt buffalo.

On the fourth day, Pius arrived with Alex's Land Cruiser, driven by Mdebie. I had hunted with Pius on previous safaris and was very impressed with his abilities. I never saw Pius when he wasn't smiling. Makanyanga and Pius are a superb team of trackers. Mdebie is an excellent driver and "woods mechanic." Our entire contingent was assembled: Makanyanga and Pius as the trackers and a functioning Land Cruiser for our use, if needed.

The hunt continued for a total of five days, confined to the opposite side of the river. Unfortunately, the cloud cover disappeared on the third day, and it became extraordinarily hot. In fact, for two days in a row I suffered from heat exhaustion.

The buffalo-tracking pace was slow enough that I had little trouble keeping up. However, when simply walking, on several occasions I became stressed to my limit and had to stop to rest. Once while I was recuperating, Makanyanga started cutting a small tree. When asked what he was doing, he informed us, "I'm making a walking stick for Bwana Babu." This staff was about five feet long and was forked at the top. Actually, this wand did help me traverse the uneven ground that had been roughened during the rainy season by the tracks of hippos, elephants, and buffaloes. As the ground hardened, it became extremely uneven and difficult to walk on.

The night of the fourth day I felt quite washed out. In fact, I felt as though "I'd been dragged through hell with my back broke." Perhaps I had exerted myself beyond my capacity for the last two days, but I felt that something else was wrong. My mouth tasted like I had eaten a copper pipe. I came to the conclusion that the

A group of fishermen camped on the riverbank drying and smoking their recent catch.

new antimalarial was causing the problem. This put me in a real quandary. Should I stop taking the drug and risk catching malaria or feel miserable for the rest of the safari? It was an easy decision to make. I figured that if I did develop malaria, I could "rest" for a few days in Duke Hospital after the trip was over. My symptoms abated in twenty-four hours. I was "up to snuff" for the rest of the trip. (In case the reader cares to know, I remain malaria-free.)

Each day, buffalo proved to be plentiful, and a number of herds manifested themselves close-by. While waiting for one herd to appear, I spotted a mature, but narrow-horned and wizened bull, sticking his head out of the long grass approximately fifteen feet from me. He looked at me, and I looked at him. Almost simultaneously, both parties decided that it would be best to part company without further interaction. He was too ugly for my taste; perhaps *mbogo* had the same impression of me. Thankfully, the bull disappeared back into the long grass.

Other than this sorry specimen, no mature bull came into contact with us. However, one cow did give us a moment's fright. When her calf walked quite close to us, Mama ran in our direction in a threatening way, but luckily for us, she decided not to pursue the issue. Using her horns, she nudged the calf in a very forceful manner and drove it away into a nearby thicket of long grass.

Although game was not plentiful on our side of the river, there were a few sables, waterbucks, hartebeests, pukus, and bushbucks; no zebras, giraffes, or impalas were to be found, however. Late one evening just as the sun was setting, we came upon a small pond and stopped to admire the view. A bushbuck, judged by Alex to have a record-book set of horns, stepped to the water's edge and began to drink. I easily overcame a momentary desire to shoot him, much preferring not to disturb this tranquil scene. About midmorning one day, our presence disturbed a pride of lions, consisting of seven or eight lionesses and one immature male, taking their noon siestas on an overgrown termite mound. They left the area without incident.

Late one evening, a small herd of elephant cows and calves appeared approximately a mile away. The matriarch got our scent and made threatening gestures in our direction: trunk up, ears extended, and screaming to high heaven. Alex said that the best plan would be to move quickly toward the safety of the boat on the river. He thought that there had been significant poaching of the animals in the area, and as a consequence, the elephants might be quite aggressive. His admonition met with unanimous approval. We quickly got the hell out of there!

During our daily excursions on the river, there were a number of fishermen nearby who were using either nets or fishing poles. The *mtumbwi* (canoes) that they paddled gave the general impression of being quite unstable and ready to disintegrate at any moment. However, the men seemed quite unconcerned about possibly being dumped into the crocodile-infested river. They had constructed several camps on the riverbank where the fish, predominantly tigerfish, were being smoked and dried. Makanyanga obtained several pounds of freshly prepared fish for the equivalent of a dime in U.S. currency. He offered to share with me. The fish was delicious, and luckily I didn't ingest any pathogens along with the meal.

These camps were serviced by men riding bicycles to bring supplies and beer as well as local gossip. On the return trip they

Makanyanga with a handful of smoked tigerfish.

took dried fish back to the villages. This weekly effort required an eight-hour round trip. The fishermen were quite talkative and seemed knowledgeable about the locale of the buffalo, as well as other game.

Once, while cruising up the river, we saw a large and very dead crocodile floating in the water. Philippe said that the cause of death was from it eating a type of fish armed with very sharp fins that perforated the diner's stomach.

Apparently, a tribe of wandering Masai had driven their cows into the lower end of the hunting area to feed on the grass. (Not good news for the indigenous lion population.) It seemed that there was considerable human activity and undoubtedly fairly heavy poaching throughout the game lands. All the game animals that we saw, including the buffalo, were very skittish.

Joey and Bill Richey had a spell of bad luck. A large old male lion began feeding on one of their baits, and Bill had an open shot, about seventy-five yards, from the blind. However, the scope on his rifle had come loose and the bullet went astray. They waited for the next two days, but the lion did not return to the bait. In addition, a large male leopard figured out how to cut the tie-down rope and absconded with another bait. This leopard was not seen again. Joey decided the area was unlucky. They decided to try to attract the pride of lions that we had seen on the opposite side of the river. Thereafter, Joey and Bill hunted on both sides of the river.

On the sixth day of the hunt, Alex made a decision for us to hunt on the camp side of the river in an area Bill and Joey had not previously explored. Our daily boat riding forays came to an end. I was in full agreement with the change of venue, for I was tired as hell from continuous walking and, more importantly, the current plan had not produced significant contact with mature buffalo bulls. Makanyanga was even happier than I with Alex's decision. He is deathly afraid of water because he can't swim. He had hunkered down in the boat, both hands holding onto the seat for dear life.

For the rest of the hunt, we rode in the Land Cruiser looking for evidence of either buffalo or their fresh tracks. The topography of our new venue was similar to the old. In addition to a belt of long grass near the river and low hills covered by *miombo* forest, there were several large lakes containing a number of hippos. Waterbucks and pukus were more numerous, and we saw several large herds of sables. The lead bull in one of these herds carried a very impressive set of horns.

As on my previous excursions to Africa, the standard ritual at the end of the day was to have a hot shower, sit by the campfire, partake of a libation, smoke a good cigar, and solve the problems of the world. This tradition was followed by an excellent meal. On this safari, our cook outdid himself. The menu ranged from broiled lobster and calamari to chicken curry and various exotic recipes for game meat. It was all superb. If I hadn't been too tired to eat most of the time, I would likely have gained ten pounds.

One evening, after drinking too much white wine, I was stumbling toward my tent. Somehow, I managed to get involved with a bunch of army ants crossing the path. The next thing I knew, they were all over me and stinging the hell out of my legs. After a spate of cursing, I tried to deal with the situation myself by mashing the critters, but to no avail. I hurried to Joey and Alex's tent and quickly stripped. Alex thoroughly doused my anatomy with Doom, a concentrated insect poison. The ants quickly gave up the ghost. However, I had been stung at least fifty times. I felt toxic the rest of the night, whether from ants or the insect poison, I know not. (I found out later that the can was clearly labeled, "Avoid Contact With Skin.") No significant aftereffects occurred from either the ants or the insect poison, but I was more careful where I put my feet in the future.

One thing of note was the excellent condition of the roads on the camp side of the river. Impressive bridges constructed from logs spanned a number of the deeper gullies; the roads were even with very few potholes. The difficulty of excavating and maintaining an adequate road is especially impressive when you consider that the work is done exclusively with shovels, machetes, and "elbow grease." Being a member of the road crew is the beginning position for nearly all of the camp staff. If individuals are tough enough to

Makanyanga and the author, "on the sticks," waiting for the herd to appear

through an opening in the long grass

last a season and perform well in this endeavor, then they are trained for other duties in the camp.

We saw plenty of buffaloes, but the dearth of trophy-size mature bulls was concerning. I began to doubt whether I would collect a suitable specimen. On the eighth day we did see three old bulls, which we stalked to within a hundred yards, but the troublesome wind shifted and our quarry quickly left. It was too late in the day to follow them. Other than that, we did not have close contact with shootable bulls. Although we hunted primarily in the long grass, we did cover a significant amount of *miombo* forest.

Two days before my safari was to end, we crossed tracks where a fairly large herd had fed early that morning. Makanyanga and Pius followed these tracks for about three hours while we followed the trackers both on foot and in the truck. About noon, we spotted the buffalo and began our stalk. The buffalo had fed out from the grass into a fairly thick *miombo* forest. We followed the trail for approximately an hour. As we got closer, it was obvious that they had lain down for an afternoon siesta. Well, we did the same. We rested within one hundred yards of the herd for about an hour and one-half. Luckily the wind, which had previously given us a lot of trouble, blew in the right direction, and the herd remained unaware of our presence.

The herd woke up and began to feed toward a more open area. We followed, the last seventy-five yards on our rear ends, emulating a crab. This approach got us to within thirty yards of the nearest cow. The herd was spread out in an open area. Only one old bull was among them. This *mbogo* was very large with reasonably wide horns and a solid boss, but the horns were not as impressive as I had hoped to find. The bull was feeding on the far side of the herd, approximately a hundred yards from where I stood.

Because of the distance, I felt more comfortable using the .375 Winchester. Makanyanga positioned the shooting sticks for me, and I got ready to shoot. Initially, cows and calves surrounded the bull, but it grazed to within eighty yards of us. He turned sideways, his head to my left, presenting an ideal shoulder shot into the "vital triangle." At the report of the rifle, *mbogo* jumped straight up, bringing his back legs forward. This reaction usually indicates the bullet has penetrated the heart-lung area. The bull ran for approximately fifty yards, and, just as Alex fired an "insurance shot," the buffalo keeled over and lay still. I did not hear a death bellow. The rest of the herd did not run off initially, but milled around for about five minutes, and then finally decamped.

Although he appeared to be quite dead, we cautiously approached the bull from his rear. (If the bull tries to get up, this technique places the hunter in the best position to quickly dispatch the animal.) No need to worry, *mbogo* was dead. *Mbogo*'s horns were much more impressive than I originally had estimated, with a wide, solid and well-worn boss. Since I only wanted a skull mount, no additional skinning was required. I hung the rifle on the shooting sticks, breathed a sigh of relief, and savored the moment.

While we rested, one thing of interest occurred. It turns out that Makanyanga had been diagnosed with hypertension two years previously and had been informed by the village "physician" that he should not eat meat. He was allowed to eat only fish, chicken, and various vegetables. For reasons totally unclear to me, testicles were on the acceptable list. Makanyanga began to remove this delicacy from the bull. When I realized what he was doing, I handed him the same pocketknife that he had used previously in Botswana to cut off my elephant's tail, and he quickly removed the testicles with it. I'm not sure if this approach is a recognized technique to prove ownership of a buffalo as with a severed elephant's tail, but I'll bet few others have a pocketknife that has been used to perform both tasks.

Joey would use the majority of the carcass for lion bait. After we secured a portion of the meat for the table, we tied a rope to the carcass and pulled it to the nearest road. There we left it for Joey's crew to cut up and hang. As we prepared to leave the buffalo, I noticed Makanyanga kneeling by the carcass sprinkling a small amount of snuff on it. Alex informed me that this ritual assured that the bait would attract a lion.

Impressive bridge. The "road crew" was excellent.

For the next two days we continued to hunt buffalo as before. We saw one herd containing only a narrow-horned old bull that I chose not to follow. On the last day we rode up and down the river photographing hippos, crocodiles, and a number of the fishermen in their canoes. One hippo gave us a momentary fright. I saw a wake as a hippo ran submerged in the river. He surfaced about a dozen feet from the boat, gave us the "evil eye," and turned in our direction. Philippe immediately turned up the throttle to full, and we rapidly exited the scene, luckily without mishap. The multiple boat excursions were a very positive feature of this safari, for they provided me an opportunity to view a different component of African ecology.

On the day before I left, Makanyanga presented me with a snuff container. He had obtained a palm nut that had traversed the innards of an elephant; thus, the outside was smooth and shiny. He had hollowed it out with his knife, put a piece of bamboo in the neck, and then carved a stopper from wood simulating the hoof of a buffalo. The container was suspended on a piece of rawhide obtained from a puku antelope and suitably cured with buffalo dung. Makanyanga had put in a supply of his own special snuff, tobacco leaves ground by him and mixed with some type of soda ash. Makanyanga is convinced that using this snuff makes him see better.

One of the most important aspects of the trip was the opportunity to spend several hours with Alex and Makanyanga and obtain a detailed description of their adventures. I thought that Alex, who had worked with Makanyanga for almost eighteen years, would be very conversant with his background, but this was not the case. Alex was quite impressed at the amount of new information that we were able to obtain from Makanyanga. This material enabled me to write a detailed description of Makanyanga's life history. (Makanyanga also gave me some new pictures of his family.)

As I was preparing to leave, Pius brought me an audiotape on which he and several of his friends and family had recorded a number of religious songs. The Christian Church in Ngorongoro provided the instruments and recording equipment. The group wrote and recorded these songs with Pius playing a major role. I cannot understand the Swahili words, but I did recognize "hallelujah." From the tunes and their singing, the message is clearly heartfelt.

The night before I left, I had heard lions roaring close-by on the other side of the river where *mbogo* had been placed as bait. (Makanyanga's snuff ritual obviously worked.) These lions serenaded me almost continually for about one hour. One male *simba* was especially vociferous: a loud roar followed by a trio of short, very low-pitched grunting sounds. In fact, he seemed to be singing the *basso profundo* while the ladies carried the melody. I had not been treated to this level of vocal outpourings from lions since my first trip to the Selous. From my standpoint, nothing is more typical of Africa. Their roaring seems to awaken in me all of the latent genetically encoded memories of eons past; it represents a major part of Africa's pull on my being. My only—and it was minor—disappointment was that I did not find any new butterflies; in fact, the butterfly net was essentially unused on this trip.

Mdebie, Pius, Kijazi, the author, Makanyanga, and mbogo. *This hunt is over.*

I said good-bye to Joey and Bill Richey and wished them good luck. The drive back to the airstrip and the flight to Dar es Salaam were uneventful. Scott, Alex, and I feasted on an excellent hamburger at a restaurant overlooking the Indian Ocean. During dinner we had a long discussion regarding the Kilombero concession. Since my plane did not leave until 11 P.M., we had ample time to hash out many of the issues regarding the management of game animals and poaching.

Miombo Safaris had recently obtained a several-year contract to hunt in that area. Scott was concerned about the amount of poaching. Since the area had been unused for professional hunting for a number of years, the poachers essentially had a free rein to ply their trade. Although poaching is clearly illegal, the government has neither the resources nor, in many cases, the interest to police the area effectively.

It is up to the safari company and its professional hunters to protect the game. This fact is poorly understood by nearly everyone not directly related to game management in Africa. It would seem logical that an unhunted area, where professional hunting is disallowed, should be teeming with game. However, the reverse is true. Since the professional hunters must have an abundance of undisturbed game for their livelihood, they develop strategies to curtail poaching. Thus, the paradox is: safari hunting = an abundance of game; no safari hunting = no game.

Scott and Alex described several interesting strategies that are employed to deal with their poaching problem. By far, the most effective way to curtail poaching by the local inhabitants is to identify the best two or three poachers in the local villages. Then, hire them to work. If the money they receive is considerably more than they could make selling biltong (dried meat), they quit poaching. Obviously, these individuals know all there is to know about the game. Usually they are first-class woodsmen and soon learn to be excellent trackers for safari hunting. In addition, they know the identity of the other local poachers and can help develop a plan to either bribe them to quit poaching or have them arrested. This strategy will nearly eliminate poaching by local individuals.

On the other hand, if the poaching is done by organized crews who come into the area from a considerable distance and are after ivory as well as biltong, then the only effective technique is to catch them and have them prosecuted to whatever degree the law will allow. If these poachers are caught at their trade, the government will usually mete out a stiff penalty. The problem is to catch them "red-handed." Luckily, poaching in Kilombero seems to be carried out entirely by local citizens.

An important strategy of game management is determining the current status of the population of game in the area. The government issues a yearly regulation regarding the quota of animals to be taken from a concession, but the inventory is frequently out-of-date. An extreme example of this problem is found in the current official hunting report document used by the game scout. The black rhinoceros still appears as a huntable species, in spite of the fact that it has been completely protected for a number of years and is essentially extinct throughout all but a few parks in Tanzania.

If the population of game is found to be inadequate, it may be necessary to significantly curtail the killing of that particular species. For example, after Miombo Safaris obtained a concession in Rungwa, they protected the pride males and for several years killed fewer lions than the permit allowed. The lions prospered. Now they have an abundant and stable population. This mechanism may need to be employed in Kilombero.

Another extremely important approach is to patrol the area continually and remove the wire snares that are invariably used by poachers to trap game near watering places. These snares are very effective. It is estimated that of the animals caught in snares, only 5 to 10 percent are actually butchered by poachers. The rest experience a horribly slow death and their bodies rot, unused. Even if the animals escape, they commonly sustain serious injuries, such as the loss of a foot, and cannot fend for themselves in the wild. Wire snares pose a major threat to the future existence of African wildlife.

I found our discussions to be extraordinarily interesting and informative. I came away with a markedly enhanced respect for the importance of the safari industry in maintaining a viable population of African game.

The trip from Dar es Salaam to Detroit was long but restful. In Detroit, I watched the carousel go round and round; it became obvious that my luggage was not present. Oh well! On the positive side, that made inspection by Customs quick. The luggage was delivered to me two days later in Durham. Most everything was intact.

This safari, to say the least, was exciting and productive, and I thoroughly enjoyed it. Obviously there are problems with poaching, but I'm sure that the situation will be well in hand within the next year or so. I couldn't ask for a better time; the opportunity to hunt with both Alex and Makanyanga was outstanding. As on previous occasions, I've proclaimed that the current trip was my "last safari." But as events have always turned out, I've been wrong every time. I'll bet I hear *simba*'s message again!

Simba's Message

Suddenly awakened from restful sleep
By roaring that shakes the ground.
Across the river the *simba* clan
Cleaves night with thunderous sound.

Their message is clear to great and small:
"This piece of land is mine."
Together the pride proclaims for all
A warning that's old as time.

Fear and love doth meld as one
While roars fill wood and glade.
Africa's essence is stamped in me
By their awesome serenade.

No sound I've heard before or since
Can hold my being in thrall.
And make me return again and again
Like the magnet of *simba*'s call.

Makanyanga

Chapter XI

Anyone interested in the history of big-game hunting in East Africa during the past century can find a plethora of excellent books that provide a wealth of information. Written by reasonably articulate professional hunters, these books detail a rich and exciting picture of their hunting experiences. The multiple topics covered include descriptions of the lives of these hunters, their clients, the geography of the region, specific aspects of various hunts, and the nature of the various game animals.

The material presented makes it very clear that professional hunters are invariably assisted by a number of outstanding native woodsmen. These individuals function as trackers to find the game and to guide the professional hunters and their clients to an appropriate location to shoot. Their expertise is especially important when hunting dangerous game. On many occasions, the actions of these trackers have saved lives. The exploits and the abilities of these woodsmen are described in detail, but there is a dearth of biographical material on them. In almost every case, the professional hunters are laudatory about their trackers and frequently emphasize that they are forevermore grateful to them. However, descriptions regarding the lives of these trackers, outside of specific hunting adventures, are essentially nonexistent.

The purpose of this chapter is to provide at least a cursory biographical sketch of one of these "living legends." As a tracker, Makanyanga Kilango Mutio is clearly at the top of the list, having hunted big game in a number of African venues for approximately forty years. His exploits have been briefly mentioned in at least three books.[1–3]

Also, he played a role as a tracker in the video production, *In the Blood*.[4] I've had the opportunity to hunt with Makanyanga on four safaris. Although I am a novice big-game hunter, I can certainly attest to his outstanding capabilities, which have been detailed in several of the chapters in this book.

I have relied on the personal observations of Alex Walker and a series of interviews with Makanyanga to provide material for this chapter. Alex, undoubtedly one of the most experienced young professional hunters in Africa today, has hunted with Makanyanga for nearly two decades. They have functioned as a very effective team and have developed a very warm and close personal relationship. Alex has been essential in the development of this treatise, both from the standpoint of his personal experiences with Makanyanga and as a translator during the interview process. Makanyanga also provided several excellent pictures depicting a number of activities in his home environment.

Perhaps, before proceeding further, a precise description of an accomplished tracker is in order: It takes years of personal experience with all types of game in every kind of cover to receive even a passing grade as a tracker. Alex indicates that the job entails far more capabilities than simply following tracks made by a specific animal. To be successful, the tracker must possess a detailed knowledge of the animal's behavior.

This is especially important when tracking wounded dangerous game. The aim is to stalk close enough to the animal so that the professional hunter and client can have a chance to shoot the

[1]Herne, Brian. *Tanzania Safaris*. Clinton: Amwell Press, 1981.

[2]Bull, Bartle. *Safari: A Chronicle of Adventure*. Middlesex, England: Penguin Books, Ltd., 1988.

[3]Hurt, Robin. *Hunting the Big Five*. Long Beach: Safari Press, Inc., 2002.

[4]Butler, George. *In the Blood*. (video) New York: Central Park Media Co., White Mountain Films, Inc., 1989.

animal, but not close enough to facilitate a charge. In addition, the tracker has to be able to spot game in all types of cover. Physically, he must have unlimited endurance. Finally, he must be completely reliable in all types of situations, including life-threatening ones. Very few individuals live up to these requirements. Makanyanga does, in fact, surpass them.

I met Alex during my safari to Rungwa and have hunted with him on three subsequent trips. Before proceeding with the account of Makanyanga's life history and exploits, I need to briefly describe Alex Walker's background, which is essential to paint a comprehensive picture of Makanyanga. In addition, Alex is sufficiently unique to have his own background described in print.

Alex comes by his love of hunting quite naturally. His father, Trevor Walker, was a farmer and part-time professional hunter, taking clients on at least two to three safaris a year. Alex was born in 1967 in Mufindi, Tanzania, moving to Ngoina, Kenya, in 1973 and then, in 1978, to Imatong, Sudan. During this period, his father also maintained a home near Nairobi, Kenya. His family returned to Kenya in 1985.

Alex began hunting as a toddler, going on a number of safaris with his father. From age six to age seventeen, he spent eight months a year in England in school, but during the time he was in Africa he was hunting continuously. He began shooting with a BB gun and later graduated to firearms. His first hunting memory is shooting a marsh bird at age five. Later on, he shot guinea fowl and at age seven killed a duiker with a .22 rifle. His primary mentor, other than his father, was Wyscogie, one of his father's trackers. Wyscogie had deforming arthritis and could hardly straighten his hands, but he spent a lot of time teaching Alex about tracking and hunting. The lessons were so well learned and enjoyed that, by age six, Alex had made up his mind that he would become a professional hunter. He never wavered from this course, although he got no encouragement from his father. It was, in fact, quite the opposite.

Alex hunted with his father on every possible occasion. He killed his first Cape buffalo at age twelve and an elephant when he was seventeen. Shortly after his seventeenth birthday, Alex decided that further education in England was not for him. Alex's father wanted him to become an English army officer, but, to say the least, this career was not Alex's "cup of tea." Instead, he became an apprentice to Danny McCallam, a professional hunter with Robin Hurt's organization. After two years, he became a fully licensed professional hunter. Initially, he hunted in the Moyowosi region of Tanzania, and for a three-year period (1987–1990) hunted bongo in the Central African Republic (C.A.R.). Makanyanga was one of the senior trackers and was assigned to "take care" of Alex during the safaris in the C.A.R.

Alex left Robin Hurt's organization in 1991 and became a freelance professional hunter. He contracted for a number of game-control positions in Kenya as well as guiding for George Angelides in Tanzania for a four-year period. In 1996, he joined Miombo Safaris as an independent professional hunter. During his entire career, he has spent approximately nine months per year in the bush as a professional hunter and guide. During much of this time, Makanyanga has hunted with Alex, beginning in the C.A.R. and more recently in Tanzania. Also, he assisted Alex with game-control activities in Kenya. Obviously, they share a rich wealth of hunting experiences.

With this information as background, let's begin the narrative about Makanyanga. Makanyanga, a member of the Wakamba tribe, was born in 1943 in a small village, containing about ten families, located on the edge of the Tsavo National Park in Kenya. One of the most important characteristics of his tribe is reverence for the family. The first-born male always takes the name of his grandfather; hence, the son and the grandfather always have the same name, so that the strong family tradition is carried on.

While subsistence farming was the main vocation, a number of the villagers were hunters, and many were involved in the safari industry. As a toddler, Makanyanga was introduced to all varieties of hunting. He became very proficient in the use of a small bow and arrow and learned to provide food for the table, beginning with guinea fowl and, later, small antelope.

Makanyanga was the eldest boy in his family. When his father died when he was ten years old, Makanyanga had to assume responsibility for procuring food for the family. Unfortunately, the family's livestock was soon stolen, leaving his mother and her other children without a source of food except what was provided by Makanyanga's hunting forays.

It was clear from the beginning that he had a penchant for tracking, learning to track both game and the wandering livestock. At least at this time, he did not use traps or snares. Killing animals was done exclusively with a bow and arrow. As he grew, he was taught woodsmanship by his uncle and instructed in the correct use of poisoned arrows. Arrows smeared with lethal poison were the mainstay of his armament throughout his hunting career. By hunting continually, he gradually became more and more proficient in the techniques of hunting large animals. He killed an oryx when he was thirteen, and a year later, his first buffalo. These were followed by a rhinoceros at age fifteen and an elephant when he was eighteen years old.

The British authorities considered the killing of rhino and elephant to be serious poaching and deemed it illegal. However, from Makanyanga's standpoint, his family had hunted these animals for untold numbers of years; he was unimpressed with the need to stop. He estimates that he killed approximately thirty rhino during his late teens. He is uncertain as to the exact number of elephants but estimates that throughout his career he's killed one hundred elephants using poisoned arrows. He can't guess the number of buffalo that fell to his arrows. In the early 1960s, he sold rhino horn to Arab traders for two shillings per pound and elephant ivory for five shillings a pound. To put this price in perspective, Alex indicated that his father hunted ivory at the same time and received ten to twelve shillings per pound, about twice as much as was paid to Makanyanga.

In describing how to place poisoned arrows properly, Makanyanga says that the appropriate location for both rhino and buffalo and all species of antelope is the fleshy part of either the leg or shoulder. However, the best location for elephant is just in front of the crease made by the hind leg with the arrow penetrating, as best I can determine, the peritoneum. If the poison is potent

Makanyanga demonstrating how, in times gone past, he hunted with a bow and poisoned arrow.

and the arrow placed correctly, it takes approximately one hour for a buffalo or rhino to die and four hours for an elephant. If incorrectly placed, death takes considerably longer or the animal survives. Just prior to expiring, the animal becomes quite wobbly on its feet and develops explosive diarrhea. These signs indicate that the animal is near death.

Since poison was the mainstay of these hunters, the techniques used to produce it are of considerable interest. Generically, it is called "Bushman's poison," and a variation is used throughout much of sub-Saharan Africa. The lethal agent of the poison is a cardiac glycoside akin to digitalis. To prepare the poison, the woody portion, not the green stems or leaves, of the bush (Acokcanthera) is placed in a pot with water and slowly simmered for a number of hours. When the extraction is complete, the resin becomes a thickened syrup that crystallizes upon cooling. A portion of the material is broken off, reheated to a liquid state, and then smeared on the arrow. To maintain potency, the arrow must be wrapped in the skin of either a Vervet monkey or caracal. Nothing else is acceptable. (Makanyanga is adamant as to the validity of this procedure.)

Another important aspect of making poison is that the poison will lose its potency if a woman is involved in any way during the process. When queried about whether women were allowed to hunt with poison arrows, Makanyanga gave a look of disdain, indicating that "women's jobs are to gather firewood and to chop weeds." (So much for feminism in the Wakamba tribe!)

The final step is to test the potency of the poison. A frog is scratched with a poisoned arrow. If it hops more than twice before dying, the poison is not potent enough.

Makanyanga indicates that it is entirely safe to eat the meat from animals poisoned in this manner. In fact, after a thorough washing, the pot the poison is made in is used for cooking! Poison stored as a crystal will retain its potency for at least several months.

One cannot overemphasize the enormous degree of woodcraft and skill necessary to stalk close enough to dangerous game to make an effective shot and then escape without being mauled or killed. The technique Makanyanga described for rhino seems quite frightening. The hunter tracks a rhino to the noon resting place, which is usually in dense cover. The rhino sleeps lying on its side, exposing a shoulder. After the hunter lodges the arrow in the shoulder, he runs a few feet from the rhino and then shouts loudly. He does this because the poison works faster on a running animal. The rhino will always charge at a sound and invariably keeps on running without turning back. The trick is to shout to attract the rhino's attention and then jump aside in time to be missed by the initial charge. Sounds like a foolish strategy to me, but apparently it works. Makanyanga could not describe any specific techniques regarding buffalo or elephant except that when the arrow is imbedded, the hunter exits as fast as possible.

After the quarry is successfully impaled with the poison arrow, the hunter must follow the animal until its demise. Depending on the nature of the game and the potency of the poison, this may require a chase of many miles, obviously taxing the tracking ability of the hunter. In addition, the hunter must correctly gauge the degree of disability of the game to avoid getting prematurely too close to a sick, but dangerous, adversary.

When Makanyanga was about eighteen, he was seriously mauled by a buffalo. That morning he had made a good stalk and placed the arrow appropriately into the *mbogo*'s shoulder. Quietly following the escaping quarry, after about an hour, he noted from examining the tracks that the animal had fallen on two occasions and was beginning to develop the telltale diarrhea, indicating an imminent death. Whether or not Makanyanga was in too great a hurry, became careless, and pressed the animal too closely is entirely conjectural. However, what happened next nearly ended Makanyanga's life.

He recalled hearing a rustling sound behind him before *mbogo* impaled the back of Makanyanga's left upper thigh on a horn and then tossed him in the air. As he fell to the ground in a heap, the buffalo began pushing him along with his horns. The buffalo ripped the inner aspect of Makanyanga's right arm from the elbow nearly to the shoulder, exposing the bone. (Forty-two years later, the scar is still quite impressive.) As he was being pushed along the ground, Makanyanga had the presence of mind to grab his skinning knife with his left hand and drive it into *mbogo*'s nose. The animal backed off a few steps. As Makanyanga waited for the mauling to continue, the buffalo's back legs buckled and he fell. The poison had finally done its job. Makanyanga gave thanks to his grandfather's spirit for saving his life.

Severely bruised, cut, and barely able to move, Makanyanga somehow managed to walk and crawl approximately four miles to the road, where he was found later that afternoon. Luckily, no bones were broken. Although it took about a month for his wounds to heal, he soon returned to hunting.

Although poison arrows were his mainstay in hunting, he did inherit two leg-hold traps from his father, which he used occasionally to trap leopards. He would place the traps in an area frequented by leopards and attach them to a heavy billet of wood. When caught, the animal went into thick cover dragging the log. The animal was dispatched either with a poison arrow or directly with a regular arrow. Makanyanga never used either a spear or a firearm. Makanyanga was unclear how many leopards he took in this manner, but he gave the impression that it was approximately thirty. In the mid-1970s, he received approximately one hundred shillings for a female and three hundred for a big male leopard skin. He did not hunt lions until he joined the safari industry. Although there were a few dogs in the village that would at least attempt to trail game, Makanyanga made little use of canine assistance in hunting.

Makanyanga acquired a reputation locally as being extremely knowledgeable about locating elephant. When he was twenty-one years old, a well-known Kenyan professional hunter, Kevin Torrens, led a safari near Makanyanga's home. Makanyanga's uncle, a gunbearer for the company, indicated that Makanyanga might know the location of an elephant. Makanyanga agreed to participate in the hunt and led the hunters to a very nice tusker. Apparently Kevin Torrens was so impressed with Makanyanga that he hired him on the spot as a tracker. Makanyanga worked in this capacity for the next thirteen years, until 1977 when hunting was closed in Kenya.

Even though safari hunting was almost continuous throughout the year, Makanyanga did spend several months at home each year and continued his poaching career in the off-season. As a professional tracker, Makanyanga was paid the handsome sum of ten shillings a month and was given a bonus of twenty-five shillings for every elephant that was killed. He hunted primarily in Kenya and the Moyowosi region of Tanzania.

In describing hunting at that time, Makanyanga explained that game was so plentiful that the amount of land to be covered to have a successful hunt was much less than in later years. In general, trucks were used to move the party and accouterments to a given area; then the hunters would pursue the animals on foot. Quite early on, Makanyanga was involved in safaris in which porters were used to carry the supplies. However, this classic technique was supplanted by vehicles in a very few years. In fact, he remembers porters being used on only one or two safaris to the Tana River area.

It was reasonably easy to obtain good trophy specimens because of the plethora of game. In order to hunt lion, the tracker would first find a kill and then track the lion to where they were taking a noon siesta. Really big elephants (greater than one hundred pounds per tusk) were always difficult to find.

Like most longtime professional hunters, Makanyanga clearly feels that *tembo* is the ultimate game animal. If given a choice, that's the only animal he would pursue. Makanyanga said that it is extremely difficult to track elephants, especially when one needs to stay on a given track in an area where many elephants are found. The tracker/hunter determines the age of the elephant from the roundness and smoothness of the track. Since each animal carries itself a little differently, it is possible to determine if a specific track is made by a given elephant. While it is a major challenge to track elephants, it is the peak of woodcraft when it's successfully done.

The longest pursuit of an elephant occurred near the Tana River. Makanyanga remembers following the elephant for four days before they were able to get in a position to shoot. The tusks weighed one hundred and one hundred two pounds. Since a feeding elephant will move as fast or faster than a man can walk, successful elephant hunting is physically very taxing. Throughout his career, Makanyanga estimates that he's been involved in the killing of approximately two hundred fifty large bull elephants while on hunting safaris.

Although the buffalo mauling was by far the most serious injury that Makanyanga sustained during his hunting experiences, he was also severely bitten by a leopard while hunting with Kevin Torrens. The leopard had been wounded in the abdomen by a client and had crawled into dense vegetation. The professional hunter and Makanyanga followed to dispatch the wounded cat. However, they misjudged the location and crept past the animal. Unseen, the leopard charged. The cat bit Makanyanga on the left knee and thigh before finally being killed by the professional hunter. Although the multiple wounds were quite painful, Makanyanga received quick medical attention and was soon back at work. (Forty years of almost continuous hunting, most of it with dangerous game, and only two life-threatening incidents—one buffalo and one leopard—is certainly a remarkable record.)

Following the close of hunting in Kenya in 1977, Makanyanga worked for Brian Herne for several years as a tracker in both Uganda and Tanzania. Brian Herne described Makanyanga as "a quiet fellow with a wry sense of humor," adding that "in the bush he was slippery as a shadow and he could track a fly across a wall. He could probably outwalk and outrun prospective Olympic contenders."[1] During the six-year period, Makanyanga also hunted intermittently with Danny McCallam in Sudan and in Zambia. Beginning in 1983, he chose to hunt exclusively with Robin Hurt's organization.

During the time he was hunting with Brian Herne, his poaching activities got him into significant trouble with the Kenyan authorities. Brian Herne briefly described the following episode.[1] While poaching rhino in the Tsavo Park (at that time rhino horn was selling for the unbelievable sum of 500 shillings a pound, which translates into about 5,000 shillings per rhino, an enormous amount of money), Makanyanga was apprehended, after being chased by a helicopter patrol, and incarcerated. He was ordered to either pay a large fine or spend two years in jail at hard labor. He had no money, so jail was the only option. He found himself in a prison named Shimo-la-Tewa (Hole of the Rock Cod). This jail had a primitive and restrictive environment; no communication to the outside world was allowed. Makanyanga did note that, not infrequently, one of the inmates would be led out and would never be seen again. The general understanding among the prisoners was that the individuals were executed.

After about a month, when he didn't make an appearance to begin the safari season (Makanyanga was usually quite punctual), Brian Herne investigated the cause for the absence. He found out from Makanyanga's brother that Makanyanga was in jail. Brian Herne arranged to pay the fine (bribe?) and sent someone to pick up Makanyanga. Makanyanga knew nothing of these proceedings. When his name was called one morning, he was convinced that he was to be summarily executed. He was led down a hall and told to go through a door. Much to his surprise and relief, when the door opened, he found himself on the outside of the jail! He quickly identified his benefactors and went back to work—a very happy individual. Whether or not this episode had any lasting effect on his poaching career is doubtful. The dearth of rhino was probably the controlling factor, at least for this species.

At age thirty-three, Makanyanga had saved enough money to pay a dowry, allowing him to marry. Although he spent very little time at home, he did obtain land for a small farm and purchased a significant amount of livestock. He tried to begin a family, but unfortunately, the first five children died. Subsequently, he had three boys and three girls, who are currently living and doing quite well. He married for the second time several years later. Apparently both wives and the growing family live together in harmony. At least family matters are congenial when Makanyanga is at home.

Although Makanyanga is not deeply religious, his religion is best described by Alex as a type of animist, which is the attribution of conscious life to nature or natural objects. His religion involves a deep sense of family history and obligation. Makanyanga lives by an impressive code of ethics. He is extremely devoted to his eldest

Plowing the land using a "live tractor."

son, who is currently working in the safari industry in a role other than hunting or tracking.

In 1984 Makanyanga went to Zaire (Congo) with Danny McCallam and Robin Hurt to hunt forest elephant. He describes this trip as one of the best experiences of his life, primarily because they were successful in finding a number of bull elephant with heavy ivory. In fact, they spotted one elephant that was estimated to carry one-hundred-sixty-pound tusks. Lady Luck did not smile. This behemoth eluded them by joining a herd of cows. Makanyanga indicated that the tusks of this elephant were by far the largest he has ever seen. A couple of days after this incident, they found tracks in the soft ground that showed gouge marks made by the enormous tusks. Stalking this *tembo* was not to be. They were notified by radio that hunting in Zaire had been officially closed, and they were forced to leave the country immediately.[3] (Apparently the activities of professional safari hunters were interfering with state-sponsored poaching

activities.) Several elephants with tusks weighing over one hundred pounds were killed on this safari.

During the early 1980s, Makanyanga had the opportunity to hunt in Botswana on several occasions. In 1986, he played a supporting role as a tracker in the video production, *In the Blood,*[4] which was filmed in the Moyowosi region of Tanzania. Makanyanga was introduced as a "former poacher." In the film he demonstrates both his tracking ability and showmanship, even testing the warmness of a "buffalo pie" with his fingers (a characteristic action). In the final scene, Makanyanga can be heard giving his patented loud warbling victory yell.

For political reasons, it became progressively difficult for Kenyan citizens to work in Tanzania, so for the 1987–90 seasons Makanyanga went with Danny McCallam to hunt in the C.A.R., primarily after bongo. It was on these safaris that he worked with Alex and developed their close long-term relationship. Although not his favorite adventure, Makanyanga took to hunting bongo with a great deal of success. The land where they hunted was fairly dense forest with "fingers" of grass separating trees. To find the bongo and to make the area more open and visible, these fingers of grass were burned.

One of Makanyanga's favorite pastimes is burning land. (I'm convinced he's a pyromaniac.) When growing up, the area around the village frequently was burned primarily to reduce the amount of vermin around the homes. He learned to burn to make tracking and finding game easier.

A very interesting incident occurred due to Makanyanga's overzealous burning. Toward the end of an unsuccessful hunt, while walking back to camp, the trail led the group through a village. However, when they arrived at the village, they found a great deal of consternation. The local constable, astride a bicycle, was quite agitated and spouting out vitriol in both French and Zande. When they finally sorted things out, they found that he was planning to arrest the entire group, or at least Makanyanga, as the primary culprit. What had happened? The village on one side of the road had been burned to the ground. Apparently, a fire that had been started either that morning or the day before gradually spread to the village. Since the villagers had seen him starting brush fires in the past, Makanyanga was judged to be responsible.

The Zande, not a particularly industrious group of citizens, had not bothered to cut the grass away near their thatch huts. When the fire arrived, it rapidly consumed half the village; only a few mud walls remained. The villagers were upset about the situation. Alex finally figured out what they really wanted: help, both physical and fiscal, in restoring the village. He arranged to provide both. The total cost of this misadventure was a few hours of labor and around two hundred dollars. Was Makanyanga guilty? Probably. But the settlement, judged adequate by the constable, saved Makanyanga from incarceration. I'm not sure how many homes were involved, but this certainly strikes me as being a rather cheap price for half a village. At any rate, this episode in no way dampened Makanyanga's enthusiasm for burning brush.

In 1991, when Alex decided to quit Robin Hurt's organization to become a freelance professional hunter, he obtained several contracts for game control on large ranches in northern Kenya. Makanyanga had developed a very close relationship with Alex and decided to work with him.

This job of game control primarily involved reducing the numbers of antelope and buffalo. Alex recalls one incident where he and Makanyanga nearly got into serious trouble. On this particular occasion, Alex was using a .30-06 rifle to shoot buffalo and a .222 rifle to shoot small antelope. They spied two buffalo and killed one readily, but the second, only wounded, ran off. When they approached this animal, still standing and dangerous, Alex discovered that he had no more .30-06 ammunition. Luckily, he killed the buffalo by shooting it in the brain with the .222.

Breathing a sigh of relief, they walked toward the dead buffalo. Suddenly they heard a loud noise in a nearby bush. A few seconds later, two fairly large lions made an appearance, running in their direction. Well, there they were . . . armed with only a .222 rifle and facing two obviously disturbed lions running straight toward them. Reflexly, Makanyanga and Alex crouched down behind the buffalo carcass. Luckily, the lions ran by about fifteen feet away from where they were hiding and disappeared.

The two were beginning to breathe again when all of a sudden, another racket occurred. A large angry rhino appeared on the scene. This beast apparently had been chasing the lions. The rhino came within fifteen feet of the buffalo carcass, but he, too, kept going. After a few minutes, Alex and Makanyanga slipped away, very happy to be unhurt.

Moral of the story: In Africa you never know what is behind the next bush, so take a big enough gun and have plenty of ammunition. After that day, Alex, who hunts with his father's .470 Westley Richards double rifle, always has this weapon with him in any area where dangerous game might be around.

Having a "sixth sense" that enables him to deal effectively with dangerous situations is a Makanyanga trademark. On many occasions this ability has been lifesaving. One morning while hunting in Masailand, he and Alex followed four old buffalo bulls through a dense field of long grass. As they approached the bulls, the fickle wind shifted. The buffalo ran off. They followed the tracks for several hundred yards and again came upon their quarry. Although unseen, they could hear the nearby buffalo breathing heavily. Again, the wind changed and the bulls quickly left. Disgusted, Alex started to follow, but Makanyanga signaled to back up quickly. They had retreated approximately twenty feet when a charging buffalo appeared at their prior location, obviously with evil intent. The buffalo stopped to locate them, but Alex luckily had a clear shot and quickly dispatched the bull. This bull had planned an ambush and had remained behind when the others left. How did Makanyanga know that something was amiss? Neither he nor Alex ever saw or heard the buffalo standing silently close-by. The buffalo was not wounded, and there was no reason to suspect that he would be so aggressive. Undoubtedly, the warning by Makanyanga's "sixth sense" saved one or both of their lives.

Control work and hunting in Tanzania with George Angelides' safari company occupied the next four years for Makanyanga and Alex. More and more, Alex became impressed with Makanyanga's capabilities.

One of the hallmarks of a good tracker is excellent eyesight. The ability to see far better than his peers is a Makanyanga trademark.[3] Alex recalls that, on one occasion, Makanyanga indicated to him that an oryx was standing near a lone tree in the distance. Alex was barely able to make the animal out using his eight-power binoculars. How Makanyanga saw the horns without the aid of optics is a mystery, but he carries out similar feats almost on a daily basis. Although Makanyanga generally spots animals without the use of any optics, he does carry binoculars and occasionally uses them. Using binoculars does not seem to be a point of honor with Makanyanga. (Many trackers seem to feel that using optics is a slur on their capabilities.)

One of Makanyanga's ever-present accouterments is a snuff container. He has used a variety of containers for snuff. The ritual of dipping snuff is always carried out as he begins tracking and occasionally a time or two throughout the process, depending on the length of the stalk. Makanyanga claims that it enhances his eyesight. The snuff is his own concoction: He buys the tobacco leaves, grinds them himself with a hot stone, and adds soda ash from the lake, which gives it a saline content. The final product is ground tobacco and soda crystal. I once tried the potion myself. A small pinch nearly knocked the top of my head off. It for damn sure didn't improve my eyesight.

I have noticed that while tracking, Makanyanga has a determined facial expression with cheeks slightly puffed out and a set jaw. I always concluded that this look indicated determination and concentration. Alternatively, maybe it's the result of the foul-tasting snuff.

As Alex indicated, one of Makanyanga's strongest points as a tracker is his unwillingness to give up. In fact, he rarely, if ever, admits that he has lost a track. This characteristic paid off on numerous occasions and was one of the reasons he became an outstanding elephant tracker. What was the longest distance they tracked a given animal? Alex recalled that one time near Kilimanjaro, Makanyanga followed the track of a wounded eland for over forty miles before they finally caught up with the animal. It was standard fare to follow animals seven to eight miles.

The elephant is by far Makanyanga's preferred quarry, but next in line is Cape buffalo. The reason for this choice is that he considers killing buffalo quite similar, if not as challenging, as elephant hunting. Makanyanga enjoys the challenge of hunting lion and leopard, but the lack of tracking markedly detracts from his enjoyment. Also, he likes to be on the move rather than sitting in a blind. I asked why he becomes so involved with the celebration following a successful lion or leopard hunt. The answer was somewhat unclear, but I have the impression that he participates in order to go along with the expected ritual. Makanyanga recognizes the necessity of hunting various species of antelope because of the client's interest, but, to be frank, he'd rather not.

Hunting crocodile from a boat is out of the question. Because he can't swim, Makanyanga is deathly afraid of the water. In fact, he would rather be anywhere than in a native *mtumbwi* (canoe). Makanyanga's aversion to hunting in a boat was graphically illustrated by an event that happened recently. At the beginning of the safari season, Joey arrived at one of the Kilombero camps where buffalo hunting is mostly done from a boat. That evening he had the opportunity to talk, via two-way radio, with Makanyanga, who was currently in Lukwika. Makanyanga was quite vociferous in his desire to hunt with Joey and indicated that he would try to rearrange his schedule.

After Joey told Makanyanga the location of the camp, there was a prolonged silence. Makanyanga whispered softly in Swahili, "It will be best if you came here." In fact, I was quite flattered that Makanyanga agreed to come to Kilombero to hunt with me knowing that he would have to ride in a boat.

Although he excelled in the use of a bow with a poison arrow to kill all varieties of game, Makanyanga never learned to shoot either a rifle or a shotgun, preferring to let the professional hunter carry out that end of the task. Alex relates an instance when he and Makanyanga followed a leopard that had been wounded by a client and had escaped into thick cover. Alex carried his .470 double rifle and Makanyanga uncharacteristically was armed with a 12-gauge over-and-under shotgun. When they first saw the leopard, it was approximately five yards away and charging. Alex's shot killed the leopard. Makanyanga was no help. He pulled both barrels at the same time, was knocked down by the recoil, and missed the quarry completely. So much for his prowess with a firearm.

In 1996, Alex joined Miombo Safaris as an independent professional hunter in several locations within Tanzania. Alex has been able to take Makanyanga into the various hunting concessions in Tanzania, with the exception of Rungwa. (The district manager would not allow Kenyans in his territory.) Until recently, they worked together for approximately nine months per year.

In 2000, Makanyanga became sick and missed the season. He was told that he had high blood pressure and was advised to stop eating meat and to eat only vegetables, fish, and chicken. Whether or not this regimen had any effect, he is fit as a fiddle, but he does continue to shun meat. Unfortunately, his new diet has precluded his favorite foods, which include eland brisket, buffalo stomach (uncooked), and his favorite, raw impala liver. In fact, Makanyanga indicates that fresh

Makanyanga's nearly completed "shopping mall" located about one mile from his home.

impala liver dipped in the contents of the antelope's stomach is by far the tastiest food imaginable.

An interesting experience occurred when Makanyanga was partaking of this feast in the presence of a client's somewhat persnickety wife. The woman was disgusted and told Alex so. Alex quickly conveyed the problem to Makanyanga who misunderstood, thinking she was upset by not being offered some of the feast. Makanyanga quickly righted this wrong and presented a large slab to the lady. She promptly turned pale and fainted. So much for variation in culinary taste between different cultures.

Makanyanga cannot relate any particular instances regarding problems with clients. He leaves all of these issues up to the professional hunter and goes on his merry way with tracking duties. To say that he is not disappointed when a client either misses an easy shot or significantly wounds the game would be untrue. However, he accepts and deals with these problems.

Makanyanga has an interesting perspective regarding the appropriate choice of a rifle, undoubtedly from long years of observation. He much prefers that the professional hunter and the client use a double rifle. He named the two barrels *Mother* and *Father* and the appropriate ammunition, *the children*.

Makanyanga's relationship to the other trackers is clearly one of leadership. He is not impressive physically, being about five feet eight inches and of medium build, but he takes charge of the proceedings and the others do precisely as he directs. Probably the best team of trackers that I have observed is Makanyanga and Singi. Makanyanga and Pius (Miombo Safaris' best young tracker) also make an outstanding pair. Alex thinks that Makanyanga's capabilities are clearly appreciated by the rest of the staff. They respect and tolerate him even if they perceive him as somewhat arrogant and abrasive.

During the stalking process, Makanyanga makes clear the appropriate position for everyone in the group. I remember when stalking a buffalo, the Tanzanian game scout, "Little Mama," stood up rather than crawl, creating a problem. The second time that she didn't follow his instructions, Makanyanga "tuned her up" in Swahili and made her sit down and wait until we returned. She didn't like it, but she obeyed him.

Makanyanga clearly has a wealth of experience that is considerably greater than those of his contemporaries. He is not bashful in stating his evaluation of a given situation. His ideas are expressed as fact, not opinion. This degree of assertiveness occasionally irritates the other hunters. However, Makanyanga does not push the issue. Whenever he is proven to be either right or wrong, he shrugs his shoulders in a characteristic way and lets the matter drop.

I saw an excellent example of his assertiveness during my first safari to the Selous. We jumped three buffalo in the long grass, and they ran toward an impenetrable thicket. Makanyanga indicated to Joey, "No need to follow, they've escaped." Joey disagreed. We followed the buffalo a few hundred yards and found them in the open, staring back at us. Although late in the day, I killed one. Makanyanga smiled and looked at us as if to say, "Well, I was wrong this time, but it doesn't happen very often." From my observation, he is exactly right.

Although essentially fearless around dangerous game, Makanyanga is deathly afraid of snakes. In fact, when he spies one, he becomes quite agitated and vocal until he has put a good distance between himself and the reptile. Makanyanga, no doubt, has seen the results of a venomous snakebite, but it is unclear why seeing a snake provokes such a response. Perhaps he had an extraordinarily bad experience as a child? Alex asked Makanyanga to explain the situation. He looked at us for a long minute and muttered quietly in Swahili, "I don't want to talk about snakes." So ended the discussion. The reason for his fear of snakes will be forever a mystery.

During the past several years Makanyanga has considerably expanded his land holdings. He owns four hundred acres of land, approximately one hundred acres of which is farmed using oxen, shovels, and hoes. The primary crops are maize and beans. He also owns a fairly impressive number of cattle and goats. Several of his children have married and live nearby, and twelve grandchildren have been added to the family.

Makanyanga has begun another project—that of building a "shopping mall" about a mile from his home on the main road. This structure is essentially complete and provides room for a number of entrepreneurs to sell their wares. It also has rooms to rent for temporary housing. The front of the building is covered with pictures of animals and a sign indicating Miombo Safaris. Makanyanga plans that the rent from this "mall" will be his means of support during his future retirement. In fact, he has done extremely well financially, by African standards, for a man who began life penniless.

For the past two years, Makanyanga has primarily hunted elephant for Miombo Safaris in the Lukwika concession near the Mozambique border. In this venture, he has tried to train the young trackers in the fine art of tracking elephant. The hunting has been reasonably successful, and Makanyanga gets a significant bonus of five hundred dollars for each elephant killed.

While the foregoing provides only a brief sketch of an extraordinary man, it should be obvious that, in his chosen area, he is clearly at the top of the heap. Having been a superior hunter for his entire life, he has spent forty years as a tracker associated with the best of professional hunters. These exploits have been carried out in much of sub-Saharan Africa including Kenya, Tanzania, Uganda, Botswana, Zaire (Congo), Sudan, the Central African Republic, and Zambia. Obviously, Makanyanga has "been there-done that." It is highly unlikely with the amount of game markedly reduced, especially dangerous game, that trackers equal to Makanyanga will ever be produced again. I consider it a privilege to have had the opportunity to watch him "on the job."

Beginning in 2006, Makanyanga's vision began to deteriorate. An ophthalmologist in Dar es Salaam diagnosed retinal degeneration, which was not amenable to therapy. Although able to see well enough to function, he was forced to give up elephant hunting. Thus ended the career of an "African legend." With the current reduction in the scope of hunting in East Africa, it is very doubtful that we will "look upon his like again."

Makanyanga Met *Mbogo*

Mbogo took my arrow
About an hour ago.
Deadly poison has done its work.
Much farther he cannot go.

Tracks show where he stumbled and fell.
(No need to follow so slow.)
Just ahead I'll find him . . .
Dead—or nearly so.

What? A noise—just behind me.
His horn pierces my leg with a blow.
I'm lifted up—as if flying.
To earth, in a heap I go!

In a moment—he's on me again.
My right arm is ripped; the bone shows!
But, I will not die without fighting.
I drive my knife through his nose.

He backs off. We glare at each other.
Our eyes transfixed in the stare.
Then, slowly his body collapses.
His death bellow answers my prayer.

"Grandfather, your Spirit has saved me."
On this day I shall not die.
I crawl four miles to the roadside.
They find me there as I lie.

* * * * *

Many days it took to heal.
Now body and spirit are together.
Though he gave me the chill of death,
I'll hunt *mbogo* forever.

Return to Rungwa

Chapter XII

For a variety of reasons, none of them very good, I elected not to hunt in Africa in 2004. However, as time passed, satisfying my obsession to hunt Cape buffalo again became almost a necessity. Accordingly, I asked Joey to book a safari. In January, the arrangements were finalized for a ten-day buffalo hunt in the Miombo Safaris concession in Rungwa, Tanzania, where I had been on one previous occasion. The license for this safari allowed me to kill two buffalo.

Since the hunt was scheduled to begin 15 September, I had almost nine months to plan for the trip. One of my colleagues, Dr. Ralph Corey, who had only a sparse hunting experience, indicated a keen desire to tag along and shoot plains game. While I had some concern that Ralph might not enjoy the proceedings, I was delighted to have him join this expedition. Prior to our safari, Ralph, an expert in infectious diseases and international health, would visit one of the medical facilities in Arusha and then meet me in Dar es Salaam.

My preparations for the safari were not particularly difficult. Luckily, I obtained a very cheap ticket to fly on KLM through Amsterdam to Dar es Salaam. The authorities at Schiphol Airport in Amsterdam had decided to enforce the requirement to have a permit in order to transport a rifle through the airport. The appropriate paperwork was sent in, but after two months I began to get concerned. I called, and after some discussion requiring translation from Dutch to "Southern" English, I was assured that everything was in order. The permit arrived the last week in August. I also had to renew my passport, obtain a visa to Tanzania, and bring my immunization status up-to-date.

My preparations also included deciding which firearms to take. Since Joey would be in Africa, I could use one of his rifles as a backup. Thus, I had to transport only one firearm, the .470 Holland & Holland double rifle, which I had used on many of my prior trips. I felt quite comfortable with its use while hunting. In order to prepare for this safari, I shot the rifle on two occasions. (The cost of approximately $10/round and the associated uncomfortable recoil reduced my enthusiasm for extensive practice.) The hard gun case and forty rounds of both soft and solid ammunition fit into the rolling duffel bag. Actually, all of my accouterments were packed and ready to go at least two weeks early.

As is my custom, I prayed that the luggage would arrive at the same time I did. On four prior occasions my prayers had not been answered. The flight over was uneventful and, wonder of wonders, all the luggage arrived in fine shape. I was met by Scott Coles, the majordomo of Miombo Safaris. I spent the night at the Sea Cliff Hotel where I was joined by Ralph and Joey.

The next day we flew by air charter to Rungwa, arriving at 2 P.M. We were met by Doudi, our chief tracker, who was a tall thin individual of Masai extraction, and according to Joey, a first-class woodsman. Martin, the other tracker; Ollie, a Tanzanian game scout; and Thomas, the truck mechanic and driver made up our contingent. We climbed into the Toyota Land Cruiser and soon arrived at a very palatial tented camp.

As he disembarked from the vehicle, Ralph severely twisted his ankle. This situation would likely slow him down in walking and would put him on par with me since I had developed painful tendonitis in my left heel. (I wouldn't necessarily be the one holding up our various stalks.)

As on my prior safaris, the staff began referring to me as *Bwana Babu* (grandfather). I am told that this is a term of endearment, but I really believe it means "decrepit old man." Joey informed the group that

Doudi, Martin, Bwana Babu, and the wide-horned old bull.

Ralph was the "top doctor" for all of Africa—a very important person. They quickly named him *Bwana Mbwa Kubwa* (Big Dog). Accordingly, they treated him with a great deal of respect. Joey continued to be known as Bwana Marlboro. (He wears a cowboy hat.)

The rest of the day was taken up with checking the rifles—no problem—and unpacking. The day ended, as did all the others, with us sitting around a small campfire, smoking cigars, imbibing sundowners, and listening to the African night sounds. Following a sumptuous meal, we retired. I, for one, slept like the proverbial log.

The next day, we began hunting at daylight. It was cool and comfortable, the temperatures ranging from fifty to seventy-five degrees as they did throughout the rest of the trip. During breakfast, Ralph inquired, "What was making all the rasping noise outside my tent about 2 A.M.?"

Joey said in an offhand manner, "That was the camp leopard."

Ralph turned slightly green around the gills and exclaimed, "Oh!" Welcome to Africa!

We got situated in the Land Cruiser and away we went. The terrain was quite hilly with interspaced flat lands, all of which had been burned, making visibility excellent. This allowed us to evaluate the trophy potential of the game without the necessity of getting close, thereby lessening the chances of having to shoot an unwanted *mbogo*. Within very short order, we started seeing buffaloes. In fact, throughout the entire ten days there were very few prolonged "dry spells." My goal was to kill a mature bull having a horn spread of greater than forty inches. We spotted a small herd of about fifty *mbogos* grazing on the side of a hill and walked a mile or so to get in front of them. No acceptable trophy bulls were present.

Then we saw four old *dagga* boys near the top of a very high hill. We circled the hill in order to cut their tracks; however, when we finished this journey, we could find no tracks. Doudi climbed the hill and signaled that they were still there, sound asleep. With Doudi's help, I managed to ascend to the top, although to say the least, it was strenuous. We found the bulls asleep in a small depression and eased to within about forty yards of them. The largest *mbogo* may have met my horn width goal. On the other hand, it was the first day of the hunt; we decided to leave them alone.

That afternoon we saw a very large herd of about two hundred fifty buffaloes moving slowly toward water. We walked parallel to them for a mile or so. They paid little attention to us, although they were clearly aware of our presence. I wondered if perhaps the members of such a large herd feel quite safe from attack by predators. It was getting late and although there were a couple of bulls near my forty-inch goal, we decided not to pursue them.

The next day, after riding for approximately an hour, Doudi spotted where two buffaloes had crossed the road earlier that morning. One of the tracks was quite large, indicating a good size bull. With a great deal of anticipation, we followed. The buffalo walked through mostly open ground where the trackers could move at a fast clip, but there were several places where the tracks became obscure, requiring the trackers to walk slowly in order to stay on the trail. Thus, Ralph and I were able to keep up and not retard the stalk. These *dagga* boys met a small herd of buffalo and a few zebra but continued by themselves. How the trackers can unerringly follow a given buffalo through a herd is always a mystery to me. I could see very little of the spoor, and on several occasions, I had the definite feeling that they were pulling my leg—a conclusion which was not justified.

After walking about five to six miles, the buffaloes were spotted moving from our right to left. The direction of the wind was such that we had to make a wide detour to get in front of them. We quickly executed this maneuver, but found ourselves surrounded by tall grass. (For me, anything over four feet is tall.) Joey aptly remembered that my short stature made visualizing game in long grass impossible. In fact, on several prior occasions he had wryly suggested that I wear "elevator shoes." A nearby large termite mound solved the problem; we quickly climbed to the top.

I had an excellent field of vision and got set up on the shooting sticks. As if by a planned script, both *dagga* boys came ambling by, and one of them clearly was a very good trophy bull. When they came to within thirty yards of our perch, they stopped, turned, and stared in our direction. The larger bull was quartering toward me.

At my shot, the buffalo emitted a loud bellow and fell. He was not paralyzed since he could move his shoulders and back legs, but he was unable to get on his feet. I quickly shot the left barrel, reloaded and shot twice more into the chest. The last shot was followed by a loud death bellow. The other buffalo turned, ran off about sixty yards, looked us over, and decamped. Joey and Doudi determined that *mbogo* was dead and started congratulating me.

This *dagga* boy, a magnificent specimen, had a number of recent wounds made by horns. My guess is that he had just been evicted from the herd. Measured out later, his horn spread was slightly greater than forty-three inches, which is a good bit wider than anything I had killed previously. I had fulfilled my primary goal for this safari. We took the usual pictures.

While the staff butchered the buffalo, I collected a few butterflies that were attracted by the blood. During the butchering, a solid was retrieved from one of the hips. This bullet had entered just under the chin. It had apparently grazed, but did not break, the spine, but it had damaged the great vessels and a lung. I had killed an outstanding trophy. What more could one ask? We returned to camp and celebrated.

The next several days were filled with numerous exciting episodes. Ralph fulfilled his trophy expectations with an excellent impala and a large warthog. As a new member of African big-game hunters, he was ecstatic. The two-hour tracking of the warthog across open ground by Doudi and Martin was among the most impressive feats I've seen.

We continued to see a number of buffaloes, both in singles and in herds. Each day was spent in following them and looking for a better trophy. Late one afternoon, we sat for at least an hour on a large termite mound while a large buffalo herd gradually grazed to within twenty yards of our location. An old cow winded us, snorted, and the herd ambled away—not really frightened, just not interested in making our acquaintance.

One day we sat on the side of a hill overlooking a water hole and spied a plethora of animals and birds coming to the water. Notable among the birds were spurwing geese, several hamerkop and a saddle-billed stork. Nearby a spring, we found a three- to four-month-old buffalo calf by himself. Probably his mother had been killed by lions and the herd abandoned him. Undoubtedly, he will fall prey to the hyenas in the next day or two. Africa is an unforgiving land.

We spied an old *dagga* boy feeding and eased to within about forty yards of him undetected. Joey was taking a picture when the buffalo became aware of our presence. *Mbogo* snorted and turned in our direction, giving us the "evil eye." Joey's camera quickly hit the dirt as he positioned his rifle for immediate use. (This encounter significantly limited further use of the camera.) The buffalo clearly didn't like our looks. Luckily, he exited without incident.

There was considerable evidence of elephants feeding—broken trees, etc. On several occasions we saw small herds of ten to fifteen cow elephants with calves and occasionally a solitary bull. One instance was almost breathtaking when a herd of about fifty elephants and a herd of about two hundred buffalo were spied running along the side of a hill. The buffaloes ran close to the

Bwana Mbwa Kubwa (Ralph) and warthog. I'm not sure which is the uglier.

elephants seemingly trying to pass them, but apparently decided that invading the pachyderms' space was not a good course of action. Buffaloes are big, but when seen together with elephants, they are dwarfed.

We also saw a number of outstanding specimens of plains game including sables, roans, elands, kudus, hartebeests, and zebras as well as numerous small antelopes, such as klipspringers, oribis, and the ever-present impalas. While driving, we saw lions on two occasions. Several lionesses were hiding in the grass near the road but left posthaste when Doudi threw a stick at one of them. Also, we spotted a small pride that included an adult male feeding on a recent giraffe kill.

On the eighth day, we spied two very old *dagga* boys on the side of a hill approximately one thousand yards off. Although their horns were severely broomed and were clearly not as wide as on the buffalo I had killed, they struck me as outstanding trophies. Joey looked at me and I at him. We both agreed. "Let's go."

Doudi and Martin made a wide circle, and, again as if by magic, we got in front of the buffaloes as they grazed in our direction. I got ready on the sticks as the larger *dagga* boy slowly walked past us at twenty-five yards, thus presenting an excellent side shot. The five-hundred-grain solid entered the "vital triangle" just behind the shoulder. *Mbogo* went down. He tried to rise. I shot again, reloaded, and shot twice more. The bull never regained his feet and shortly issued a soft moaning death bellow. I reloaded.

His buddy came over to investigate, stopping about thirty yards from us and giving us the once-over. Joey was on my left and Doudi on my right. I covered the bull with my rifle, but I was not expecting any trouble. Joey and Doudi both shouted and clapped their hands, and Doudi started waving a small tree to entice *mbogo* to leave. In my limited experience and in Joey's, who has had a lot of experience with similar situations, this approach always works. Well, it didn't this time.

At this juncture, I made a very stupid mistake: I took my eyes off the buffalo and looked at Doudi. A second or so later I heard a shot. I looked back at the bull who was running at nearly a right angle to us. Apparently, instead of exiting, he took a couple of determined strides in our direction. To stop the charge, Joey had shot him.

The 570-grain bullet from his .500 double rifle entered just under the right eye and exited above the spine on the left side. The path of the bullet went just under the brain and just above the spinal cord. Clearly, it should have dropped the bull in his tracks, but it didn't. However, the shock of the bullet changed *mbogo*'s direction so that he ran *from* rather than *at* us. Joey shot the bull's rear-end, reloaded, and we shot twice more. The buffalo turned to face us and received two more bullets . . . again, without apparent effect. While Joey continued to shoot, *mbogo* ran approximately one hundred yards, stopped and again turned in our direction. Joey, who was nearly out of ammunition, grabbed my rifle and he and Doudi ran toward the buffalo. By this time the buffalo was quite weak but still on his feet, and several more frontal shots were necessary to end the affair.

I counted a total of fourteen shots to finally bring this old *dagga* boy down. I would never have believed this scenario if I hadn't seen it for myself. Also, I felt very chagrined that, in the proximity to a dangerous animal, I was stupid enough to take my eyes off of *mbogo*. That mistake won't be repeated! Joey made a smart-assed, but correct remark: "That's why I needed him."

Why did the old *dagga* boy decide to charge? When we examined both buffaloes, we saw that they had been clawed up badly, evidence of a fight with lions within the past couple of days. Perhaps the old bull realized that his buddy had just been killed, and since he was in considerable pain from a lion fight he decided enough was enough. I'll never really know why he charged. The extent of the damage done by the bullets was amazing. In addition to the head wound, his chest looked like a pincushion. Both lungs and the heart were essentially destroyed, but he was still able to run—luckily not at us. The game scout observed all the proceedings and was perfectly comfortable with our killing the third buffalo. He listed the incident as a necessity.

The last day we spent game viewing. I wanted to visit an area of sedimentary rocks that contained tracks from a long forgotten era. Doudi knew where these rocks were located. We found a number of tracks embedded in a slab of rock one hundred feet wide, which were made by different animals ranging in size from small-hoofed ones to large elephantlike imprints. I'm not sure of the geologic date, but these tracks document the fact that this Rungwa territory has been home to game for untold eons.

Doudi presented Ralph and me with Masai shields made from the buffalo skins and demonstrated their use in battle. Although

Two old dagga *boys. The one on the left charged rather than run away. Obviously, he hadn't read the manual, "Buffalo Etiquette."*

Doudi didn't have a Masai spear, he employed a machete. Clearly, he would be a very formidable opponent. I, for one, would not like to engage in hostilities with him.

The night before we left, the staff put on quite an extremely impressive ritual celebration with singing and dancing. The jest of the singing was to celebrate that they had all returned alive and well from hunting dangerous game. I don't know what either "booby kabooby" or "gotacha" means, but the associated vigorous movement of the hips during the dancing gives one the impression that procreation was probably part of the agenda.

One final exciting event occurred as we were packing to leave. I heard a noise outside my tent and looked out. There stood a young bull elephant, probably fifteen to twenty yards away, giving me the once-over. I took one picture, grabbed the double rifle, and kept very still. I watched as he slowly trudged between my tent and Ralph's, breaking the railings beside the path. After feeding on a small tree for about ten minutes, he wandered off. I looked towards Ralph's tent. There he stood, looking as though he had swallowed a live frog. What an ending for this safari!

Everything about this trip was memorable. Both Doudi and Martin are outstanding woodsmen and trackers; indeed, it was a joy to see them at work. Buffalo and other game were everywhere. As always, I told Joey that this would be my last trip to Africa. He gave me the usual, "I know better look." Certainly, the opportunity to hunt with him again was one of the highlights of the trip. Also, rather than being bored, Ralph thoroughly enjoyed every minute of the experience and wants to return.

I'm certain that in the near future, Africa will call me again.

Ralph Becomes a Hunter

When Ralph first came to Africa,
He had to learn a lot:
Like, how to work a safety
And that trees must not be shot.

But he caught on very quickly,
Killing impala and warthog.
Soon he was known by everyone
As Bwana the Big Dog.

So, here's a toast to Dr. Corey
And to the hunter he became.
(I taught him well.) He'll soon be back
To hunt for dangerous game.

Hunting Leopards with Hounds in Namibia

Chapter XIII

I never met Arturo. In fact, I don't know his full name or anything about him other than he is from South America and very wealthy. However, without him, this hunt would not have taken place; thus, I owe Arturo a debt of gratitude. Let me explain.

Following a very successful buffalo hunt in Rungwa, Tanzania (2005), I indicated to Joey that I would like to try for a "rerun" in September 2006. Several months later, I was somewhat taken aback when Joey informed me that Arturo's safari had been finalized, so no openings were left for me in Rungwa. Well, damn! I accepted this somewhat surprising turn of events with only a modicum of disenchantment, recognizing that it proved a time-honored adage: Money always wins. However, when May of 2006 rolled around and the stark reality of my remaining "Out of Africa" for this year became evident, I decided to pursue a new course of action.

Although I had never hunted in Africa without Joey's companionship, I decided that I was "old enough" to go it alone. Accordingly, I contacted Cabela's Outdoor Adventures and spoke with Mr. Frank Cole. I indicated to him that I would like to hunt leopard with hounds somewhere other than in Zimbabwe. Both the political unrest and the desire not to support Mugabe's dictatorship made me very wary of this venue. I've never liked still-hunting from a blind, the technique used to hunt leopard in Tanzania—which I equate as having all of the excitement of watching paint dry.

Bwana Babu, Moshile, Alex, and Barry along with several of the dogs

including the Jack Russell, admiring the leopard

Hunting leopard with a well-trained pack of hounds sounded much more to my liking. Several days later, Mr. Cole contacted me and proposed a fifteen-day leopard hunt beginning in late September at Trudia Game Ranch in Namibia with Mr. Barry Burchell of Frontier Safaris. Although Barry had not previously hunted leopard at Trudia, leopard tracks were reported to be abundant. Another very positive feature was the extremely low cost of this venture when compared to leopard hunting in Tanzania. Although I could have conjured up multiple reasons not to participate, the proposal sounded too good to be true. I signed up.

Although the time was shorter than usual for detailed planning for this safari (one of my favorite aspects of these ventures), there were a number of issues that needed to be addressed. First, what rifle should I use? My .470 Holland & Holland double rifle certainly would be "enough gun"—probably too much. Also, my .375 H&H Winchester Model 70 would certainly get the job done, but a smaller caliber rifle would be adequate. When Barry suggested that I borrow his Remington Model 700 in 7mm magnum, I accepted his offer. I owned a similar rifle and could practice with it at home. Thus, all the difficulties in transporting firearms by the airways, especially dealing with the new regulations at the Johannesburg airport, were obviated. First issue solved.

I chose Cabela's Travel Service to make the appropriate travel arrangements. The coach class international flight on South African Airways flew from Dulles to Johannesburg and thence to Windhoek. I was to leave home at 4 A.M. on Wednesday, 20 September and arrive at Windhoek at 5:30 P.M. on Thursday. Cabela's also arranged for a VIP service to shepherd me through the Johannesburg airport. In addition, I obtained flight cancellation insurance that provided air evacuation in case I became ill. All in all, travel arrangements were a very painless process.

Late September in Namibia is at the end of winter but before the rains set in. Thus, the temperature would be in the fifties at night and warming up to ninety degrees plus by early afternoon. The chance of rain was very slight. I chose my clothes accordingly and packed a two-tiered duffel bag that weighed forty-five pounds (limit fifty pounds). I also had a carry-on that contained at least one change of clothing and all the essential equipment. Thus, if the checked baggage didn't make it, I could hunt anyway.

A new health issue had manifested itself since my prior safari. On two occasions, I had developed a rapid regular tachycardia (about one hundred sixty b.p.m.) lasting about thirty minutes. The precise diagnosis was never made but nothing of note turned up on a cardiac evaluation except a mild degree of mitral-valve insufficiency. Other than having Metoprolol available in case of need, the cardiac situation was put aside. Although I would be at the edge of endemic malaria, I chose to take prophylaxis anyway. In view of the dreams and potential arrhythmogenic effects of Lariam, I decided to give Malarone another try. I took the drug for five days in August and remained asymptomatic. I guess the prior problems of malaise and nausea in Kilombero were unrelated to Malarone.

In August, I began my thrice weekly, two-mile walking exercises; by departure time I felt I was in pretty good shape. I also rented a satellite phone ($8/day) so that I could communicate if necessary. Since a lot of time would be spent in the air, I convinced myself to foster my education by reading Dickens. I obtained abridged versions of *David Copperfield, Oliver Twist,* and the *Pickwick Papers.* With all of these tasks completed, I was ready to go two weeks before departure—overly compulsive as usual.

After a long, somewhat exhausting flight, I arrived in Windhoek along with the luggage. Barry met me at the airport. At 6 feet, 3 inches tall, Barry turned out to be very personable, and I liked him immediately. We checked in at the Safari Inn Hotel, which had very nice accommodations.

At supper, I met Mr. Roy Sparks, who had just driven from South Africa with the dogs. He filled me in on all the particulars. Roy has been hunting primarily stock-killing leopards essentially full-time since the mid-1980s. During that time he officiated the demise of approximately one hundred fifty leopards. Certainly, this is an experience that is unlikely to be exceeded. Roy obtained his hound stock from the Lee Brothers in Arizona, who supplied primarily treeing Walker and bluetick hounds. He has bred these

Mr. Spots stretched out on an uprooted tree trunk. Even in death, he is quite majestic.

Barry and Bwana Babu. Barry is 6'3" tall. The huge leopard is quite a handful, even for him.

dogs selectively to hunt leopard for a number of years and now has an outstanding pack. In fact, a number of individuals interested in "dry-ground" cat hunting have purchased dogs from him.

Another and extremely important member of his contingent was Moshile, a Xhosa tribesman (originally of Zulu lineage). He described Moshile not only as very talented but also as an outstanding tracker and dog handler. This description turned out to be a major understatement of Moshile's abilities.

On Friday morning, after purchasing several items that were needed for the camp, we started our trip northward. Trudia Game Ranch, approximately thirty thousand acres in size, is located about ten miles south of Etosha National Park and was originally a cattle ranch. (It is currently surrounded by cattle ranches.) Purchased in 1996 by Barry's family, it has been developed as a game ranch, primarily for kudu and gemsbok along with numerous other plains game.

Our drive was on a two-lane paved road having minimal traffic. The country we traversed was generally brown, desolate in appearance, and very rocky. It was somewhat hilly, and during the three-hundred-mile drive, we passed several fairly impressive mountains. The topography reminded me of Wyoming where I had hunted sage grouse. The terrain was covered with thornbushes, scrub trees, brown grass, and straw. A significant portion of the land was covered by dark red sand. Barry indicated that it was actually quite good cattle country. About thirty miles from camp, we turned onto a gravel road and arrived about 5 P.M.

My living quarters turned out to be a standard two-room tent covered by a thatched roof, which provided adequate shade. The bathroom in the tent had a flush toilet. Electric lights were present until the generator was turned off about 10 P.M. In fact, I had all the comforts of home. The main complex, including the kitchen, was housed in a permanent structure surrounded by a number of flowers: good butterfly hunting?

After unpacking, we got in the Land Cruiser and drove to a field to sight-in the armament. The Model 700 Remington was equipped with a fluted barrel and a Leopold scope. Barry also had shooting sticks for me to use. The rifle was "dead on" with a custom load that he had handloaded, so there were no problems there. We went for a drive on a woods road, which are typically covered with shale. Barry shot a female gemsbok, which was cut in half and hung for bait in two locations.

Interestingly enough, there were no vultures in the sky and few, if any, hyenas on the ranch. Thus, it is not necessary to hang bait high off the ground or to camouflage it. Barry stated that leopards in this area, seldom if ever, come to bait. Perhaps this is the result of the local ranchers putting poison on any carcass that they find in order to kill all the predators. The surviving leopards obviously have learned to stay away from a free meal.

At dinner I met Barry's father, Fred, and his mother, Laura. Fred was guiding a gentleman from Atlanta who was hunting plains game. Laura is a delightful individual who was supervising the cooking and housekeeping activities. The meals were excellent, served family style, and proceeded by a heartfelt blessing.

At 4:30 A.M. the next day, we started to hunt in earnest. The modus operandi was to have Moshile and Alex (Barry's tracker) ride on the hood of the Land Cruiser as we slowly drove along the woods roads. During the dark, Moshile used a spotlight to locate leopard spoor, which he hooked up to the battery of the truck. It seemed like an impossible task, but that's what he did. It was light about 6:15 A.M. and we could continue this method of hunting until about 10 A.M. After that it became too hot for the dogs to smell scent satisfactorily, even if fresh tracks were found.

During the first morning, we traversed an area of about six miles. Moshile pointed out a number of old leopard tracks along with areas where the leopard had scratched and marked the ground with scent and scat. Moshile and Roy were convinced that a fairly large male leopard was using this area. We stopped hunting and returned to camp about 11 A.M., had lunch, and relaxed until 4 P.M. I used this time for a nap and to engage in a successful butterfly hunt that added several new specimens to my collection.

That afternoon, we took four baits from the plains game killed by the other hunter and hung them along the same road where we had found tracks in the morning. During the afternoon, a number of plains game were in evidence: kudus, gemsboks, zebras, hartebeests, and dik-diks, to name a few. We saw cheetah tracks on two occasions. Also, we scouted several watering areas to look for tracks. These consisted of a deep well from which water was pumped into a cistern. Originally developed for cattle, these wells provide the primary source of water for the game. We also saw tracks made by a large bull elephant sometime during the past week. (Apparently, elephants occasionally visit the ranch.) Bird life was not particularly abundant except for large flocks of guineas. The characteristic call of the ubiquitous African ringneck doves reinforced the fact that I was "home again."

The next morning, we drove along the same road. None of the baits were touched and no fresh tracks were spotted. We did find the remains of a gemsbok killed by a leopard approximately two weeks before. That afternoon we went to another area and found several old leopard tracks and hung additional bait. Moshile felt that we were wasting time to hunt elsewhere. He knew that we would contact a large leopard within two to three days in the area where we had hunted in the morning.

So far, the dogs had remained in the truck but did not seem to mind being hauled around together. Roy occasionally turned out a Jack Russell terrier and let him run around. He was somewhat larger than the ones I have seen in Florida. Roy indicated that he employs this dog to go into holes to rout out leopards that have taken refuge underground. This concept doesn't seem to me to be compatible with a long life, but at least this particular dog was still alive.

The next morning, we began our trek at the same time. We traversed the majority of the six-mile stretch and passed all the untouched baits before entering a very rocky area. Suddenly Moshile's hand went up, signaling for us to stop. He became quite animated and smiling, for he had seen fresh tracks made by a large leopard. Since there was no moon, the tracks either had to be made earlier that morning or not long after sundown. Roy agreed with Moshile's assessment that the tracks were fresh. They got tracking collars from the truck and put them on three hounds. The hunt began! Moshile, who carried a two-way radio to keep in contact with us, along with Alex took the dogs in the direction the leopard appeared to be traveling.

They went toward a ravine situated between a fairly high hill covered with large boulders and shale and our location, which was on a low hill covered very thickly by thorny brush, low trees, and brown grass. After about ten minutes, Moshile indicated that he had found a fresh track in a dried streambed. About this time, one of the dogs gave tongue. Another one opened a couple of minutes later.

For the next hour or so, the trackers and the hounds gradually unraveled the trail, moving perhaps a mile. We kept ahead of the direction of their travel in the Land Cruiser. As the tracks became fresher, the dogs began to bark more frequently. At this juncture, Roy turned out another hound. When he struck, Roy smiled and indicated that the track was very fresh since this dog would not give tongue on a cold track. Roy felt the leopard would probably be hiding on the hill among the rocks, but this was not the case.

All of a sudden, Moshile began communicating on the radio in a high-pitched staccato voice. He had seen the leopard! The hounds began running in earnest. The tailgate of the truck was dropped and the other six dogs joined the chase. They were obviously very well trained. No barking occurred until they got to where they were supposed to be.

The sign on the tailgate of the truck that stated "The B.S. stops when the tailgate drops" was prophetic. For the next ten or fifteen minutes, the air was filled with a high volume of hound music as they ran behind the leopard who was coming in our direction. About two hundred yards from our location, the leopard stopped and the dogs bayed, letting the world know of his stand. It was time for us to join the fracas.

Just as I grabbed the rifle and prepared to walk, my heart rate suddenly accelerated dramatically—the damned arrhythmia manifested itself. For fifteen seconds I was quite woozy, but I adjusted to the problem, and my head cleared quickly. I had to make a decision. Should I stop, take the Metoprolol, and try to control the rate, or go ahead? Not really a decision! I wouldn't have missed these proceedings unless I was completely incapacitated. Away we went! I kept up fairly well in spite of the fact that my heart was racing. (Actually, I ignored this problem.)

When we got to within about sixty-five yards of the leopard, we could hear him snarling and emitting low-pitched coughing growls. He clearly was not happy with the contingent of dogs surrounding him. He changed his location and, after running about one hundred yards, stopped again. We got within thirty yards of the cat. At first, I did not see the leopard who was surrounded by thick brush, but I could hear his guttural vocal outpourings. We slowly moved forward. I was able to make out an area of yellow covered with black spots three feet behind a dog named Charlie, who was letting the world know that he was looking at the leopard.

I eased the rifle up on the sticks and waited. When Charlie moved, I had a clear view of the leopard's chest. At the report of the rifle, the leopard snarled, ran to my left about five yards, and crouched behind a bush. Completely hidden, he became quiet. The hounds continued to bay but seemed to back off farther from the leopard than before. Roy on the far left, Barry in the middle, and I approximately three feet to Barry's right and slightly behind, gradually moved toward the leopard. Barry, because of his height, saw the leopard first and exclaimed, "He's dying. No need to shoot again."

The words were scarcely out of his mouth when "Mr. Spots" disproved this assessment of the situation. Without uttering a sound, he charged toward Roy. Both Roy and Barry shot simultaneously. The leopard piled up about six feet in front of Roy, the object of his attentions. Well, this time the leopard really was dead. Both bullets had grazed the right cheek and made a substantial hole in the front of his chest.

All the dogs were there with the exception of the Jack Russell. (We found him later back at the truck.) They looked the leopard over and licked some of his blood but did not worry the carcass. (This is quite different from the hounds I've seen that are used to hunt raccoon or hog in the United States.) Undoubtedly, these dogs have learned that mouthing the carcass of a supposedly dead leopard might not be compatible with longevity. At any rate, they left "Mr. Spots" pretty much alone.

Moshile easily carrying the massive leopard back to the truck along with four the, apparently, quite satisfied hounds.

Moshile, who was smiling and as happy as could be, reached down and easily hauled the leopard up onto his shoulders. We walked back toward an open area where the truck was parked. Moshile deposited the leopard on the ground and we began to take pictures. It became quite apparent that this was a very large, majestic animal. Interestingly, most dead animals lose their persona. A dead elephant is certainly a very depressing sight. Not true for this leopard. He retained all the splendor that he had exhibited during life.

By the way, my arrhythmia disappeared sometime during the final few minutes of the encounter. I felt fine.

In discussing the climax of the episode, Roy indicated that about half the time leopards will bay on the ground rather than climb a tree or hide in rocks. If a leopard bayed on the ground sees a man, it invariably culminates the hunt by charging. This one was no exception. Barry confided in me that he had made an error, dictated primarily by his desire not to puncture the leopard skin with too many holes. When he first saw the leopard, it was lying on its side and barely breathing. He concluded that the leopard was terminal. Undoubtedly, he learned that a "nearly dead" leopard can still create a world of trouble. I'll bet Barry won't refrain from shooting a "dying" leopard in the future.

After taking pictures and watering the dogs, it was about 11:00 A.M. and beginning to be warm. Roy wanted to get the skin off the leopard as soon as possible. We drove back to the camp and Moshile went to work with his knife. The skinning took thirty minutes or so. He spent the next two hours carefully removing all the flesh so that the hide could be put into the salt. When the chest was opened, it was filled with blood. My bullet had penetrated through the edge of the heart. Clearly, the leopard would not have lived more than two or three minutes. How he had the strength to charge is amazing, but charge he did!

Typical of desert leopards, the background color of the hide was a pale yellow. He was measured to be 7 feet, 5 inches long. Although we did not have scales, Roy estimated the weight to be 75 kilos, or 165 pounds. Rough measurements of the skull gave a combined total of 15 10/16 inches. Obviously, this was an exceptionally large leopard.

Since I killed the leopard on the third day of the hunt, I had twelve more days to view game: look at kudus, gemsboks, dik-diks, and so on. Instead, I made a decision to come home early; the flights were changed. Two days later we left camp, after saying good-bye to Roy, Moshile, and the Burchells. Barry and I arrived in Windhoek about 5 P.M. We celebrated at the Safari Inn with an outstanding dinner. I caught the plane the next day and had a reasonably quiet and uninterrupted flight back to Durham. I finished the Dickens novels, perhaps significantly enhancing my erudition.

In summary, I traveled to Africa and returned by myself. I had an outstanding adventure, killing a very large male leopard. It is number four in my quest for a record-book "Big Five" animal. (The only thing left is a white rhinoceros.) By any measure, this was an outstanding episode in the saga of my African hunting. Arturo, thanks. I hope that your safari was half as exciting as mine.

Him

For ten long seasons, I've been wild and free.
My only worry: to look after Me.
With antelope aplenty and cattle about,
Filling my belly is never in doubt.

For the past few days, I've seen more of Him
Riding the roads; tying meat to a limb.
Keeping away from Him is easy for Me:
Hiding in caves or high in the trees.

Today is no different. I hunt before dawn.
I hear a dog bark near where I've just gone.
Two more join in as they follow my path.
Soon I may have a fresh canine repast.

Closer they come. I'm ready to kill.
But I see Him stalking slowly downhill.
I'd best be off and leave them behind.
There's lots easier prey for Me to find.

Just after I start, I hear Him yell.
More dogs join in as I run pell-mell.
As fast as I go, they're gaining on Me.
I'll stop and fight them under this tree.

They're all around Me. There's no chance to hide.
How many will die? I'll soon decide.
The dogs come close to my fangs and claws.
Flirting with death, they feint — they pause.

He's here! A loud noise—then pain in My chest.
My life's blood flows from the wound in My breast.
He smiles in triumph as I die at His feet.
Now I know. He's the one to defeat.

He's my enemy. Now I must kill!
Quickly I charge . . .
Then, everything's still.

White Rhinoceros, The End of My Quest for the Big Five

Chapter XIV

Although previously I had not entertained the possibility that I would acquire the African Big Five, shooting a "picture book" leopard in Namibia dramatically changed my outlook. Now I had killed four of this group. Thus, I began to investigate the available options for hunting a southern white rhinoceros.

I had seen rhinos in the wild on two prior occasions while hunting elephants in Timbavati, South Africa, and on the Zuka Game Ranch in KwaZulu-Natal. Neither of these experiences whetted my appetite to hunt these behemoths. At least in these locations, they appeared to be reasonably docile and easily approachable, which meant that they were not likely to provide a challenging hunting experience.

However, the major drawback to my killing a rhinoceros was not sport, but money. Although available for hunting, the trophy fee for a white rhinoceros was approximately $50,000. (Acquiring the Big Five wasn't worth an investment of this amount to me.) During my leopard hunt, Barry Burchell, the professional hunter, indicated that he could make arrangements for me to dart a rhino near his game ranch on the Eastern Cape. This fee, which included a simulated rhino horn trophy and insurance in case a mishap to the rhino occurred, was $6,000—a far cry from the trophy fee for killing one. After I returned home, I mulled over the situation for a couple of weeks and decided to give it a try.

Accordingly, I booked a seven-day trip with Frontier Safaris and Barry Burchell as the PH. Frank Cole of Cabela's Outdoor

Bwana Babu and the immobilized white rhinoceros. Note the impressive horn.

Bwana Babu, Barry, and the rhinoceros. The dart is still in place. Note the long barrel of the dart gun.

Adventures again made all the arrangements. Although darting a rhino was the primary goal, the opportunity to hunt caracal with a pack of trained hounds was a very attractive option. An additional very positive feature was that my daughter, Ruth Ann, could accompany me and perhaps try her hand at hunting plains game. The description of the beautiful country in the Eastern Cape, where the ranch was located, assured me that she would thoroughly enjoy being a tourist in that area, if nothing else.

Although her interest in actually shooting plains game seemed to wax and wane, she did practice with a Remington Model 700 bolt-action rifle in .257 Roberts caliber. She shot enough to become comfortable with both the rifle and the use of shooting sticks.

Our trip to the thirty-thousand-acre game ranch was quite uneventful. We left the Raleigh-Durham airport at 12:30 P.M. and boarded a South African Airways flight at 5:30 P.M. at Dulles Airport.

After our arrival in Johannesburg, South Africa, we boarded another plane for Port Elizabeth and arrived at 9 P.M. the next day. We were promptly met by Barry, who drove us to the game ranch.

We were in for a real surprise. To say the least, we were not going to "rough it." Each of us had a very well-appointed stone chalet, which had been constructed near the top of a hill. From the porch, there was a view of the valley and adjacent hills. What a spectacular sight: They were covered by green vegetation and trees. After a few hours of sleep, we were awakened at 5 A.M. to begin the day's hunt.

The initial adventure was to hunt caracal with a pack of hounds. Barry owned a number of hounds that were hunted almost daily on his ranch and adjoining territories. Their primary task was to keep under control the number of small predators, i.e., caracals, foxes, jackals, aardwolves, and so on, that could decimate the newborn plains game. Like the leopard-hunting hounds I had seen in Namibia, these dogs were primarily bred from strains of hounds that were used to hunt big game (cougars, bobcats, and bears) in the western United States. Since Barry hunted with his pack on a daily basis, they were well behaved and tractable.

Ruth Ann and I rode in a Toyota Land Cruiser with Barry. The dogs and the two dog handlers occupied another truck. We drove about fifteen miles to another ranch where they had recently reported seeing a number of caracals. The dog handlers walked with the dogs through a valley while we followed their progress from a high ridge. They quickly struck a hot track that had been made by a bat-eared fox. The hounds chased the fox for twenty minutes until it went into an underground den. After that, they hunted for approximately two hours, but they did not pick up another hot scent. We retrieved the dogs and went back to the game ranch about 11 A.M.

The weather on that day and for the rest of the trip was quite comfortable. In the early morning, the temperature was about fifty degrees, then warming up to about seventy-five degrees by midafternoon. It did not rain during the time that we were there.

In the early afternoon, Barry took us to the range to familiarize Ruth Ann with a Ruger Model 77 in .270 caliber rifle that he would loan her to use on this trip. The target of choice was a number of small brown rocks placed on a board. From a distance of approximately seventy-five yards, Ruth Ann was quite proficient in breaking the rocks. Barry seemed satisfied with her performance.

After rifle practice, we went plains game hunting. Ruth Ann decided that she would like to shoot one of the large, and two of the medium-size, antelopes. The standard hunting procedure is to drive along the roads on the tops of the hills, intermittently looking into the valleys and up to the next hill while using binoculars to spot game. Shortly after we began hunting, Barry saw a small herd of Cape kudus that contained a couple of very nice bulls. He decided that we should try to stalk this group.

Accordingly, we walked down the hill, keeping in contact via radio with our tracker, Neeba, who remained at the truck. Neeba watched the movement of the kudu herd and was able to tell us in which direction to walk. After beginning the ascent on the next hill, we saw the group of kudus coming in our direction. Ruth Ann positioned the rifle on the shooting sticks and got ready to shoot. The herd walked across a road approximately one hundred fifty yards from us. A large bull stopped in the road long enough for her to shoot, but it moved just as she fired. The path of the bullet angled forward into the chest.

The bull, obviously hit, jumped out of the road, then turned around and came back across the road. The rest of the herd decamped. Neeba arrived quickly with the truck and turned out two dogs that were used to follow blood trails. One was a pure Jack Russell terrier and the other a "Heinz 57" containing some bulldog. They quickly picked up the track and found the wounded kudu about sixty yards from the road where the brush was extremely thick. Although the bull was severely wounded and sick, he moved on two occasions, but each time he was followed by the dogs. Finally, we saw a horn tip in the dense undergrowth and ended the affair. Ruth Ann, who had been quite upset after wounding the animal, was elated by the final outcome.

Ruth Ann and a large springbok.

That night we were entertained by a local dancing group at the very impressive lodge. The dining area contained an inside raised fireplace where all the cooking was done. Lizelle, Barry's wife, and their four children joined us. Obviously, on this game ranch, they had the facilities for a large operation. For example, during the previous week, twenty-eight hunters along with fourteen PHs had hunted there and had killed approximately three hundred animals.

The next morning we drove approximately thirty miles through heavy fog to the Lalibela Game Reserve. We arrived about 7:30 A.M. and met Carl van Zyl, the owner's son, who was to be our guide. Shortly thereafter, a veterinarian arrived with all of the appropriate accouterments for the darting process. The dart gun had a very long barrel with a red-dot Holosight and a maximum range of fifty yards.

Since the parabolic trajectory of the dart was high, the precise distance to the target had to be known. If the animal was twenty yards away and the sight was set for fifty yards, the dart would go too high. Conversely, if the sight was set for twenty yards and the

Bwana Babu, a large Cape bushbuck, and Ruth Ann. Note the spectacular sunset.

animal was at fifty yards, the dart would go into the dirt and not reach the quarry.

Another important factor is that the dart must go into the thick skin perpendicularly in order to penetrate to the underlying tissue. If the drug is injected into the skin, it will not be absorbed fast enough to immobilize the animal. I practiced eight or ten times, and at thirty yards I was able to hit the target, a cardboard box. The veterinarian indicated that he had been involved in darting a number of rhino. Carl noted that they had only one rhino that had been darted recently, but several others provided good options for me. They only dart a given rhino once a year.

Our group piled into a Land Cruiser: Carl, Barry, the veterinarian, a driver, Ruth Ann, and I. A scouting party in another Land Cruiser went in another direction to help locate rhinos.

As we drove along, it became quite obvious that the reserve was very heavily stocked with a variety of game. Although no hunting was allowed, the reserve was used for game viewing by a number of photographic safari parties. We saw numerous herds of impalas, waterbucks, gemsboks, zebras, and a pod of hippos. The terrain was much like Barry's game ranch. Although quite hilly, it did have a number of open areas covered with grass.

Our first contact with a rhino was a female accompanied by an approximately two-week-old calf. She didn't seem too perturbed at our presence, but it was obvious that she preferred for us to move on, which we did! About 10 A.M., the other scouting party contacted us to say that they had located five rhinos in an open field of approximately thirty to forty acres. We quickly drove to that area and saw the rhino. At least one of them had a very impressive horn, so we decided to get close to this behemoth.

Accordingly, Barry, Carl, and I stalked the rhino by crawling along a row of thornbushes at the edge of the meadow. Ruth Ann and the veterinarian remained approximately seventy-five yards behind us, hidden behind a tree. When we got to the edge of the meadow, we were lucky. The wind was in the right direction; the rhinos were totally oblivious to our presence. They were feeding approximately one hundred yards from our location. (When grazing, they move their head from side to side and seem to be mowing the grass. They ingest a prodigious amount of green groceries.)

We got into position, and waited behind a row of bushes. Initially, the rhinos grazed away from us but then turned and gradually fed in our direction. Two of them came within the accepted fifty yards and then, for some reason, stood without moving for what seemed like one hour but was probably no more than five minutes. They were unaware of our presence and were facing perpendicular from my left to right. One of the rhinos, the smaller one, was approximately twenty yards off, while the larger, our quarry, was fifty yards off.

They started to move again, and I was afraid that the closer rhinoceros would obscure my view of the large one. However, Lady Luck smiled. The small rhinoceros stopped, giving me a clear shot. Barry was behind me, armed with a Krieghoff Classic .470 double rifle, just in case of trouble. I aimed at the rhino's shoulder and a whooshing sound occurred as the dart left the barrel. It was easy to

Large male caracal and Bwana Baby

see the dart as it went toward the rhino. It hit and stuck about the middle of the way up on the right shoulder.

The rhino exited at full speed to our right and was joined by the others. They left the field, and ran into a wooded valley. The other truck had been perched on a high hill, so the occupants had seen all of the action. They indicated that the rhino had fallen approximately seven hundred and fifty yards from us in a ravine. We arrived very quickly, jumped out of the truck, and examined the rhino.

The behemoth was resting on his abdomen with all four legs tucked under him, completely immobile. Its breathing appeared somewhat labored. The veterinarian went to work drawing blood samples, giving the rhino an antibiotic, and making measurements. (The large horn was about thirty inches in length.) The rest of the crew cleared the brush away so that we could take photographs. The entire episode required approximately fifteen minutes.

At that juncture, we all got back into the Land Cruiser and turned to leave. The veterinarian gave an antidote and hotfooted it back to the truck. About the time he got to the truck, the rhino started getting up. Within five minutes, it was stumbling off to find its compatriots. We saw the critter one hour later, grazing as though nothing had happened.

Well, now, I had successfully acquired the African Big Five. Certainly, hunting a white rhinoceros was not nearly as exciting as I have had with the other four, but the darting process was far more interesting than I had ever imagined. In fact, it would have been quite easy and anticlimactic, upon arriving at the meadow, to take Barry's .470 double rifle and kill the rhino. On the other hand, waiting, hoping, etc., for the rhino to get close enough for me to use the dart was quite an exciting adventure. After visiting the very palatial lodge and eating lunch, we returned to our home base.

That afternoon, about 3 P.M., we drove toward the high hills looking for smaller plains game. The scenery was absolutely spectacular. We saw a number of different species of plains game. Ruth Ann shot at and missed a blesbok. Just as the sun began to set, Barry decided to drive through an area of pines that looked much like Virginia spruce pine. Just as we got to the other end, Barry told us that there was a bushbuck in this area that was shy from having been shot at previously. It had very impressive horns.

We got out of the truck and walked along the ridge. Barry spotted the animal approximately one hundred twenty yards off. Ruth Ann put the rifle on the sticks, but couldn't visualize the bushbuck in spite of Barry's directions. Finally, he said, "Do you see that brown rock?"

She concurred.

"Shoot the rock!"

She did, and the bushbuck promptly fell. Whether she actually saw anything but a brown apparition resembling a rock, I'm not sure. She had taken a very impressive animal. We obtained a beautiful picture with the setting sun as the background.

We got an early start the next morning to hunt caracal. On this occasion, we released the hounds close to the lodge where two caracals had been seen crossing the road the day before. Barry, Ruth Ann, and I were in the Land Cruiser and the dog handlers and Neeba, along with the hounds, were in another truck. They released the hounds and walked with them in a brush-covered valley while we remained on the crest of the hill watching their progress.

After about thirty minutes, we heard the dogs strike. It soon became quite clear that they had jumped a predator. They ran in full cry for about thirty minutes. They finally bayed a caracal within three hundred yards of our location. When we arrived at the tree, a large male caracal clung to a branch that was densely covered by leaves.

Although quite visible when I was close, if I had moved more than ten feet away, the cat would have been totally obscured by the foliage. This created a difficult situation. The rifle had a telescopic sight mounted close to the receiver. If I moved far enough away to see clearly through the telescope, the leaves obscured the caracal. At a short range, when the cat was visible, the scope could not be focused.

In desperation, I sighted down the left side of the barrel and guessed where the bullet should travel. By sheer luck I killed the

Unique sign in the Addo Elephant National Park.

caracal. The cat fell out of the tree and was immediately retrieved by Neeba so that the hounds didn't tear the hide. The caracal, a very large male, was placed on a tree limb and photographed, along with a number of the hounds.

Then, the dog handlers resumed hunting and walked with the pack along the hillside. About thirty minutes later, the hounds began running. Again, they were in full cry for about fifteen minutes, and then shut off. They did not bay. When we arrived, we found that they had caught an aardwolf, a creature that looks a lot like a large fuzzy fox. Unfortunately, the hounds ripped the skin in a number of places so that the hide was unusable. At that juncture, we "called it quits" and returned to the lodge.

That afternoon, we drove to a ranch, approximately seventy-five miles northwest, that was located on the edge of the Karoo drylands. This land is flatter and the vegetation sparse, making it an ideal location for springbok. Our destination was a ranch that

A somewhat bedraggled aardwolf.

was used primarily for sheep and ostrich; in fact, we saw several thousand ostriches.

Shortly after we arrived, we saw a large group of springboks and were able to stalk to within two hundred fifty yards of the herd. They initially trotted off, but then they turned around and came back in our direction—stopping to within one hundred seventy-five yards. Ruth Ann shot at a very large male.

Initially, Barry thought that she had missed. However, when the herd ran off, the springbok collapsed after running about seventy-five yards. The bullet had gone through his chest. He was a very impressive animal. Barry pointed out that the hairs on the back of springboks when they are excited or run a lot exude a particular odor much like cotton candy. I had my doubts, but he was right. With this springbok, Ruth Ann had completed her goal to acquire three antelopes.

The next day, we drove to Addo Elephant National Park, which is an enormous refuge funded by the government. There are a number of different animals in the park, but the primary attraction is the elephants. Interestingly enough, on one of the paved roads there was a sign with a very unusual message: "Dung Beetles Have Right Of Way." We concurred with this request. We did see a number of animals, including a Cape buffalo that fed within ten yards of the truck. A very large bull elephant passed us on the road. It is extremely impressive to see at close range such a massive animal. As the elephant walked by us, we looked through his legs, but could not see his body. The bottom of his chest was above the roof of the Land Cruiser. I estimated that each tusk weighed approximately sixty pounds.

Although we had not spent the entire seven days hunting, we had accomplished everything we had planned, and made a decision to come home early. Accordingly, we left the next day, caught a plane in Port Elizabeth, and began our arduous, but uneventful, trip back home.

Although I have no desire to dart another rhinoceros or to kill one, I thoroughly enjoyed the experience. A very positive feature: I am certain that the rhinoceros approved of this approach rather than the alternative. I am doubtful if Ruth Ann will ever become a "Diana," but she did thoroughly enjoy her experience.

In fulfilling my quest for the African Big Five, my dreams have all come true. This safari was a fitting end to my goal.

Cape Buffalo Finale

Chapter XV

"Jambo, Bwana Babu!" This salutation, along with the pungent odor of African coffee, awoke me at predawn. Ahead lay the eighth day hunting Cape buffaloes. The hilly part of the Miombo Safaris' Rungwa concession was teeming with buffaloes, and the preceding week had been filled with multiple encounters. We had tracked and stalked small herds, large herds, single *dagga* boys, and groups of *dagga* boys, and we had come close enough to shoot on many occasions. However, except for one *mbogo*, none had met my requirements: at least a forty-three-inch horn width with a solid boss, similar to the one I had killed in Rungwa two years before.

After a prolonged stalk, a qualified *mbogo* now faced me at a distance of approximately fifty yards. Although I could see his head and upper shoulders clearly, the lower half of his body was obscured by brush. I didn't shoot. I know that Joey, the professional hunter, Sampson, the head tracker, Martin and Joebere, the other two trackers, were somewhat disgruntled at my reticence. However, I had made a pact with myself, several years before, regarding shooting at Cape buffalo: "If I can't see it, I ain't gonna shoot at it." I am convinced that following this maxim has helped to keep me out of serious trouble.

We had followed three large herds, and from a distance, had seen several bulls that might have qualified. On each occasion though, either nearby giraffes or zebras had given the alarm;

these herds had left posthaste. One stalk was called off when we determined that a pride of lions also was following this herd. The amazing ability of the trackers was demonstrated on a number of occasions in both woody and grass-covered terrain.

Since every day had brought different and exciting encounters with *mbogo,* I was certain that my expectations would eventually come to fruition. (Frankly, my primary reason to set such a high standard was not to kill the two licensed buffalo on the first days of the hunt and, thereby, spending the rest of the time game viewing!)

Somewhat tired of body, but by no means disheartened, I quickly made ready to begin this day's activities. At 7:15 A.M., our contingent began traversing the woods roads in the Land Cruiser. A few minutes after leaving camp, we saw a small herd of buffaloes, about fifteen or twenty, cross the road. It was impossible to determine whether there was a shootable bull among them. We followed for about ten minutes and saw this herd crossing a small clearing. At that point we could clearly see there were no acceptable bulls.

On the way back to the truck, we came upon a group of approximately twenty-five bulls. We made a protracted stalk, requiring a long detour to get the wind blowing in the correct direction. We closed to within seventy-five yards before we could again estimate that none of the bulls with a solid boss had a horn width greater than thirty-nine inches. We left them undisturbed. (I believe that we had seen this same group earlier.) At any rate, we walked back to the truck.

The driver informed us that he had just seen a small herd of buffaloes cross right in front of the truck. We followed their tracks. Just as we closed to within about seventy yards, a bird, either an oxpecker or a honey guide, made a warning noise. The buffalo left posthaste. So far, the morning had been filled with a lot of excitement and continuous tracking and stalking, but my criteria remained unmet.

On the way back to the truck, we spotted another herd of about sixty buffaloes. They had just finished feeding for the morning and

We're not interested in friendship. Don't come any closer!

were milling around in a fairly open area. The wind direction was ideal. We got close enough to determine that the herd contained several bulls, but as before, none of them appeared to be of trophy quality. However, we followed as they slowly walked toward a shaded area.

They started preparing for their noon nap, several of them lying down and the others standing under the shade of some large trees. We were able to stalk within sixty yards of the herd. (I accomplished the last twenty yards by sliding on my rear-end.) Joey saw what appeared to be a wide-horned bull with a solid boss right in the middle of the herd. He positioned the shooting sticks for me. While I gazed through the telescope, as if by magic, the herd seemed to divide—shades of the Red Sea. Suddenly, I was looking directly down a corridor, buffaloes on each side, at a very impressive *mbogo*. He was standing quartering slightly to my left, with his entire chest clearly visible.

I squeezed the trigger on the right barrel of the .470 Holland and Holland. The Woodleigh 500-grain solid went into *mbogo*'s lower left shoulder region several inches to the right of where I had aimed—undoubtedly a mortal wound, but it failed to anchor him. This bull, along with the rest of the herd, quickly left, but after running no more than three hundred yards, they all stopped. The wounded *mbogo*, still on his feet, was on our side of the herd.

Although he appeared sick, he was functional and potentially very dangerous. We stalked to within seventy-five yards, but the bull trotted another one hundred yards and stopped again. We eased into position within sixty yards of *mbogo*. He stood facing from my right to left. Luckily, the bull never saw us. Although mortally wounded, any eye contact would have resulted in a world of trouble for us. Sampson quickly set up the sticks for me, and I shot. Joey shot twice with his .500 Perugini-Visini double rifle. We heard the impact as these three bullets hit *mbogo* in the chest. He showed no effect whatsoever. Following the discharge of my left barrel, the solid bullet traversed his chest and broke the right shoulder. *Mbogo* fell, and emitted a mournful bellow. We quickly advanced and ended the affair. The herd rapidly exited. Even a cursory examination

Tracks resembling those made by elephants deeply embedded in rock.

This happens to be my territory!

made it abundantly clear that my criteria for the horns had been met. The horns had a solid boss and curved downward, as well as being quite wide. What an awesome animal.

The truck soon arrived at the scene. A number of vultures lit in nearby trees, obviously anticipating lunch. We took the usual pictures. Since I only wanted a skull mount, skinning and processing the carcass was over in a hurry. Sampson made good use of the knife I had assembled and given to him. My contribution to this work: relax in an easy chair and drink a Diet Coke. In less than an hour, the buffalo was skinned, quartered, and all of the edible meat, horns, and hide were packed into the truck. In fact, the only thing left were the contents of both the stomach and large intestine, along with the small intestine and the rib cage, which had been stripped of all but a minimal amount of meat. I would say, offhand, that the vultures were disappointed.

We arrived back at camp and decided not to hunt that afternoon so that the meat could be cut up into biltong. In fact, this operation was completed by dark. It is amazing how much motivated people can accomplish who know what they are doing. I had a bowl of tasty buffalo tail soup for supper. A better hunt could not have been choreographed.

With two days left to find a second buffalo, I decided not to be so particular regarding horn width, but instead I would look for an old, hard-bossed bull. The next morning, we drove to a grass-covered meadow containing several water holes. While looking for tracks, Sampson spotted a small herd approximately three hundred yards from us. We made a quick detour to get the wind blowing in our direction. Luckily, there were several contiguous termite mounds approximately fifty yards to our front. The buffalo herd elected to walk between these mounds and us. Thus, they were only thirty yards away.

We quickly spotted one very large *mbogo*. Sampson put the sticks down; I got ready to shoot. Initially, it looked as though a nearby cow would obscure his "vital triangle" as he was walking by. However, just at the right moment, he stopped. The cow moved on, giving me a clear shot. At the report of the rifle, *mbogo* immediately dropped. Sampson was so elated that he pounded me on the back with enough force to damn near flatten me as well. At any rate, although the buffalo tried, he could not get up. He was not paralyzed and able to move all four legs. We quickly ended his life.

It seems that the bullet, a solid, broke both shoulders. (I had always assumed that only a bullet damaging either the spine or brain could cause the animal to drop and not be able to rise. Wrong again!) He was an old bull, with a relatively smooth boss having a lot of character and a horn width of approximately thirty-nine inches. We saw that a bullet had entered the right horn near the skull and the resulting wound had begun to fester. This is the type of situation that can result in an unprovoked charge from a buffalo. The unfortunate person would be unaware that a wounded *mbogo* was in the vicinity.

After taking several pictures, the team rapidly dismembered the carcass. We returned to camp, arriving about 11:30 A.M. As before, the afternoon was spent preparing biltong. As a matter of fact, the next day I visited the biltong operation and was impressed to see how much meat had been obtained from the two buffaloes. (Since none of the meat was used for bait, the entire carcass was available.) However, with Sampson's five children and Martin's eight, I am sure that all of this meat will be put to good use.

No one could have asked for a better safari hunting Cape buffalo. The entire ten days was filled with one exciting episode after another. The performance of the trackers was superb and the amenities at camp outstanding. Having the opportunity to go on my seventh safari hunting Cape buffalo with Joey was "just plain fun." As a chapter in my experiences of hunting Africa's premier dangerous game, the Cape buffalo, this hunt could not have been better.

However, reflecting upon the situation, I had the overwhelming feeling that this was my final hunt for *mbogo.* It was impossible to precisely define why I reached this conclusion, but in my heart, I knew this was the case. On all my previous safaris, I had always

A very impressive mbogo with wide horns. In the background, the .470 Holland & Holland double rifle can be seen hanging on the shooting sticks.

Biltong from the two bulls hanging on a line to dry, as well as in piles, ready to be stored.

anticipated and eagerly looked forward to the next hunt, but not this time. I tried to conjure up definitive reasons for my feeling: the dramatic increase in hunting costs recently mandated by the Tanzanian government; my age (seventy-seven); and my fulfillment of having successfully hunted a total of fourteen trophy-quality *mbogos*. All these factors undoubtedly played some role, but, try as I might, I have failed to formulate a comprehensive understanding of why I feel this way. At any rate, the conclusion remains the same. The final curtain has come down on *mbogo* and Bwana Babu.

Last Hour Leopard, The Rest of the Story

Chapter XVI

The genesis for this safari began soon after I returned from the "Hounded Leopard" saga in September of 2006. Every aspect of that encounter had been so exciting that I wanted to have a repeat performance and to take Joey with me. Although Joey had worked as a professional hunter (PH) in Tanzania and had guided a number of clients to leopards over bait, he had never had the opportunity to hunt leopards with hounds, nor had he killed his own leopard. After we discussed this situation, plans for our safari were initiated. Joey would be designated as the hunter and I as an observer. In addition to the leopard, he wanted to shoot several of the larger African antelopes as well.

Our safari to the Trudia Game Reserve in northern Namibia was booked through Frank Cole at Cabela's. Barry Burchell of Frontier Safaris would be our PH, and our safari was set for May of 2008, which meant that we would be the first hunters for the 2008 season. Although I would have preferred to hunt at the end of winter—September or October—our fifteen-day hunt was booked for May. During the 2007 season, Barry had killed seven leopards in the area, so the eight-month period between the two seasons should allow leopards to repopulate.

In January, I spoke at length with Barry at the Safari Club International convention in Reno regarding our upcoming hunt. He was very upbeat about the outlook for our leopard hunt. He had two separate packs of leopard hounds in Namibia. In large measure,

Mike holding fresh leopard scat.

these hounds had been trained in South Africa by hunting caracal. In addition, he had purchased several experienced leopard-hunting hounds from Roy Sparks. Thus, it was feasible for two groups of hunters to hunt leopards simultaneously in the area.

Our travel plans were finalized. In order to avoid a hurried schedule, I booked an early flight to Dulles International Airport where I would meet Joey. We would fly via South African Airways to Johannesburg and then on to Windhoek, Namibia. I thought everything was in order, but shortly before I arrived at the Raleigh-Durham airport, I was told my flight had been canceled and that I was rebooked for a 7 P.M. flight to Dulles. Well, the South African Airways flight left at 5 P.M. To say the least, I arrived at the airport in a somewhat agitated state.

The 2:30 P.M. flight was full and overbooked. The agent who either felt sorry for me or didn't want the problem of dealing with a "seasoned" citizen having a nervous breakdown, bumped a passenger and gave me a seat on the 2:30 P.M. flight. Although there were weather problems that caused a delay with the departure of that plane, I arrived at the gate of South African Airways at 4:30 P.M. I met Joey and began calming down, which took nearly the entire fourteen-hour trip.

We transferred planes in Johannesburg, arrived at Windhoek, and were met by Barry. Joey had brought his .500 NE Perugini-Visini double rifle and a 10-gauge shotgun for me to use in case we had to deal with a leopard at close quarters. Both firearms arrived in fine shape. After rewriting the gun permit request, using the proper colored ink and tipping (bribing) the agent, Joey took possession of the weapons.

The next morning, we drove north to the Trudia Game Ranch in Barry's brand-new Toyota Land Cruiser. (It was new, but by the end of the safari all the "newness" had completely worn off!) During the five-hour trip to the game ranch, Barry informed us that we would have to deal with a potentially serious problem: The ground was covered with green grass. Apparently, they had suffered a major drought, lasting until the latter part of February. Then abundant rains began. In fact, it rained every day until two weeks prior to our arrival. There was a total rainfall of twenty-nine inches—the average rainfall for this area is fourteen inches a year. Thus, all the trees and shrubs remained fully "leafed-out" and grass and brush covered much of the terrain. The dense undergrowth markedly limited the ability to find leopard tracks. In addition, the rain-filled springs and creeks made locating a leopard more difficult, since game was dispersed and not concentrated around the few areas containing water.

On arrival at the camp, I found that a number of building projects had been completed. Four additional thatched-covered tents and a very large dining area with an open roof in the center had been constructed. In addition, there were several flower gardens in which a number of butterflies were evident. I concluded that, even if I didn't see a leopard, I would go home with a good collection of Lepidoptera.

Barry informed us that another hunter was coming the next day to hunt plains game and leopard. Barry's father, Fred Burchell, would function as his PH.

About 4 P.M., Barry, Joey, Corporal, our primary tracker, and I got into the Land Cruiser. (I informed Corporal early on that, if we got a nice leopard, we would promote him to at least a staff

Joey and Bwana Babu along with Corporal, Esau, Alex, and Mike—a superb group of trackers.

sergeant, and maybe as high as a captain.) As we drove on a number of the ranch roads, Barry's concern became obvious. Very little of the surfaces of the roads were not covered with grass. In addition, the adjoining brush was thick and green. In fact, I would not have believed that it was the same territory that I had hunted in eighteen months before.

At any rate, we found one large male leopard track several days old on the road near the entrance gate, and one smaller female track near a water cistern. We did see a number of plains game including gemsboks, kudus, hartebeests, wildebeests, zebras, klipspringers, steenboks, and dik-diks. At supper, I told Barry that, although I was an observer, I would like to try to shoot two of the African small cats, as well as a genet. Barry said that this would not be a problem. We would hunt them at dusk on the way back to camp.

The next morning at 4 A.M., we started hunting leopard in earnest using the following modus operandi. We began riding on the woods roads before daylight with Corporal perched on the hood of the truck and using a spotlight to try to find leopard tracks. We would continue this exercise until 10:30 A.M., come back to camp, and have brunch. After a nap and a brief butterfly-collecting episode, we began hunting again at 4 P.M. In the afternoon, we would cover the area looking for leopard spoor and sign as well as hunting for plains game. The first day, we carried out this exercise on the Trudia Game Ranch. On the way back to camp, we spotted a very large male wildcat. It became our first trophy.

The weather was approximately the same throughout the entire fifteen days: cold in the morning, in the forty-five to fifty-five degree range, and warming up to about ninety degrees by noon. The skies were generally clear, and although scattered showers occurred, none of the rain fell in the areas where we hunted.

The next day we drove approximately forty miles to a cattle ranch about ten miles north of Outjo. The owner of the ranch had a major problem with a leopard that was killing cattle and goats. He had asked Barry to "Please eliminate the perpetrator." We arrived at the ten-thousand-acre ranch at daylight. Although the house seemed to be very well-constructed, made of concrete blocks, the owners were living in small tents in the yard. Why? I never found out. When we arrived, they were asleep, but they soon appeared and encouraged us to hunt anywhere we liked.

There was a dried riverbed approximately one mile from the house where the leopard had been seen frequently. Barry, Joey, Corporal, and I rode in the Land Cruiser while Wentzel Coetzer, a student in game management from South Africa who was working with Barry, drove a Toyota truck containing Mike, the dog handler, and the hounds. Soon we found tracks that were made two days before by a very large leopard. Joey estimated the leopard to be at least seven and one-half feet long. We also saw the tracks of several female leopards. On returning to the owner's home, we saw a calf that had been caught by the leopard. For some unknown reason, the mama cow had been able to run off the leopard. The calf did have fairly deep scratches on the neck, which had been covered by gentian violet, but it didn't look to be much worse off from the episode.

Rocky terrain used by the stock-killing leopard.

A very elated Joey with an armful. Note that the leopard has a full belly.

That afternoon, we drove to a very large adjoining cattle ranch to check on the situation regarding leopards. The ranch home was very palatial and the surrounding grounds were immaculate. We were entertained, at teatime, by the rancher and his wife. He indicated that they didn't have too much of a problem with stock-killing leopards, since they were either shot or trapped. He was very vocal about his recent problems with cheetahs, however, and he told us that they had lost a number of sheep. Apparently, the cheetahs got into a pen with the sheep and slaughtered a large number before they quit. "Please come kill the cheetahs"!

(Cheetahs were not on our list of desired game since it is illegal to run them with hounds, and the trophies cannot be brought into the U.S.A.) To put into perspective the number of leopards killed by cattle ranchers, Barry estimated that last year, about one hundred and fifty leopards either were killed or trapped within a fifty-mile radius of the Trudia Ranch.

For the next several mornings, the scenario was essentially the same as described. At 4 A.M. we would drive to the ranch at Outjo, ride up and down the dried riverbed, and look for tracks. One incident that added some excitement to this drive occurred when a large owl flew into the windshield, shattering most of the glass on the right side. Although still intact and functional, the broken window made the vehicle lose all appearances of being "new."

On the third day, we found tracks made by a male leopard that appeared to be reasonably fresh. Mike and Corporal, along with the dogs, followed the spoor for approximately a mile and one-half through fairly rough terrain. The dogs opened occasionally, but never really got on a hot scent. Ninety percent of the work following the spoor was carried out by Corporal and Mike. (Frankly, this is an amazing feat.) They tracked the leopard farther to a hilly area that contained a number of cliffs and caves. Near a watering hole, they saw evidence of several of the leopard's old kills. In addition, they found a tree that the leopard had frequently used as a lookout. However, they saw no fresh spoor.

For the next several days, we hunted along the riverbed and then drove to the area described above. Corporal and Mike walked

The fresh leopard track began the final episode. Note the relative size of the leopard track and the shoe prints on the right.

the dogs through the territory hoping to jump a leopard. However, these excursions were to no avail. On one occasion, the hounds did run an animal, but it turned out to be a black-back jackal. We did see numerous tracks and diggings made by an aardvark in the riverbed.

The other client and Mr. Burchell hunted on the Trudia ranch exclusively. On one occasion, they did follow a track into a very rocky area, but they didn't spy the leopard.

The afternoons of each day were taken up with hunting for leopard sign and plains game on either the Trudia Game Ranch or on adjoining cattle ranches. On the fourth day of the hunt, Joey killed a very impressive gemsbok after a reasonably long stalk. The next day, he shot a large warthog.

On the fifth day, Barry got a call from another nearby rancher who had found a dead calf that a leopard had killed two days earlier. The next day, after our morning's adventures, we went to that area, found the tracks, and changed our plans accordingly. Each morning, Wentzel and Mike checked out that area on their way to our other venue. On the seventh day, Wentzel called to say that they had "found fresh tracks."

We diverted and went to that area, arriving just at daylight. The leopard had walked down the road for approximately one-half mile. Corporal followed the tracks almost at a dead run and found where the leopard had left the road. He and Mike took the pack and followed the leopard spoor for approximately two miles up a high hill. The dogs started opening at that juncture, and the leopard turned and came back in our direction. Although the dogs never found a hot track, they were able to follow the spoor. At one point, the trackers found where the leopard had lain. However, about 11:30 A.M., when it became quite hot, they lost the track on a rocky hill. I estimated that they had followed the leopard for at least six miles. The entire episode was very exciting, but to say the least, disappointing.

On the way back to camp, we got a call from a nearby rancher saying that, "A leopard had been caught in a leg-hold trap but had carried off the trap. Please come and shoot the critter"!

It was approximately 9 P.M. by that time, so we decided to delay the adventure until the morning. Early the next morning, we found the tracks. They had been made by a cheetah, not a leopard. We did follow the drag marks made by the trap for about a mile and found the trap, but the cheetah was nowhere in sight. The trap contained a few hairs from the foot. It is likely that the cheetah had not been seriously hurt.

Barry decided that we should try to entice a leopard using bait, although he had not had any luck baiting leopards in the past. We used the quarters from the plains game shot by Joey and the other client to accomplish this task. We spent a considerable amount of time hanging bait along the trails on the Trudia ranch—all to no avail.

On the ninth day, we concluded that the leopard in the dried riverbed had moved somewhere else. It was time to quit that morning exercise. Accordingly, we moved our activities primarily to the Trudia Game Ranch.

That afternoon, we had an interesting experience on the adjoining cattle ranch. We saw a large number of vultures in the trees. I had assumed that there were not any vultures in the area because I had never seen any previously. However, in looking around, we found a carcass of a giraffe that had died recently. We went to inform the rancher of the situation. When we returned to the area, the vultures had left. They never touched the carcass, either that day or on subsequent days. What they feed on and why they didn't engulf the giraffe is an unsolved mystery.

One afternoon, while we were looking for plains game, Corporal spotted a black mamba in a tree near the road. Barry promptly killed it. Mike had reported that they had seen another one not too far from the area. I have noted throughout my travels in Africa that trackers are deathly afraid of snakes, and this was a case in point. Both Corporal and Mike showed no interest in going close to the dead reptile. Also, we killed a very large puff adder on the same day.

During the last hunting season, Joey had discussed "snakeaphobia" with Pius, the head tracker for Miombo Safaris in the Selous Reserve in Tanzania. Pius, who essentially exhibits no fear of dangerous big game—elephants, buffaloes, or lions—quickly vanishes if a poisonous snake is encountered. Pius had this very simple observation: "Bwana, elephant, buffalo, and lion have big heads. I know your bullet will hit them. Snake has a very little head. You might miss!" Undoubtedly, this explains his disappearing act.

On the afternoon of the tenth day, we saw a very large kudu, which Joey shot. My daily quest for a civet cat and a genet continued to be unsuccessful. On the thirteenth day of our hunt, the other client left, having killed a number of plains game, but without seeing a leopard. I know that both he and Fred Burchell were disappointed.

One evening, I discussed the Burchell gemsbok with Fred, who has a reasonably stable breeding population at his other ranch in southern Namibia. The Burchell has been recognized as a distinct subspecies of gemsbok, and Fred was very conversant with the genetics. Apparently, a recessive gene causes the features that make a gemsbok a Burchell gemsbok, and he has bred enough of them so that he has established a reasonably good breeding population. The basic difference between a Burchell and a regular gemsbok is the color: black in the regular gemsbok and a light brown in the Burchell. They are very impressive animals, at least in the pictures. Fred is offering limited trophy shooting for a $10,000 trophy fee.

By the thirteenth day, I would say that our temperament, although still upbeat, was beginning to be slightly frayed. Our happiness quotient was boosted dramatically when, nearly at dusk, Joey saw an enormous kudu with wide and massive horns, the largest that he had ever seen. He was able to kill it with his double rifle. He was ecstatic.

The departure of the other client put us in the position of having another group of dogs to look for leopard tracks. The tracker in the other truck was Alex, with whom I had hunted on my prior trip, and Esau, who functioned primarily as a dog handler.

An uneventful day fourteen came and went as did the morning of the fifteenth day. We finished our hunt for tracks about 7:30 A.M. Although Joey had killed a very large black-back jackal earlier, it looked as though we would soon be on our way home without finding a leopard. We sat on one of the hills overlooking a deep valley, a spectacular scene, drinking a cup of coffee. Although clearly disappointed, we put a happy face on the situation.

The ringing of the telephone interrupted our morose thoughts. It was Alex. In rapid-fire Afrikaans (the language spoken by the natives), he told us that they had found fresh leopard tracks by a water cistern near the area where I had killed my leopard last year. "Please come quickly"! he urged.

To say the least, Barry complied with the request. (He has three speeds in the Land Cruiser: fast, excessively fast, and too damn fast.) We got there in about fifteen minutes. Both dog trucks were already at the site. Corporal pointed out the distinct spoor to me so that I was able to decipher what they were excited about. They felt that a fairly large male leopard walking around the cistern that night had made it. The half moon was in the waxing part of its cycle, which meant that after 1 A.M. there wasn't any moonlight. The precise time that the leopard had made the track could not be further delineated.

The leopard just after the kill.

However, the four trackers and the hounds from both trucks combed the area looking for spoor.

Corporal found where the leopard had left the area, going in a generally westward direction, and was able to follow the tracks. The hounds, however, gave no indication that they had perceived any scent.

The terrain was not in our favor, either. We were positioned on a long ridge covered with dense brush and small trees. In front, there was a fairly deep ravine that was bordered on the far side by a reasonably high hill. The leopard had walked for approximately a mile and one-half, and then he had turned back in our direction using the ravine. We had moved the Land Cruiser toward the ravine.

At that juncture, Mike appeared and showed me some fresh scat that he had found in the ravine. He and the other trackers thought that the track was very fresh and that they would be able to follow it. (How they can find such an indistinct spoor in terrain like that is impossible for me to understand. Personally, I am in awe of their abilities.)

The leopard then went eastward, and after approximately one-half mile, the dogs began to open occasionally, an indication that the spoor was fresher. At last they were able to help the trackers follow the leopard. Mr. Spots went up the far hill and then turned around and came back toward us. By that time, it was approximately 10:30 A.M. and the dogs began to open more frequently. Corporal called on the radio and excitedly told us that he had seen the leopard in a tree, but he didn't have any of the hounds with him.

It took approximately five to ten minutes to get several of the pack to take the track where the leopard had jumped out of the tree. Corporal was approximately one mile from where we were located, but was coming in our direction. Although the dogs were in full cry following the leopard, they were not moving nearly as rapidly as I would have expected with a fresh track. I'm certain that the excessive heat was responsible for making the scent faint.

Then, Joey made a very prophetic remark: "I believe the leopard is very close-by."

A few seconds later, the Jack Russell terrier began to bark. As we found later, the terrier was looking at the leopard when it treed again. Corporal and the other three trackers, along with the majority of the pack, soon arrived at the tree and let us know that the leopard was there. He had treed approximately three quarters of the way up the high hill. We took off posthaste. I must say it taxed all of my ability to keep up; however, I was able to get to the tree in time to see the leopard.

Joey was attempting to get into position to shoot, and I was trying to take a picture when the leopard again sailed out—this time right into the middle of the pack of hounds. He remained silent and did not offer to fight, but took off running up the hill to the other side. The hounds took off after him in hot pursuit. Within a few minutes, we heard them bay again. I barely made it to the top of the hill when I heard a shot from approximately seventy-five yards away. Joey and Barry had found the leopard!

Although they would have preferred for me to have seen the final action (I think?), Joey killed the leopard without waiting for me to catch up. Well, I didn't mind. (Really?) I started to stage a major pout, but it would have been anticlimactic. At any rate, Joey had his leopard, and his quest was fulfilled.

Bwana Babu with a large South African wildcat, the ancestor of the domestic cat.

Alex hoisted Mr. Spots onto his shoulders, and he walked back to the Land Cruiser. Everyone was elated. The trackers and dogs were almost completely exhausted; many of the dogs had bloody feet from running on the shale. We drove to the same area where I had taken the pictures of my leopard. Mr. Spots was positioned on the trunk of the same downed tree that I had used. We took a number of pictures. As with all leopards, even in death, he was a beautiful animal. Interestingly enough, the leopard had eaten a full meal as judged by the size of his belly. Perhaps this had something to do with his lack of desire to fight with the dogs. Perhaps, he had rather sleep than fight?

We drove back to the camp and skinned the leopard, which weighed 145 pounds and was 7 feet, ½ inch long. (Luckily, it was smaller than mine, so Joey could not get a "swelled head.") We gave our heartfelt thanks to the trackers. I suggested that Corporal be promoted to a full General!

These activities were over around 3 P.M. We bathed, packed our gear, and said good-bye to all the staff. I must say, it's difficult to put into words how elated everyone was over this final "last-hour" episode.

I had one small disappointment: My quest for a genet and a civet cat went unfulfilled. However, butterfly collecting lived up to my initial expectations. I acquired at least fifteen new species for my African Lepidoptera collection.

We drove rapidly, but without incident, and arrived at 10 P.M. in Windhoek. We said good-bye to Barry. The next day, I began the arduous trip from Windhoek to Durham. Although long, it was made much easier by our fairy tale ending on the last day of the safari.

I've learned "never to say never," but at least for now, this twelfth safari put a wonderful cap on my African adventures. It has been an unbelievable and rewarding chapter in my life. I doubt that I will return. . . .

Pursuing Leopards with Hounds, The Epitome of Hunting Dangerous Game

Chapter XVII

There are many techniques employed to hunt the majestic Big Five of Africa. When pursuing the nocturnal and wary leopard, two methods are generally used. The first is to hang bait from a tree and shoot from a blind, with or without the use of artificial light. The second is to use hounds and/or trackers to follow and locate the quarry. Although it was not always the case, the former technique currently predominates. In fact, leopard hunting with hounds is available in only a few African countries.

I was surprised and somewhat dismayed by a recent spate of articles that characterized leopard hunting with hounds as not only nonsporting but even unethical. A series of opinions regarding the pros and cons of hunting leopards with dogs has been recently published.[1] The logic stated by the negative mavens is that, in this situation, the leopard is "easy pickings." They conclude that the leopard population would be decimated if this approach were widely used.

Since I wholeheartedly disagree with their conclusion, I would like to make a strong case for hunting leopards with hounds. My arguments contain two components: To extol the excitement

[1]Egger, Mark & Christine, NAPHA, and Collin Welensky. "Hunting Dogs with Cats in Namibia," "NAPHA Policy on Hunting Leopards with Hounds in Namibia," and "Hunting Leopard with Dogs." *African Sporting Gazette*, vol 13, nos 1 (2007), 2 & 4 (2008).

Four of the hounds methodically following a faint scent from the leopard spoor, Namibia, 2008.

associated with the chase and to characterize hunting with hounds as unquestionably ethical.

The argument as to the ethics of this situation is aimed only at hunters who believe that big-game hunting, when carried out in an appropriate manner, is highly ethical. Certainly, there will be little purpose in trying to convince the antihunting zealots that any aspect of hunting is ethical.

In order to proceed, I first should outline my credentials as an evaluator of this approach to leopard hunting. For the past sixty-five-plus years, I have had a torrid and continuous love affair with pointer bird dogs and the pursuit of bobwhite quail. I have developed an appreciation for high-quality dog work as well as a keen insight as to the importance of scenting conditions in the pursuit of game. At first blush it would appear that this sport is unrelated to hunting leopards with hounds, but I will endeavor to convince you otherwise.

Moshile watering the dogs at one of the cisterns, Namibia, 2006.

Early in my life, I hunted rabbits with my own pack of beagles and was initiated into trailing game by these diminutive hounds. For a number of years, I hunted foxes, red and gray, with my own pack of Walker and July hounds using the Southern tradition (listening to the hounds run at night and following their progress, if needed, in a pickup truck). Also, I sporadically hunted raccoons using a variety of hounds that bayed the quarry in a tree. For three to four years, before urban sprawl took over and made the local situation impossible, I hunted deer with hounds. Finally, for the past several years, I have hunted feral hogs with hounds in Florida. These experiences have given me a reasonable appreciation for the issues involved in pursuing game with trail hounds.

Specifically, I have developed an understanding of how difficult it can be for a trail hound to follow a spoor when the scenting conditions are poor due to dry conditions and heat. More importantly, all of these experiences have awakened in me a love of the chase that is undoubtedly rooted in my ancestral being. Listening to a pack of hounds work out a difficult track and, as the scent improves, rapidly follow the trail is an experience that cannot be surpassed. The music produced by these hounds rivals anything man can create.

On two of my twelve African safaris, I have hunted lions from a blind using bait. Thus, I have had the "opportunity" to sit for hours waiting for a lion to show up. In fact, one large male did arrive and was shot by a close friend of mine. I must say that these experiences, at least to me, were boring in the extreme and, as I have said earlier, somewhat akin to watching paint dry. Perhaps my dislike of hunting from a blind stems from my early experiences while still-hunting for deer or squirrel. I grew to detest this sedentary approach.

I have had the opportunity on two recent safaris in Namibia to hunt male leopards successfully using a pack of well-trained hounds. I could not have asked for more exciting adventures. The technique involved the expertise of outstanding trackers, in conjunction with a pack of hounds, who were able to pick up leopard spoor in a rocky terrain and follow the trail.

On one of these hunts, the initial spoor was fairly fresh, and the hounds took the trail and rapidly followed the trail for a mile before jumping the leopard. The next fifteen minutes were filled with a musical symphony equal to anything Beethoven ever composed. The exceptionally big leopard was brought to bay, and although he shifted locations twice, he was killed after a determined charge.

During the second safari, tracks made by large male leopards were identified and followed on three occasions. In the first episode, both the trackers and the hounds followed the leopard for five or six miles, but they could not close the gap. The leopard escaped. The second hunt began in a dried riverbed and ended after a three-mile ordeal following the spoor through rocky terrain. Again, the leopard escaped. In the final episode, the trackers followed the trail

Mr. Spots's determined charge ended here a few moments before, Namibia, 2006.

for perhaps three miles before the scent became hot enough for the hounds to open. The pack ran the leopard for perhaps a mile and bayed him in trees on three occasions before we were able to put an end to the affair successfully.

All of this trail work was done under very adverse scenting conditions with temperatures in the range of eighty-five to ninety degrees and with very dry humidity. At least from my prior experiences, it takes outstanding hounds with a very keen nose to function adequately under these conditions. Certainly, the skills of the trackers were of the highest quality. Being a part of this endeavor allowed me to participate in the epitome of quality hunting.

Another very positive aspect of leopard hunting with hounds is that the tracks are not followed unless they are deemed to be made by a large male leopard. If the hounds inadvertently bay a female or a small male leopard, they can be called off and the animal allowed to escape unscathed.

While, obviously, I am a novice at the sport of leopard hunting with hounds, I can find absolutely no reason to paint this activity as unfair or unsportsmanlike. Certainly, the leopard can and frequently does escape. Without question, it is far more strenuous and dangerous for the hunter than shooting from a blind. It is not the purpose of this discussion for me to denigrate the sporting aspects of shooting a leopard from a hidden blind while it is enjoying a free dinner. Certainly, increasing the chances of success by using artificial light cannot be deemed as enhancing the sporting quality. Enough said.

For me, I have no interest in participating in this boring, sedentary approach to leopard hunting. However, it is beyond my understanding why a knowledgeable hunter would conclude that the pursuit of leopards with trackers and trail hounds is less than a high-quality and ethical sport.

Perhaps the key word is knowledgeable. I am very doubtful if most individuals who hunt dangerous game in Africa have had an in-depth opportunity to hunt with hounds, or to develop an understanding of the superior quality of an effective dry-ground trail hound. Certainly, they have not acquired a love of listening to the music that floats from a pack of hounds in full cry. They may or may not appreciate the expertise demonstrated by premier trackers. Thus, I believe that it is individuals who are not fully conversant with the various aspects of this approach who write most of the articles denigrating hunting leopards with hounds. I hope so. Perhaps an admonition from Pope[2] would be worthwhile.

[2]Pope, Alexander. "An Essay on Criticism" published anonymously on 15 May 1711.

A little learning is a dang'rous thing;
Drink deep, or taste not the Pierian spring:
There shallow draughts intoxicate the brain,
And drinking largely sobers us again.

At any rate, leopard hunting with hounds is unquestionably ethical. Also, it is difficult, exciting, and should be placed on the highest pinnacle of hunting dangerous game.

My Big Five, Serendipity Pays Off

Chapter XVIII

As with most worthwhile ventures, serendipity plays some part. In fact, in this case, it was the dominant factor. When I made my initial trip to Africa to hunt Cape buffalo, I certainly had no aspirations of successfully hunting the Big Five. In fact, this thought never entered my mind. That was thirteen years ago. Guess what? Now I have obtained an SCI record-book-quality trophy (three silver and two bronze) of each of these magnificent animals. This story will outline the uneven steps in my journey to this end.

Having been convinced by Joey, my quail-hunting partner of many years, to try my hand at hunting Cape buffalo, I made my initial trip to the Serengeti. Like so many other sportsmen, I was hooked. It's often stated: You cannot go to Africa just one time! In my situation, this prophetic tenet proved to be entirely correct. The successful killing of two *mbogos* "cast the die" for future hunts. However, at that time, I had little interest in hunting anything but Cape buffalo.

I tried to repeat my initial experience by placing a bid to hunt *mbogo* in Timbavati, South Africa. Although this offer was unsuccessful, the lottery gave me a chance to shoot a bull elephant. Since I had already paid for the safari, I shrugged my shoulders and made the journey. What an experience I had! Clearly, bull elephants are by far the most magnificent of the African animals. I thoroughly enjoyed the hunt, although I must admit having a very guilty feeling while admiring the fallen monarch. The next year I resumed hunting Cape buffalo.

"I am the right of way," South Africa, 2007.

On my fourth safari, there were a series of mix-ups as to where I was to go. Because my first choice was denied, as a consolation I was given a license to hunt both lion and Cape buffalo in the Selous. At least as far as I was concerned, the latter was the primary reason for the trip. For the first few days, *mbogos* were nowhere around, and the time was consumed by hanging bait for lions. This approach was unsuccessful.

Makanyanga, Africa's top tracker, devised a new plan. Since lions were roaring close to camp each night, we would go to them. Although I seriously questioned the sanity of this idea, before daylight we crept to the area where the lions were vocalizing. Just as the rising sun barely illuminated the surroundings, a very large male lion became visible close-by. A few short moments later, I had killed the third of the Big Five. Talk about serendipity!

For the next few safaris, I continued my quest to hunt Cape buffalo in Tanzania with one sojourn to Botswana for another elephant. Although I had seen leopards on two occasions, I did not entertain the notion that I would ever hunt for a leopard. This was for two reasons: leopard hunting in Tanzania is from a blind, which I detest, and since one must commit to a twenty-one-day hunt, it is extraordinarily expensive. However, when my plans for hunting *mbogo* in Tanzania fell apart, I was faced with the reality of not going to Africa at all that year. This did not suit me at all. I signed on for a different type of safari, pursuing leopards using trail hounds in the dry region of northern Namibia. Again, Lady Luck smiled. This exciting adventure yielded an outstanding and very large male leopard. Chalk things up to serendipity. I had shot four of the Big Five.

Now I had to decide if climbing the final rung of the ladder was worthwhile. White rhinoceroses are available to hunt in several African countries (primarily South Africa), but the cost is, to say the least, excessive. However, darting a rhino was well within my budgetary limit. Again, it never occurred to me that I would even remotely be interested in this approach. But, the more I pondered the situation, the more it became evident that I really wanted to join the fraternity of hunters who have successfully taken the Big Five. So, I traveled to the Eastern Cape with Barry Burchell as the professional hunter. This successful rhino hunt turned out to be far more exciting than I had anticipated and was a fitting end to my final challenge.

In reflecting on this twelve-year unplanned journey, I must conclude that every episode has been more thrilling than I had ever imagined. Certainly, I am by no means alone as a successful hunter of the African Big Five, although beginning these safaris after age sixty-five must be somewhat unusual.

What have I accomplished? Looking at each of these outstanding trophies brings a deep sense of pride. More importantly, they irrevocably tie me to the majesty of the treasures on the African continent. A powerful bond has been forged between me and those hunters who have from time immemorial stood in the same unique part of the globe and had similar experiences.

Yes, I owe a great deal to serendipity, or more likely, to the "guiding hand of Providence."

White rhinoceros and companion tick birds, South Africa, 1997

The Big Five

Though fields and fens in Africa
Hold Noah's Ark alive,
The stars of all those chosen
Are crowned as the Big Five.

Elephant, lion, leopard,
Buffalo and rhino as well—
Each wields a unique feature
For all of God's world to tell.

The ivory tusks of *tembo*
Store Africa's white gold.
Simba's roaring challenge
Makes the blood run cold.

The spotted coat of *chui*
Holds beauty at its best.
The steely stare of *mbogo*
Mirrors the eyes of death.

Kifaro's horn is touted
To return the magic of youth.
With tusk, fang, claw or horn
These Five give "moments of truth."

Yes, danger, the age-old challenge
Brings hunters from near and far
To face the reality of death
From Africa's Big Five stars.

The Double Rifle, a Necessity?

Chapter XIX

There is voluminous literature penned by knowledgeable hunters (as well as many whose opinions are of questionable sagacity) on the appropriate weapon for hunting African dangerous game. These writers discuss the pros and cons of bolt-action vs. double rifles extensively. In the end, I believe, the majority vote would favor the classic double rifle. Having perused much of this literature, I accept the majority opinion. My conclusion, however, is not totally objective but was influenced by my love for double-barrel shotguns. In fact, I had purchased a .465 Holland & Holland sidelock double rifle—when it was relatively cheap—many years before I decided to hunt in Africa. It functioned solely as a "play toy."

One of the recurring themes throughout the descriptions of my various trips to the Dark Continent revolves around whether or not to take my Holland. Using the Holland would undoubtedly add to the adventure, but I initially concluded that the risk of having this valuable weapon either damaged or stolen was far too great. On my first safari, the rifle stayed at home. It was the only time I used a bolt-action rifle exclusively. On my next trip, to hunt elephant in South Africa, I overcame my concern, and the Holland went along. Prior to my third trip, I concluded that the possibility of mischief in Tanzania was too great to risk taking the Holland. I wanted a double rifle, so I obtained a .500 Krieghoff. Although functional, it was a poor substitute for my Holland.

After much soul-searching, I finally "bit the bullet." To hell with the potential problems. I planned to take the Holland on all my remaining safaris. I had to reverse this decision when monolithic solids destroyed its rifling, requiring that the rifle be rebored to a .470. For my fifth trip I substituted a .470 Krieghoff double rifle. The Holland did participate in my recent hunts for elephant in Botswana and Cape buffalo in Kilombero, Tanzania.

Agonizing over whether or not to take the Holland and, if not, spending the effort to find a suitable substitute occupied a considerable amount of my time during the planning phase of each trip. I frequently asked myself, *Why bother? What is it about a double rifle that adds to the mystique of an African safari?* Let's examine the possible reasons to choose a double rifle over a bolt-action.

Is the ammunition available only for a double rifle superior to the various loads available for a bolt-action rifle? No. The .465, .470, or similar nitro-express cartridges that were designed in the early part of the last century have withstood the test of time for killing dangerous game. On the other hand, cartridges with similar ballistics as well as some with enhanced velocity of the bullet are currently available.

Is the double rifle more accurate? Of course not. The double rifle is accurate enough to perform adequately with the short ranges typical when hunting dangerous game. However, it is in no way as accurate as a better-grade bolt-action rifle.

Are double rifles more reliable? Perhaps. A double rifle does provide two separate rifles in one; if problems occur with one, the hunter has a second mechanism to rely on. This conclusion requires that the double rifle be a sidelock with two triggers.

Does the double rifle fire more rapidly? Yes. The standard double rifle, although heavier, is better balanced and can be brought into action somewhat faster for the first shot. For the second shot, obviously the double rifle provides a major advantage over a bolt-action rifle. This has been widely heralded by most sages as the primary reason to use a double rifle, as a "stopper" for rapid close-range shooting. This concept makes sense, but whether it elevates the double rifle as the overwhelming choice for all hunters is questionable. A double rifle encumbered by a scope loses much of its advantage for close-up use on charging dangerous game. Unfortunately, my ocular accommodation has deteriorated with age. In a word, I see iron sights very poorly and must use a scope. Consequently, at least for me, this aspect of bolt-action vs. double rifles is a draw.

Is the double rifle cost effective? Certainly not. The cheapest acceptable double rifle available today (in the range of $7,000 to $10,000) is several fold more expensive than a high-grade, bolt-action rifle. The better class double rifles are similar in cost to an average house. In addition, ammunition for many of the classic double rifles is very difficult to obtain. Even when commercially available, the high cost of the cartridges makes sufficient practice with these weapons an extremely expensive proposition.

Are double rifles the overwhelming choice of knowledgeable hunters of dangerous game? Were they employed by all the well-known professional hunters in the past? Not really. While a double rifle was used by a number of these famed hunters, many with similar credentials swore by a bolt-action rifle. Many well-known African hunters initially used a less-expensive bolt-action rifle because of financial reasons, graduating to a double rifle when they could afford one.

Do I conclude that a double rifle is essential to hunt dangerous game? Truthfully, no. When one adds up the pluses and the minuses, it would seem that any logical individual, including myself, would opt for a bolt-action rifle. The choice of a double rifle cannot be strongly defended by any analytical evaluation.

On the other hand, why be so damn analytical? For me, the decision to use a double rifle is quite easy. I'm quite enamored of high-grade, double-barrel shotguns and wouldn't hunt quail with anything else. It logically follows that I have a similar feeling regarding a double rifle. My Holland is a graceful and artistic weapon. A bolt-action rifle, while obviously serviceable, can never remotely be as attractive or have the same graceful feeling when in use. A bolt-action rifle can get the job done but pales in

Double rifles ready to go, from left: .500-465 Holland & Holland and .470 Rigby.

comparison to the double rifle, and the same can be said of a mule when compared to a thoroughbred horse. To put it another way, hunting buffaloes, lions, and elephants would not be the same unless I used a double rifle. Anything else "just ain't right."

My Double Rifle

While I clean my double rifle,
(Perhaps for the last time?)
My thoughts are sharply focused
By Hoppes' No. 9.

Crafted by Holland and Holland
With skill that brought them fame,
This London Best .470
Can kill all dangerous game.

Elephant, lion, and buffalo
Have fallen to its 500-grain shell.
Never once has it failed to deliver
So these stories I can tell.

Spotless and well-oiled,
In a gun safe now it will rest.
Ready to go to Africa
To flirt again with death.

But I've finished my African adventures.
Twelve safaris are all "has-beens."
Now my double rifle must wait
For another to use it again.

I Choose Hunting

Chapter XX

I never thought about the question "Why hunt?" until recently. Undoubtedly, if asked, I would have quickly answered, "Because I enjoy it." During the past year, while in a somewhat reflective mood, I have attempted to explore the reasons for the preservation of a hunting ethos in modern society. The specific question to be addressed is "Why are some men (myself included), living in an industrialized society in the twenty-first century, enamored by hunting?"

From the onset, I need to clarify the subject of this treatise: It is not a defense of hunting. I won't take the militant antihunting genre to task or outline the multiple reasons why hunting is an environmentally sound practice. Rather, I explore the "whys" that drive the human animal to hunt.

To begin, let me define what is meant by hunting. The noted philosopher, José Ortega y Gasset, the most widely acclaimed proponent of hunting as a necessary component of the ethos of modern man, defines hunting as "What an animal does to take possession, dead or alive, of some other being that belongs to a species basically inferior to his own."[1] He outlines a compelling argument that hunting must include the rendering of the prey animal either dead, or at least captured, and restrained. Thus, photography is ruled out as true hunting.

The latter part of this definition implies that predators belong to a species superior to their prey. A golden eagle killing a young pronghorn antelope or a peregrine falcon capturing a

Joey and the author break for lunch—it was a hard life, Rungwa, Tanzania, 1998.

hare represents hunting at the highest level. Whether or not avian predators are superior in the general order of life to their mammalian prey is certainly doubtful. From my vantage point, the following encompasses a better definition of hunting: The actions involved in the pursuit of an animal, when successful, culminates in either killing or taking possession of the prey.

Note that the methods used are not constrained by any concern for the prey. In order to elevate hunting to a sporting activity suitable for the modern human, it must include an ethical component. Thus, the definition of hunting becomes: The actions involved in the ethical pursuit of an animal, when successful, culminates in either killing or taking possession of the prey. The difficult issue that immediately arises is to define precisely the meaning of the word ethical as it relates to hunting. Actions that are way off the mark and thus, truly unethical, can be generally agreed upon—for example, killing a deer on purpose

A herd of giraffe staring at us, unconcerned, Botswana, 2001.

with a car, shooting big game from a helicopter, or in the case of bird hunting, shooting quail on the ground. However, there are many activities that are considered borderline or actually unethical by one hunter but are embraced by another. A uniform consensus of ethical is, therefore, unlikely to be achieved. Since this is the case, fairly wide latitude must be accepted, and, thus, the definition of ethical as it applies to hunting must come down to individual choice.

Having developed a reasonable definition of hunting, the next issue is to explore the drive to hunt in the human animal. Hunting to provide food for subsistence is no longer a plausible reason, nor has it been since the development of agrarian culture several thousand years ago. Hunters today pursue their avocation in spite of the negative opinion held by many of their fellow humans that hunting, an atavistic and improper pastime, has no place in modern society. In fact, a hunter is often characterized as a throwback to *Homo erectus,* a species long since extinct. I confess to a lifetime of being enthralled by quail hunting and, more recently, by hunting dangerous game in Africa. Why then, have I chosen to be an exception to the accepted norm?

A considerable body of writing[1-7] has attempted to explain the strong desire to hunt still found in many citizens of modern society. The following is one of the hypotheses that have emerged from these writings: Twenty-first-century man descended from ancestors in whom hunting during the course of many eons was necessary for survival. Thus, hunting as a way of life is genetically transmitted to all of us. Perhaps, at least to some extent, this is the case. However, as with all complex inherited traits, the degree of penetration or effect on a given individual can vary dramatically. Hence, the desire to be a hunter, even if genetically encoded, may manifest itself in only a small number of the total population.

Undoubtedly, the environment of the individual during formative years plays an important role in nurturing the latent desire to hunt. Two people with the same genetic predisposition to hunt may be markedly influenced by their upbringing. The more the individual is exposed to hunting, the more likely this latent drive will be positively influenced. To succinctly state the proposition: If the parents are hunters, the more likely the children will follow in their footsteps.

However, the degree to which genetic makeup vs. environmental factors (i.e., nature vs. nurture) primarily dictates the desire to hunt in a given individual is not quantifiable. Further examination of

[1]Gasset, José Ortega y. *Meditations on Hunting.* Bozeman: Wilderness Adventures, 1995.

[2]Jones, Robert F. (editor) *On Killing.* Guilford, CT: The Lyons Press, 2001.

[3]Swan, James A. *In Defense of Hunting.* San Francisco, CA: Harper Collins Publishers, 1995.

[4]Petersen, David. *Heartsblood.* Washington, DC: Island Press, 2000.

[5]Nugent, Ted. *God, Guns and Rock 'n Roll.* Washington, DC: Regnery Publishing, Inc., 2001.

[6]Leopold, Aldo. *A Sand County Almanac.* New York: Oxford University Press, 1949.

[7]Brander, Michael. *The Hunting Instinct.* Edinburgh and London: Oliver and Boyd, 1964.

the issue is not likely to be fruitful. That said, let's put aside the root causes of the hunting instinct and attempt to characterize a "philosophy of hunting" as espoused by three individuals with very different ideas.

David Petersen[4] describes in great detail his own reason for hunting. When boiled down to its essence, he seems to place hunting in a nearly spiritual context—to worship the "earth goddess" by hunting. In order to be recognized by this deity, he has chosen a primitive bow (slightly recurved is acceptable) and arrow. I'm assuming this choice of weaponry and the associated still-hunting makes him an acolyte. On the other hand, if the deer or elk were caught in a primitive snare and subdued with a rock, he would undoubtedly be dubbed a high priest. Conversely, use of a modern high-powered rifle would label the individual as a heretic, and the "earth goddess" would not be impressed. This seems like sheer nonsense to me, but at least it defines Petersen's philosophy regarding hunting.

A more straightforward explanation for hunting is given by Ted Nugent.[5] Nugent likes to kill "critters." Bow and arrow, pistol, and rifle are all acceptable tools. He is unimpressed by any ethical arguments why this is not perfectly reasonable behavior. Frankly, I like his straightforward approach.

One of the more articulate and often quoted proponents of hunting, Aldo Leopold,[6] places hunting as a major component in the larger spectacle of man's involvement in the great outdoors. The hunter then becomes a participant in the ever-changing and exciting face of nature. The totality of the desire to hunt represented by the divergent opinions of Petersen, Leopold, and Nugent provides ample room for most hunters to find a comfortable niche.

To analyze the spectrum of hunting further, let's outline the methods employed by different hunters. The actions taken by the hunter to pursue game can take many forms: sitting in a duck blind on a lake or on a butt in a grouse moor, waiting in a tree stand for deer, following a pair of pointers searching for quail, or walking through a hostile environment pursuing dangerous game. All are very different but clearly all qualify as hunting.

How do I fit into the wide landscape of hunting? Specifically, why do I hunt? My love of the outdoors began at an early age. I lived close to a large tract of woods and fields bordering Peachtree Creek near Atlanta. I spent many happy hours exploring and enjoying nature. When at age seven or eight I was allowed to carry a .22 rifle on these expeditions, it seemed a natural step to begin hunting squirrels. Maggie Belle, our cook, deemed fried squirrel as the best of nature's bounties, so the "fruits" of my hunting labors were appreciated.

My defining moment as a hunter came when, at age ten, I accompanied my father on a quail hunt in South Georgia. A somewhat obstreperous bird dog finally pointed quail, and I was allowed to shoot my grandfather's 20-gauge Parker shotgun. The gods smiled and the bird crumpled to earth. My future as a hunter was sealed.

Dogs, first beagles, and then pointers, soon became an inseparable part of my hunting experiences. (Both Ortega y Gasset[1] and Brander[7] have dealt, in some detail, with this aspect of hunting.) Personally, I know of no more enthralling sight than watching a pair of stylish pointer bird dogs hunt quail and finally point their quarry. To me, this provides unequaled excitement, especially if I have been involved in the training of the bird dog. A secondary, but necessary, aspect of quail hunting, the killing, enforces my love of fine double-barrel shotguns. For more than sixty-five years, quail hunting has been a major part of my life. I look forward with anticipation to the opening day of each season.

I've become quite enamored with hunting dangerous game (elephant, lion, rhinoceros, Cape buffalo, and leopard). How can this experience be reconciled as similar, or at least compatible, with my desire to hunt quail? Parenthetically, I've tried shooting a variety of game birds in Africa without the companionship of pointer bird dogs, but I didn't enjoy it at all.

Reflecting on my reasons for becoming a hunter of dangerous game, the answer became perfectly obvious. I have thoroughly enjoyed watching an experienced tracker and professional hunter perform their unique roles. For a "babe in woods" compared to them, the opportunity to observe expert trackers follow these animals for several hours and unerringly find the quarry affords me excitement of the highest order. In addition, the knowledge and craft necessary to place me safely in the correct position to attempt a killing shot is truly remarkable. I am not discounting the high level of excitement or "adrenaline rush" associated with hunting these magnificent animals. However, without the association of these woodsmen, I am certain that I would have been only lukewarm to the experience.

Is it possible to synthesize from my experiences and the writings of others a tight framework that can completely encompass the desire to hunt? I doubt it. The reasons people hunt are multifactorial—heredity, environmental, cultural, and, as with most aspects of life, monetary, to name a few. Each hunter, if he desires to address this issue, must develop his own unique philosophy.

Why do I hunt? No other activity affords me the opportunity to play a role, even a small one, along with outstanding actors, both canine and human, on nature's magnificent stage.

Trophies on Display

Chapter XXI

Although the opportunity to accumulate trophies did not enter into my decision to engage in African big-game hunting, I have acquired a large number of these treasures after twelve safaris. In addition, my hunting escapades over a number of years in the United States have inevitably produced a variety of mounted animals. By pure serendipity, I had an excellent place to display these treasures—a log cabin with an abundance of wall space.

Let me outline the genesis of this structure. In 1970 I purchased twenty-eight acres of land completely surrounded by Duke Forest. A locked gate restricted access to this property. During the ensuing years, I gradually developed the property—impounding a two-acre lake and constructing a number of utility buildings. I used a small trailer as temporary housing.

In 1991, a close friend, Larry Williams, constructed a thirteen-hundred-square-foot log cabin. The western hemlock logs and other building materials were obtained from Hearthstone, Inc. The architecture consisted of a single large room with a twenty-foot-high ceiling in the center. Part of the first level was enclosed to provide a bathroom and two small rooms, which were covered by a loft. The large room functions as a kitchen, dining, and living area.

A fireplace was constructed utilizing locally quarried stone, which had been salvaged from a renovation project at Duke Hospital. This unique stone had been part of the original material used to construct a clinic building sixty years ago. The wall occupied

Snarling leopard in a fighting pose. The gemsbok skull was salvaged from his last kill.

by the fireplace has a center height of twenty feet, no windows, and provides an ideal place for the display of my trophies. In addition, a wide, covered porch spans the width of the structure. Thus, the rear wall of the house is protected from the elements by the roof of the porch and provides an ideal location to display trophies consisting of horns and/or bone.

Prior to the arrival of the trophies, the wall in the cabin was essentially uncovered except for four display cases containing a portion of my butterfly and moth collection. Collecting Lepidoptera began while I was a Boy Scout, and with many irregular stops and starts, continues to the present. A collection of butterflies that I caught in Africa has recently been added to this display.

Probably my most impressive and rare trophy resulted from the quick thinking by a colleague of mine, Marvin Rozear. Marvin was discussing my cabin and the trophies with his neighbor, Mrs. Lynn Dilts. During the course of this conversation, she questioned

Marvin as to whether he thought I might like to have Ivan. It turns out that Ivan is a tiger rug that she had stored in a trunk in her attic for many years. Marvin enthusiastically stated, "I know he would be very interested in Ivan."

How Ivan the tiger ended up in Mrs. Lynn Dilts's attic trunk is an interesting story. This is what she told Marvin. Her grandfather, John Symington, became a missionary after graduating from medical school in 1902. He immediately began a series of missionary ventures to India. He had a number of posts, including Gwailor, Mysore, and Landour. In 1919 he accepted a position in Duars, Bengal, in charge of the health (and I'm assuming the salvation) of fourteen thousand tea plantation workers. Very few of the natives had seen a white man before.

Shortly after he arrived at his new position, the villagers requested that he help rid the area of a tiger that had killed and eaten several of the local citizenry. (The exact number is unknown.) Although not a hunter, he was able to shoot the tiger. (Mrs. Dilts knew nothing of the particulars.) The skin was sent to a taxidermist in Mysore in 1920 and made into a rug.

Whether or not it had actually been displayed before, I'm not certain, but at least for many years it was kept in a sealed trunk. Did I want Ivan? Absolutely! When the rug was delivered, it was amazingly preserved. In fact, the local taxidermist who cleaned the rug told me that he had never seen any trophy of this age (approximately eighty years) so well preserved. The mount contained the original skull with an open mouth. The tongue was cast from metal, presumably an alloy of lead, and painted. The rug is labeled Mysore, India.

(As it turns out, Ivan is actually a medium-size female. Man-eating tigers predominantly are of the "weaker sex." Kipling once wrote, ". . . for the female of the species is more deadly than the male."[1])

[1]Kipling, Rudyard. *"The Female of the Species"* in *Rudyard Kipling's Verse.* (Definitive Edition) New York: Doubleday, Doran & Co., Inc., 1940.

Ivan quickly occupied the center of the cabin wall, stretching from approximately eight feet above the floor to the roof. She is, to say the least, spectacular.

Following my initial safari to the Serengeti, I had one of the buffaloes preserved as a shoulder mount and the other as a skull, or English, mount. Interestingly, when the shoulder mount was delivered, I initially hung it directly over the fireplace. I was very disappointed. The entire room seemed to be filled by buffaloes. However, moving the mount higher by approximately four feet dramatically changed the perspective, and it looked just fine. The skull mount also was hung on the same wall nearby.

I killed Cape buffaloes on seven of my twelve safaris. My third Cape buffalo, *Mbogo*, was preserved as a shoulder mount also. I hung *Mbogo* on the opposite side of the wall from the fireplace at the same height as the other buffalo shoulder mount. In preparing this mount, I had given Bucky Flowers of Skins and Scales Taxidermy, Naples, Florida, a very strange request. I asked him to put a contented expression on the face of *Mbogo* instead of reproducing the usual malevolent stare of a Cape buffalo. I explained to Bucky the reason for this bizarre request. He did his best and, I think, the result turned out rather well.

The two shoulder mounts occupied a considerable amount of space, and it became obvious that additional shoulder mounts could not be accommodated. Also, I really like skull mounts. Accordingly, except for the horns from a young buffalo that I crafted into a pair of unique bookends, the fourteen Cape buffaloes I killed during these seven trips resulted in ten skull mounts. All of these are distributed on the same wall or on the wall of the porch. In addition, skull mounts from two of the three water buffaloes I killed at J&R Outfitters in Indiantown, Florida, are displayed in the same location.

Following the trials and tribulations of obtaining the ivory from the Timbavati elephant, I initially tried to display the tusks in pedestal mounts on each side of the fireplace. (This seems to be a standard procedure.) At least from my perspective, the tusks took up floor space and added nothing to the appearance of the room. However, when hung directly over the fireplace under the buffalo shoulder mount, they looked outstanding. I had the front foot of this elephant made

Ivan surrounded by skulls. To say the least, she is frightening.

into an umbrella stand. I didn't like the stand, so I covered the top with a four-inch section from the trunk of a black walnut tree. By sheer coincidence, this slab of wood turned out to be the exact circumference of the foot. After finishing the wood, the foot became a unique end table. The left ear, which resembles a map of Africa, was mounted on a board, and Clive Kay, the illustrator for both *Bwana Babu* and *Bwana Babu Kwaheri,* painted an authentic representation of the African Big Five on it. This treasure also adorns the cabin wall.

The tusks from the Botswana elephant, although much heavier and more massive, are not as long as their predecessor's. Again, I agonized on how to display them. However, I finally decided to hang them by chains under *Mbogo*'s shoulder mount.

Three other trophies resulted from this elephant. One of the ears, mounted on a board, served as "canvas" on which a Botswana elephant was painted by an accomplished young artist, James Young, in Zimbabwe. This striking artwork is mounted on the stairway to the loft.

African butterflies collected in Tanzania, Botswana and Namibia.

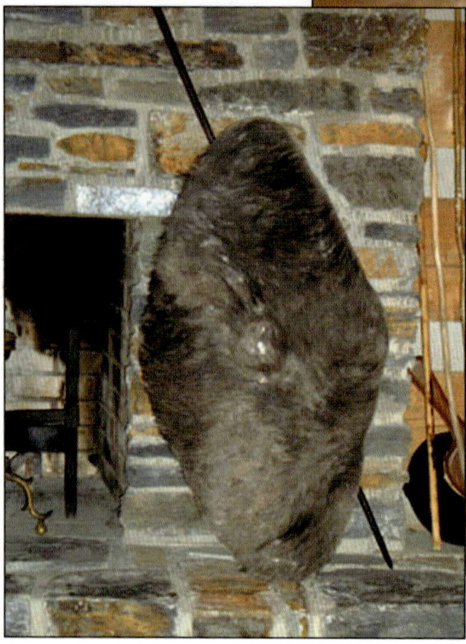

Masai shield and spear. Doudi made the shield from buffalo rawhide.

The Big Five painted by Clive Kay. As the background, he used the ear from the elephant that I killed in Timbavati.

A second and very interesting acquisition from this elephant was the skull. Since the ivory was extracted by burying the skull and removing the tusks a month later, the skull was left completely intact. Although the lower jaw remained in Botswana in order to age the elephant, the rest of the skull made it unscathed to my cabin. Placed on a wooden base, it functions very nicely as a side table on the porch; it is quite a conversation piece. Both long leg bones (femurs) are mounted vertically on the two wooden columns that hold up the porch roof. Also, the tail, with all the hair intact, hangs in the trophy room.

One of my most impressive trophies is the large old male lion, with sparse mane, that I killed in the Selous. The great room has a small covered closet that serves as a pantry. The full-body lion mount fits perfectly on the top of this pantry. Bucky was kind enough to fly from Florida, look at the situation, and obtain the exact dimensions of the room so that the lion could be mounted correctly. He did an outstanding job. His creation has the mouth partially open and one front paw extended to show the claws. Occasionally this mount does create some consternation. People who are not familiar with the lion's presence walk into the room, look up, and find themselves only a few feet away from an extremely large, open-mouth lion.

An alcove in the room contains the kitchen. On the left is the trophy wall and on the right, the pantry where the lion resides. The shelf above the kitchen cabinets displays the leopard killed in Namibia. It is mounted in a pose just as I first visualized him. Here he's fighting the dogs with a snarl on his mouth, his left leg raised, and his claws extended. Behind the leopard is the gemsbok skull salvaged from its last kill.

The shelves connecting the lion and the leopard contain a caracal resting on a rock, a South African wildcat, a black-back jackal, and a shoulder mount of a warthog having exceptionally large tusks. The final member of the Big Five is a replica of the two horns from the white rhinoceros darted in South Africa. The horns are mounted on a beautiful plaque made of red *miombo* wood.

Gracing the wall is the bow, arrows, and quiver crafted by Makanyanga and given to me. In addition, the shooting sticks that he made stand by the fireplace. Makanyanga fashioned a snuff box from a hollowed-out nut that had been "cleaned" by passing through an elephant's intestines. He carved the stopper from *miombo* wood to simulate the hoof of a small antelope. Doudi, who is a member of one of the Masai tribes, made a shield from the rawhide of one of the buffaloes I killed in Rungwa. This shield as well as a Masai spear are displayed by the door of the gun room.

I have been very lucky in obtaining outstanding woodcarvings of a buffalo, two lions fighting, and an elephant. Carved in Zimbabwe from ironwood, they are outstanding examples of African art. One of the best features of the collection was the price. They were cheap. Joey had contracted a provider to furnish African carvings to be sold to his clients in Florida. Fortunately for me, several of the best carvings had been severely damaged during shipping. After examining the broken specimens, I was certain that I could repair them to their original quality and took them home. With a little effort and some epoxy glue, it's essentially impossible to discover the damage. They dramatically enhance the trophy room.

A collection of butterflies from Tanzania, Botswana, and Namibia are displayed in two glass-covered cases.

I was given a whole body mount of a large male mountain lion killed in Idaho by Ron Clark. Ron guided clients on mountain lion hunts for several years. He had displayed this mount at various hunting shows to advertise the outstanding specimens available in his territory. After Ron quit hunting, he agreed to trade the mountain lion mount to Joey for a mule. Joey gave the mount to me.

This lion is a splendid specimen. It was quite old when it was shot, and it has a number of scars that attest to a long life. Its ears have been chewed in a manner fairly typical of a mountain lion that has been through the "wars." In fact, at the time Ron shot him, there was a very large fresh cut on the back legs—the result of fighting with another male. This trophy resides on the staircase directly opposite the tiger and seems to be gazing directly at it.

Another cat trophy displayed in this room is a large male Florida bobcat that I killed while quail hunting. This critter is mounted asleep, and it lies on a log about eight feet from the floor. Before his demise, this predator accounted for an untold number of bobwhite quail. A raucous crow, perched on a limb, looks down on this sleeping predator. An impressive red fox, a raccoon, and both gray and fox squirrels occupy the loft area. A shoulder mount of a feral hog, armed with impressive teeth, adorns the wall over the entrance door. Several species of local ducks, a Canadian goose, a woodcock, a snipe, and a dove are mounted on the walls and beams in simulated flight.

A covey of Florida bobwhite quail is displayed in a glass-enclosed end table that I constructed. This realistic scene also contains a baby cottontail rabbit that is so realistic it appears to be alive.

The skin from a six-foot-long Eastern diamondback rattlesnake and the rattles from six similar snakes are displayed. These exhibits are to remind me that hunting in Florida is not totally without danger. A full-body mount of an armadillo and the head of an eight-foot alligator round out the collection of Florida fauna.

My perception of the reason for having a trophy room has evolved dramatically over the last few years. When I first began collecting these mounts, my reason for displaying them resulted from a simple choice—show them or throw them away. I had given little or no thought as to other causes to initiate this endeavor. Being somewhat of a curmudgeon, my perception of palatial trophy rooms is that they allow ego-driven big-game hunters a place to "show off" to others and perhaps to gain a modicum of immortality. John Webster has eloquently expressed his views on trophy collecting:

> "Who seeke by trophies and dead things,
> To leave a living name behind,
> And weave but nets to catch the wind."[2]

However, for me, these reasons have little or no bearing. My trophies are reserved essentially for my own pleasure. During

[2]Webster, John. "All the Flowers of the Spring," in *The Devil's Law Case. The Oxford Book of Seventeenth Verse,* H. J. C. Grierson and G. Bullough, eds. Oxford: Clarendon Press, 1934, pps 204–205.

the past several years, I've finally come to understand how much my collection means to me. Now, I sit by the hour gazing and reminiscing about the wonderful experiences associated with each one of them.

Trophies–Why?

What role does the finest trophies play
In fulfilling your lifetime quest?
Will high scores in the record book
Make you eternally blessed?

If size is your goal as a hunter,
Fulfillment will never be gained.
And all your efforts will be wasted,
On the will-o'-the-wisp of fame.

But the sight of the trophies can focus
Your thoughts regarding the chase.
And make you always remember
The excitement of time and place.

So collect all trophies needed
To bring to your mind anew,
That magical moment on safari
When the quarry became part of you.

* * * * *

But, after the death of the hunter,
The trophies cannot survive—
For no one else has the memories
Which kept these trophies alive.

Tiger
Red-striped, majestic, foe of man,
Your hourglass is out of sand.
No longer will your roar strike fear
Into the hearts of all who hear.

Yet when you depart this earthly host.
Man himself will lose the most:
We'll remember your glory in word and song,
But forget our greed is why you're gone.

Joey O'Bannon, African Professional Hunter

Chapter XXII

Joey O'Bannon has functioned as the professional hunter on many of my Tanzanian forays. By any criteria, he is considered to be one of the best of the current African guides. Since it is unusual for an American to be certified, I would like to describe both his path to becoming a licensed PH in Tanzania and to relate a few of his hunting experiences.

At a very early age, Joey was introduced to the outdoors by his grandfather, and he spent many hours learning to hunt the indigenous game in Florida. In the late 1970s, Joey was working as a cowboy for the Red Cattle Company near LaBelle, Florida. Derek Evans, an African PH, had hunted quail on the ranch as a guest during his annual business trip to the United States. Joey and Derek developed a good relationship, and he invited Joey to come to Africa. Excited by this opportunity, Joey raised the money by selling several horses. In 1981, he was able to hunt with Mr. Evans in the Luangwa Valley in Zambia for a three-week period. Joey thoroughly enjoyed the experience, especially hunting Cape buffalo, and looked forward to future African adventures.

In 1990, when J&R Outfitters (Joey's quail hunting operation) had been firmly established, he decided to accompany several of his clients to South Africa during the summers after quail hunting had ceased. For advice and help, he contacted Derek Evans who, by then, had retired from hunting. Derek introduced him to Graham Jones, a South African PH, who operated hunting concessions on several large game ranches in South Africa. Joey obtained a South African PH's license and booked a number of his clients to hunt plains game on these ranches, including the Zuka Ranch owned by Anton Wienand. (Anton led the safari to hunt elephant in Timbavati with Joey and me in 1997.) In 1996, Graham contracted with Hunters and Guides Africa to hunt on a concession in the Fort Ikoma region of Tanzania. I accompanied Joey on this trip, his first Cape buffalo safari in Tanzania.

The next year, Joey met Alex Walker, who, at that time, was associated with Miombo Safaris in Dar es Salaam. Joey decided that the opportunities to hunt, especially dangerous game, were far better in Tanzania than in South Africa, so he set about obtaining a Tanzanian PH license. In order to function properly as a PH, Joey became reasonably fluent in Swahili. (Undoubtedly, a mixture of Florida "cracker" dialect and African Swahili.)

During the first year, Joey served as an apprentice, but in 1998 he became fully licensed. Since that time, he has spent approximately three months a year, July through September, in Tanzania employed by Miombo Safaris. During this period, he has hunted in all the Miombo concessions—Selous, Rungwa, Kilombero (Mlimba and Mgeta), Msanjesi, and Lukwika, which borders Mozambique. He has hunted on several occasions near Fort Ikoma on the Grumeti River as well as north of Arusha in Tanzania. In addition, he made several safaris to hunt elephant in the Chobe area of Botswana. However, his primary activities have been in Miombo concessions.

During the past ten years, Joey has hunted with a number of trackers. Makanyanga and Singi worked both in the Selous as well as in Msanjesi and Lukwika where Joey primarily hunted elephant. In addition, he hunted elephant with Little Juma, Mtoto Tembo, and Chumbo in Msanjesi and Lukwika. Pius and Fabian were his primary trackers for the Selous concession. Doudi, Sampson, and more recently Martin work in Rungwa. Pius and Martin, along with Chalimbo, were the primary trackers in the Kilombero concession.

All of the trackers are outstanding. Makanyanga has the most experience, but as a group, they clearly are among the best in Africa. Joey has absolutely nothing but good things to say about their abilities as trackers, game spotters, and hunting confidantes—especially when hunting dangerous game.

Approximately 90 percent of Joey's clients from J&R Outfitters had hunted with him in Florida before traveling to Africa. This is obviously a major advantage not enjoyed by many African PHs. He knows his clients, their wants, and abilities prior to their arrival in Africa. This has essentially eliminated problems in developing a good client-PH relationship. In fact, the only "less than optimal situations" have occurred with clients who have been assigned to him during the open times in his schedule.

Obtaining a mixed bag that includes plains game (especially eland, roan, sable, and kudu) has been the goal of most of his clients. However, their primary activities have centered on hunting dangerous game. In this endeavor, Joey has been quite successful. He has guided clients to approximately thirty-five elephants, thirty lions, a similar number of leopards, two-hundred-plus Cape buffaloes, and several hippos. Primarily due to his consummate professionalism, these hunts have been carried out without the occurrence of an uncontrollable serious incident. However, there have been numerous occasions in which the situation can best be described as "tense."

Joey enjoys hunting elephant, lion, and buffalo, and it would be difficult for him to choose which one he most likes to hunt. His clients' success rate for these three has been better than 90 percent. He put the leopard at the bottom of the dangerous game list, especially hunting leopard from a blind, which he considers far from exciting.

One of the important issues for a PH and the client to agree on is when should the PH back up the client's shot. Following Derek Evans' example, Joey prefers, as do many PHs, to back up the client after the initial shot. The majority of Joey's clients have concurred, myself included, in this strategy. However, a few did not want him to shoot unless a dangerous situation developed. The choice regarding an initial backup shot is clearly up to the client.

From the beginning, Joey has used a double rifle. Initially, he used a .470 NE Krieghoff, followed by a .470 NE Rigby, and more recently a .500 NE Perugini-Visini double. To say the least, he has become quite proficient in the use of these rifles. One misadventure with a rifle significantly impaired his hearing. This was caused when a client, to reduce recoil, had a muzzle brake installed on his rifle. Joey had no prior experience with the excessive noise from the muzzle brake and was too close when the rifle was fired. The loud explosion deafened and nearly knocked him down. Although his hearing had been slightly impaired previously, from that moment on, he has had a significant hearing deficit requiring him to wear hearing aids. Unfortunately, even with these aids his hearing has deteriorated.

The following will briefly describe some of the episodes that Joey has experienced while hunting dangerous game. I will not include those hunts with Joey and me since these are described in other chapters.

The majority of the lions that Joey's clients have killed were obtained using a variety of baits—buffalo, zebra, and hartebeest. These baits were hung in trees and checked daily. They were looking for the presence of long hair, which indicates that a male lion is feeding. A blind is constructed and then Joey and the client wait for the male to make an appearance, either early in the morning or late in the afternoon.

After the shot, if the lion runs off, he is followed. Joey estimates that about 75 percent of the lions run some distance, but the majority are found dead. If an animal is shot late in the afternoon when the light is bad, follow-up can produce a high level of excitement. As a general rule, the client does not accompany Joey and the tracker on these endeavors unless he insists on participating. Joey makes it quite clear that if he and the client are walking side by side, he cannot adequately protect the client from a charge on his far side. When apprised of this situation, most of the clients decide to remain in the vehicle. Following up lions in poor light seems foolhardy, but waiting until morning also has its drawbacks. If hyenas find the wounded or dead animal, they will destroy the trophy.

Moments of excitement can occur during these follow-ups. Recently, Joey was following a wounded lion in the dark. He hadn't

An old dagga boy, Bwana Babu, and Joey in Rungwa, Tanzania, 2007.

gone one hundred yards when his flashlight illuminated a lion's eyes approximately fifteen yards to the front. He promptly shot the animal. The lion roared, jumped to the side, and hid behind a thorn thicket, growling furiously. Joey walked to the left to get around the thicket for a follow-up shot. He nearly stepped on a male lion . . . the one that had actually been shot over the bait. Luckily, *simba* was dead! He quickly killed the wounded lion. Now he had two dead male lions and only one license. Fortunately, the game scout was fully aware of the situation, so Joey was not penalized.

The terrain in the Kilombero-Mgeta concession is flat and covered with dense tall grass. Access to the hunting area is through one of the river's tributaries. Since there aren't any trees, the bait is staked to the ground near one of the streams. The usual scenario is for the hunters to wait in the blind all night and hope that the lions will not consume the bait and depart before daylight. (One cannot use an artificial light when hunting in Tanzania.) If possible, the blind is constructed on the other side of the water; this establishes a barrier between the hunters and the feeding lions. Hunters can also wait in a boat, but they must be very wary of feeding hippos and elephants walking in the stream. When neither of these options is possible, the blind is constructed on a low platform within approximately fifty yards of the bait.

Joey with a large black-backed jackal, Namibia, 2008.

Although the Kilombero concession has some of the largest lions in Africa, they have been hunted very little due to the difficult terrain. Thus, they have little innate fear of man. In fact, they not uncommonly include some of the local fishermen as part of their diet. That situation, along with the tall grass, makes for some very exciting and dangerous adventures.

Perhaps Joey's most frightening incident regarding lion hunting occurred in this venue. While waiting near the bait on a six-foot-high platform, a small pride of lions arrived just after dark and began feeding. Soon, they were joined by another larger pride. As Joey described it, "We had one hell of a cat fight going on all around us." One of the large males, who had been significantly chewed up, almost jumped into the blind to escape his tormentors. Luckily, he changed his mind and sought refuge elsewhere. With lions fighting and growling all around them, the rest of the night was spent praying for daylight. To cap it off, by morning all of the lions had left. Thus, this terrifying experience went unrewarded. At least they escaped mauling, or worse!

Elephant hunting has been a very exciting component of Joey's experiences. The classic elephant hunting was carried out primarily in Lukwika, although he has killed elephants in Msanjesi and recently in Rungwa. The time-honored technique is to find a fresh track made by an old bull and to follow until the animal is spotted. Then the hunters must decide whether the tusks are of trophy size. Many of the elephants in Lukwika come across from Mozambique to feed on the trees in a former cashew plantation. If they are disturbed, they make tracks for the border and cannot be followed. The terrain is often dense bamboo thickets, so by the time visual contact is made the quarry is only several yards away. Luckily, all of these episodes have gone well, and Joey has not had to deal with a charging bull at close quarters. The largest ivory that a client obtained was seventy pounds per side. However, since ivory in Tanzania tends to be quite narrow, the tusks are very long. In fact, fifty-pound tusks are impressive trophies. Cow elephants rank at the top of dangerous game animals. A serious incident occurred in Rungwa with an undisturbed group of cow elephants. A herd of approximately fifteen cows and calves was crossing the road approximately one hundred yards from the Land Cruiser. The last cow took umbrage to their presence and charged. Usually, this turns out to be only a demonstration or a false charge. Not the case with this old lady! The client was taking photographs and did not realize what was going on until Joey, having failed to stop the elephant by shooting over her head, had to kill the elephant within three feet of the bumper!

Joey has hunted elephants in Botswana on three occasions. There, the technique for hunting bull elephants is either to ride and glass or to wait at a water hole. Joey feels that neither of these activities is as exciting as the time-honored method of tracking.

The technique used in hunting leopards is similar to that described for baiting lions. Again, baits are hung and checked daily until evidence of a male leopard is found, indicated by large tracks near the bait. The leopard is killed while feeding on the bait either early in the morning or late in the evening. Joey has had to follow wounded leopards on numerous occasions, but has not had a significant problem. He uses a 10-gauge, double-barrel shotgun loaded with buckshot. Joey has used this weapon to good advantage to kill several charging leopards. The closest was only five feet away.

Joey has had two interesting incidents happen while following a wounded leopard. A couple of years ago, he and Makanyanga were following a wounded leopard in fairly thick grass. Joey spotted the leopard and realized it was dead. He pointed it out to Makanyanga. Makanyanga, who had been having some difficulty with decreased vision, smiled. In his flamboyant way, he saluted Joey and said, "Bwana, I will hunt no more." What Makanyanga meant was that if Joey could see an animal before he did, it was time to quit.

The second situation occurred this year and enforced Joey's decision to stop hunting in Africa. He and Sampson had been following a wounded leopard when Sampson indicated that the leopard was just in front and to the left. Joey looked at Sampson and said, "Sampson, I can't see anything." Smiling, Sampson said, "Neither can I, but I can hear him growling." Joey had

An ecstatic Joey, Bwana Babu, and a kudu with massive, wide horns, Namibia, 2008.

not heard anything. He quickly decided that if his hearing was that bad, it was time to let someone else hunt dangerous game. (Let's hope he sticks to that decision.)

Joey has clearly preferred to hunt Cape buffaloes over other dangerous game, and he has had a number of hair-raising episodes. (A number of these have been detailed in my safaris with Joey.) Although many of the buffaloes have been killed to provide bait for either lions or leopards, good trophy bulls have comprised a large number of the total. He will not let a client shoot unless the boss is judged to be solid, which is the characteristic of an old bull. Of all his trophies, the widest horns were forty-six inches, but several clients have killed buffaloes in the forty-two to forty-five inch range. The Rungwa concession contains the largest number of wide-horned buffalo.

In hunting single *dagga* boys, small herds of bulls, and large herds of cows and bulls, Joey has developed a very, very healthy respect for the Cape buffalo. He believes that as long as the animal is on his feet or able to get up, he is dangerous as hell. Eye contact with a wounded *mbogo* guarantees a determined charge. Joey exerts great care in approaching a wounded or downed buffalo. His primary strategy in avoiding trouble is to make sure the client does not shoot unless he is certain that the bullet will enter a vital area. This means, of course, that they need to be as close to the buffalo as possible. After the first shot, as long as the animal is on his feet, the client is told, "Keep shooting."

As a general rule, only about 20 percent of the buffaloes are anchored by the initial shot. The rest run off. Following the tracks obviously produces an intense level of excitement and tests the mettle of both the tracker and the PH. Although he has had to deal with a number of charging buffaloes, to date Joey either has been extremely lucky or damned good (probably the latter).

He and his clients have not experienced any of the catastrophic episodes that are frequently described when *mbogo* decides to avenge his hurt. Frankly, many of these problems are caused by careless mistakes in underestimating the malevolence and tenacity of the wounded buffalo. Because of his meticulous attention to potential danger, Joey and his clients have accounted for over two hundred bull buffaloes without a major adverse incident.

Joey, who is considered one of the top PHs in his field, has recently decided to curtail his time in Africa. Will he really stop hunting dangerous game? Only time will tell.

The African Campfire

Chapter XXIII

I am a convert. Being mesmerized by a small bright red fire at the end of the day's activities is, to me, one of the most notable aspects of an African safari. Such was not always the case. On my first safari, the campfire seemed to have one diabolical purpose, which was to blow smoke in my direction. This annoyance, accompanied by the incessant and mindless chatter emanating from a senior partner in the safari company was sufficient to make me retire to bed early. However, by the end of this safari and on my ensuing trips, my attitude completely reversed. (I've made certain that no unwanted visitors intrude on the scene.) Now I look forward eagerly to spending the evenings gazing into the embers, smoke be damned.

I've never been a firebug. In fact, I have a very nice stone fireplace at home that is used infrequently—about every other year. My choice is to turn up the thermostat and avoid the hassles of building a fire, keeping it burning, and cleaning out the mess.

Why, then, is the African campfire so different? Certainly, in days past there were numerous practical reasons to build a fire. Depending on the location, the most obvious was to keep warm. However, heat from a fire has not been needed or, in fact, welcomed in the locations I've hunted. Fires give off light, but gas lanterns do a better job. Fires also play a protective role, warding off unwanted visits from potentially dangerous animals. While occasionally this may still be the case, there is little real need in the currently more secure campsites. A campfire was once needed for cooking, but, again, this is no longer a valid reason.

Hello there! I'm paying you a neighborly visit. Rungwa, Tanzania, 2005

What's the big deal? A campfire is not really needed for utilitarian purposes anymore. Should this scenario be relegated to the same useless category as wearing a highly starched stiff collar for appearance's sake? A valid conclusion, perhaps, is to characterize a campfire as a formality provided to the modern hunter to maintain the mystique of African adventure.

So, why do I eagerly look forward to this evening ritual? There are several reasons. Sitting near the campfire focuses my attention on the innumerable sounds emanating from the nearby bush. These sounds clearly highlight the fact that the evening's activities between predator and prey are going on full blast.

"This is the hour of pride and power
Of talon and tush and claw."[1]

While mesmerized by the ever-changing "Red Flower," I can experience the continuous fight for survival in the African bush.

More importantly, the glowing coals concentrate my thoughts and provide a bridge to let my imagination blossom. I feel the presence of other human hunters, from the dawn of history through the ensuing millennia as they perform the same ritual of gazing into the embers of a campfire. Early on, the ability to make a communal fire was the primary distinction between man and beast. I share the exhilaration of our ancestors as they realized how their lives had been changed by this gift from the Gods. The fact that their lives also were spent on the same small piece of the globe in East Africa in which I hunt makes the connection far more realistic.

As I gaze into the fire and smell the pungent smoke from *miombo* or acacia wood, I think back on those European and American adventurers to East Africa. In my imagination I become part of the succession of explorer-hunters such as Selous, ivory hunters like Bell and Neumann, game rangers like Percival, safari guides such

[1]Kipling, Rudyard. *The Two Jungle Books.* Garden City, NY: Garden City Publishing Co., Inc., 1940.

as Cunninghame and Cottar, and more recently abundant hunters and guides. All are here.

Every one of them sat by a fire similar to mine, looked at the embers, and relived their daily experiences. Exploits described in books by and about them become infinitely more vivid as the flames erase both time and distance between us. I can share their emotions unleashed by a charging bull elephant and relive the fright generated when tracking wounded buffaloes, lions, or leopards. Furthermore, I can enjoy their descriptions of the grandeur of Africa. The campfire provides a continuum—a unifying force that draws all of our lives together.

Without a small red fire, a safari would lose much of its meaning. Yes, the African campfire is very special!

The African Campfire

The campfire burns. Its flames leap up
To quell the chill of night.
Close-by I sit and gaze, enthralled
By the ever-changing sight.

From a tree nearby old *chui* coughs.
Simba roars on the distant plain.
The evening pageant of life and death
Is in full force again.

I've hunted *tembo* from dawn to dusk.
Tomorrow again I'll try.
This day has lost its race with night.
The stars now dress the sky.

Too tired to eat or even talk,
My mind is ruled by the flame.
How many campfires have burned before
On this same African plain?

Hunters, from man's dawn till now
Look into the fire with me.
Their thoughts are mine. In the burning coals
Each face I clearly see.

The flame does bind us all as one.
Our lives are now entwined.
A toast! To those who share with me,
A campfire throughout time.

Why Africa?

Chapter XXIV

I frequently reflect on my experiences hunting in the Serengeti, Rungwa, Selous, and Kilombero in Tanzania; the Okavango Delta in Botswana; the Timbavati and Eastern Cape in South Africa; and in Namibia during the past dozen years. I struggle to answer the fundamental question of why I have become so enamored of Africa. Without a doubt, I am "hooked" on Africa. The transformation from a reluctant participant at the beginning of my first Cape buffalo hunt to a totally committed zealot is obvious. I can't hide my enthusiasm.

When did I become a convert? No doubt it occurred as the small airplane flew over the airstrip near Fort Ikoma in the Serengeti. The landing field was covered with animals: topis, wildebeests, zebras, and impalas, to name a few. The pilot had to buzz the field two or three times to frighten them into moving off the runway so the plane could land. When I stepped onto the field, a complex emotion raced through my being: Had I returned to Eden?

Examining the perspectives of others regarding the magnetic pull of Africa might help to understand my own commitment. Obviously, exploration or ivory hunting, which drew a number of men to Africa in the nineteenth and early twentieth centuries, is no longer a valid possibility.

Hemingway dealt with this issue in *Green Hills of Africa*:[1] "I would come back to Africa . . . to where it pleased me to live; to really live. And not just let my life pass." This statement was made in the context that, while America had been a good country at one time, "We've made a bloody mess of it." Africa made his life worthwhile.

In "I've Got to Go Back,"[2] Ruark contrasted the life he led as a successful writer in New York City, spending his time going from one cocktail party to another, with the peace and quiet of Africa. It was an escape for him. Not so for me. I'm content with who I am and what I do in North Carolina. America is a great country to live in. Obviously, it would be a lot better if the current crop of vociferous socialists went somewhere else or at least shut up. However, in spite of obnoxious pronouncements by the left-wing media, I don't need an escape.

My background as a totally dedicated quail hunter who derives little or no pleasure from deer hunting and who, in fact, treats this aspect of hunting with disdain would not seem to be a reasonable starting point for being bitten by the African big-game hunting bug. I still don't like deer hunting. Last year I killed a large deer (eight points) to provide meat for a sick friend and felt no excitement at all. On my annual trips to Wyoming to hunt sage grouse, I saw large numbers of pronghorn antelope, a few mule deer, and elk. I have participated as an observer in several hunts but have not developed any desire to hunt these animals. I remain "set in my ways" regarding my dislike of big-game hunting in America.

What aspect of African hunting has smitten me? I tried transferring my love of bird hunting to Africa, but it didn't work. The two times I carried a shotgun I had reasonable success shooting francolin and

[1]Hemingway, Ernest. *Green Hills of Africa.* New York: Charles Scribner's Sons, 1935.

[2]Ruark, Robert C. *Robert Ruark's Africa.* Edited by Michael McIntosh. Traverse City, MI: Countrysport Press, 1991.

Along with the elephant, this remarkable baobab tree symbolizes the quintessence of Africa for the author.

guinea fowl, but I didn't enjoy the experience, for, to me, bird hunting without my pointer bird dogs just isn't bird hunting!

Taking or collecting (whichever is the currently appropriate term) a large number of different species holds no interest for me. Having the largest or the heaviest trophy does not impress me. I've let pass the opportunity to shoot a number of spectacular African antelope.

Travel is not an enjoyable pastime for me. In fact, I avoid it at every turn. On my first trip, nothing could have been less fun than arriving in the Dar es Salaam airport and finding that my baggage had been pilfered and the gentleman who was supposed to meet me didn't show. I had to fend for myself in what I considered a hostile environment. I should have been "turned off" from that moment on and stayed at home.

I truly believe the answer to "Why Africa?" is buried deep within my being. One of my colleagues, who spent several months at the Muhimbili Hospital in Dar es Salaam, described his emotions on seeing Mount Kilimanjaro in the moonlight. He asked, "What were the thoughts of the first man to walk the earth several million years ago when he saw the same sight?"

Could the magnetic attraction of Africa be inborn?

I like every aspect of the bush. The sky, both night and day, is spectacular. The air is free from pollution. No noise emanates from cars, planes, or the other "toys" of the industrial human society. The multifaceted landscape contains a variety of distinct plant life, none more unique than the baobab tree. The unbelievable plethora of animal life comes in all shapes, sizes, and colors. The people whom I've met at every level are distinct and picturesque. The professional hunters and the trackers are an unbelievably talented group, and watching them perform has been a vibrant experience for me.

Much has been written about the unique night sounds of Africa. These are heard nowhere else. The rasping made by a leopard close-by, the roaring of lions in the distance, the breaking of tree branches as elephants feed, the grunting of hippos in a nearby river, the chattering of hyenas on the plains, and the barking of zebras fleeing for their life ratchet through one's being, evoking a perplexing combination of fear and contentment. Both these sounds and the resulting emotions are amplified by gazing into a small, bright red campfire. Perhaps these sensations awaken memories quiescent since the dawn of man.

Hunting dangerous game provides an adrenaline rush that is hard to equal. It is the pinnacle of excitement to follow tracks and to stalk undetected near to a majestic bull elephant; to approach Cape buffaloes and experience their malevolent stare; to hunt at daylight in an area frequented by lions, hoping to "stumble" upon one; and to close with an angry leopard bayed by a pack of hounds.

The reality of one's fragile mortality is brought sharply into focus by these experiences.

Dangerous game can kill, so am I just trying to commit suicide? Why am I so smitten by the magic of the African bush? The simple answer may be a combination of the positive reasons I've enumerated. However, I believe that all of these factors fall far short of painting a compelling picture. Africa's pull is encoded into my genes. I feel, in fact, I know that I've lived there before. After many millennia, I'm home.

Africa . . . *Kwaheri*

Chapter XXV

As the title *Kwaheri* indicates, I have said "good-bye" to my excursions to hunt dangerous game on the Dark Continent. I recognize that on several prior occasions I have made the same statement, and to date, have always changed my mind and returned. In fact, when I told several of my colleagues that I was finished with Africa, their standard response was to smile, roll their eyes upward, and nod. Clearly, they had heard this tale before. "Crying wolf" is not a worthwhile activity. Well, I really mean it this time.

There are a number of factors that have entered into this decision. Certainly, the recent dramatic escalation of the cost involved plays some role. Furthermore, I detest the mandatory twenty-four-hour exhausting travel, both going and coming, which not infrequently has been associated with lost luggage. The increased difficulty in transporting firearms and ammunition also is a factor. Finally, the increasingly unstable political situation in much of sub-Saharan Africa raises concern for any traveler's safety to the region.

However, if I really wanted to go, I would deal with all these problems. The reason is, simply, that I have no desire to kill another member of the African Big Five. On my initial safari, I made a decision not to hunt any of the multitudes of plains game except to provide camp meat or bait. I have seen no reason on subsequent safaris to alter this plan. Everything put together adds up to the realization that I've done all I desire to do in Africa. I have had unbelievable experiences. I would take nothing for them, but it's time to stop.

In reflecting on my twelve safaris, the first thing that should be explained is why I began hunting in Africa in the first place. For more than sixty-five years, I have been an avid quail hunter, and for all that time I have felt that watching the machinations of pointer bird dogs is an experience without equal.

My first safari to the Serengeti was done reluctantly at the behest of Joey, my quail-hunting partner and friend. He convinced me that I would thoroughly enjoy hunting Cape buffalo. He was right. This first safari set the wheels in motion for the subsequent eleven. Initially, I wanted a repeat performance with Black Death. Later, I gradually developed a desire to hunt the African Big Five.

Fortuitously, the first safari occurred at a time when I had relinquished my duties as chairman of the Department of Medicine at Duke University Medical Center. Thus, I had considerable "time on my hands." In casting around for activities that might be enjoyable, as well as productive, I examined what my colleagues, in similar situations, had done. Although I continued to enjoy reading electrocardiograms and teaching, I had no interest in expanding my role in the area of patient care. Basic research in cardiovascular physiology, which I had done for a number of years prior to becoming chairman, while still exciting, did not beckon me as it had once done. Functioning as a consultant, or becoming involved in the politics of medicine, was clearly not something I would find challenging. I examined the possibilities of obtaining an advanced degree to further my intellectual growth. After due consideration, I felt that obtaining an MBA or an MPH would not be a worthwhile use of my time. It was about that time I hit upon the notion of working toward an MMBA: miles and miles of bloody Africa. Never have I regretted this decision.

What experiences have been the most memorable and what have I learned on these safaris? First and foremost, on my initial foray into Africa, I had an overwhelming feeling of déjà vu. I knew, without a doubt, I had been there before. Obviously, the only way that this could have occurred was that I was genetically programmed

The author relaxing in the dining tent after an adventurous day, Selous, Tanzania, 1999.

to remember being in the "cradle" of humanity many eons ago. Africa was home!

The African landscape is truly remarkable. The terrain of Tanzania, South Africa, Botswana, and Namibia is strikingly beautiful with their dense forests, open plains, and sparsely covered deserts. Nowhere is the sky nearly as blue as in Africa. The enormous plethora of fauna, including the annual wildebeest migration, is etched in my memory. I have been lucky enough to witness all the large African antelopes, as well as the Big Five, in their native habitats.

I have been amazed by the expertise of the native trackers with whom I have hunted. Certainly, Makanyanga was premier in this regard, but not far behind him were Simon, Pius, Singi, Doudi, Martin, Sampson, Moshile, Corporal, and Alex. All of these individuals performed amazing feats of spotting and unerringly following the spoor of dangerous game. They not only tracked the quarry, but they also placed me in the best position to be able to kill the animals.

The other major component of my experiences has been the close association with outstanding professional hunters (PHs). Joey, my longtime colleague, has developed into one of the best of the current PHs in Africa. I have, on numerous occasions, put my life into his capable hands, and at least twice, he kept me from becoming a statistic! Also, I have been very lucky to have had the opportunity to hunt with Alex Walker, Gordon Church, Anton Wienand, and more recently Barry Burchell.

The list of the animals I have hunted successfully is impressive: fifteen Cape buffalo, two large bull elephants, a massive lion, an impressive white rhinoceros, and a large, charging leopard. In addition, I was in the blind when Joey killed a lion, and I accompanied him on another successful leopard hunt. Thus, my experiences with hunting dangerous game, especially Cape buffaloes, have been reasonably extensive. Which do I consider the most challenging and dangerous? All of them!

While hunting Cape buffaloes, I have never been hurt. However, I have, on at least four occasions, had the opportunity to reflect upon my own fragile mortality. Cape buffaloes have a well-deserved reputation for being tough and difficult to kill. I concur with this assessment. I have used the following cartridges in dealing with fifteen *mbogo*s: a .375 Holland & Holland (three), a .458 Lott (one), a .465 (two), a .470 (seven), and a .500 (two). On eight occasions, the first shot anchored the animal, although I fired at least once again. In seven cases, *mbogo* ran at least seventy-five yards after being hit. On one occasion, although mortally wounded, he escaped. Of the other six, two made a determined charge. The total number of bullets striking a vital area while *mbogo* was still standing ranged from six to fourteen. Yes, unless knocked down with the first shot, he can soak up an unbelievable amount of lead in his vitals! My respect for him as an adversary is limitless. (By the way, I also killed three water buffaloes at J&R Outfitters in Florida using a .465 (one), a .470 (one), and a .500 (one). They all were immobilized by the first shot.)

The sun dips below the horizon on the Mnyera River.

Undoubtedly, I have experienced excitement at the highest level. All in all, I believe that I have earned the MMBA degree.

Luckily, I have been able to surround myself with a number of trophies from these hunts. Now, I can spend as much time as I like gazing at these animals—and remembering the exciting moments that were involved between me and them.

I have made a strong case for the immutable pull of Africa on my being. Obviously, one might wonder "How will I be able to resist it in the future?" Good question! I have no doubt that I can withstand this "tug" by mentally reliving my experiences. Further incursions into the Dark Continent are not mandatory. I must admit that in the category of hunting dangerous game, shooting snapping turtles in my pond is a very poor substitute for coping with Cape buffalo on the African veld.

As the book on my safari life ends, I must thank a kind Providence for giving me the opportunity to experience Africa at its very best.

Africa, *Kwaheri*!

Africa, *Kwaheri!*

When first I set foot in Africa
I was engulfed by déjà vu
That I was in my ancestral home
Without a doubt. I knew.

The primal pull of Africa
Lured me by its siren spell;
To Tanzania, Botswana, Namibia,
And South Africa as well.

To stalk the majestic Big Five
Enthralled my very soul.
The thrill of imminent danger
By words cannot be told.

Africa . . . *Kwaheri*

For twelve event-filled years
I've savored Africa's best.
But now I know the time has come
For me to end my quest.

In Africa, a major part of me
Always will remain.
And maybe in another life
I shall return again.

But for now, I'll bid farewell
To this land of mystery.
The sun now sets. It's time to cry
Africa . . . *Kwaheri.*

Published Magazine Stories

The following stories have either been published or are in press in outdoor journals. One tale does not appear in the main body of this book, and four are abridged versions of stories you have already read.

Mbogo's Choice

This story is a shortened version of chapter five. It was published in *Big Game Adventures*, Winter 2006.

Mbogo, Swahili for a male African Cape buffalo, is one hell of a critter. Black Death or Horned Death (his other names) is a charter member of the Big Five of dangerous game (lion, leopard, buffalo, elephant, and rhinoceros). He has been responsible for the demise of many hunters, both professional and novice.

Mbogo is usually peaceful and leaves well enough alone, but if wounded, watch out. He will charge with just one purpose in mind—to kill. An adult male may weigh up to eighteen hundred pounds, which is small compared to the other wild oxen such as the American bison or the Indian gaur. Possessing blinding speed and armed with a pair of curved horns, Africa's Black Death deserves respect. Getting run over by this animal, even without being gored or tossed, may be fatal. He can be very crafty, waiting silently in long grass until the pursuing hunter comes close . . . then he charges in for the kill. When really enraged, *mbogo* finishes the job by pounding his enemy's remains into a pulpy mass.

Male buffalo fight viciously among themselves for the right to breed. The young bull growing up in the herd is kept in check by the leader bull. If strong enough once mature, the younger bull will replace the leader, driving him from the herd. After a time, this cycle is repeated. Eventually he will be forced out to fend for himself, either alone or with the companionship of several other banished bulls. Finally, as with all creatures of Africa, *mbogo* usually meets a violent end, either from lions or hyenas.

The author with "contented" mbogo

One of the most striking characteristics of Africa's Black Death is his chilling stare, which can best be described as cold fury. *Mbogo*'s eyes have brought more sportsmen to hunt in Africa than all the other dangerous game combined. Like nothing else, these eyes mesmerize. They haunt the hunter, drawing him back to Africa . . . again and again.

I came under *mbogo*'s spell on a prior trip to the Serengeti when I hunted near Fort Ikoma, Tanzania. There I survived a somewhat harrowing experience, and, like many people with little sense, I had to try it again. Joey O'Bannon had spent the previous season in Rungwa, Tanzania, and reported that the Cape buffalo hunting there was excellent. Through the auspices of Miombo Safaris, Joey arranged for me to hunt Black Death in this concession in August 1998.

Armed with a new .500 Krieghoff Classic double rifle and other necessary accoutrements, I journeyed on KLM to Dar es Salaam, where Joey and Gordon Church met me. Gordon, the chief professional hunter and a wiry six-foot-five individual, exuded an air of confidence. I concluded immediately that I would be in safe hands.

We flew by air charter to Rungwa in western Tanzania and found our camp to be in an ideal location. It was hilly country sparsely covered with *miombo* and acacia trees as well as brush and grass, and a major portion of it had been recently burned, making for reasonable visibility. After sighting-in the rifles, our crew—Joey, Gordon, Pius the chief tracker, the Tanzanian game scout, and two general factotums—climbed aboard a Toyota Land Cruiser and rode along a dusty, well-laid-out road. Our hunt had begun! Game was plentiful. We saw zebras, giraffes, hartebeests, sables, roan, elands, and a variety of small antelopes.

About 5:30 P.M., just as the African sun began to dip below the horizon of the nearby hills, that magic time of day arrived when colors fade, the air becomes damp, and the land seems alive with animals. Just at that moment, Pius whispered, "*Mbogo*."

The Land Cruiser abruptly stopped. I didn't see anything in the fading light at first, but, with Gordon's help, I finally spotted the bull about one hundred yards on our left in the low brush and grass, near a large thicket of long grass. What followed seems almost mystical.

The bull was grazing, and the wind blew from him to us. We slipped out of the truck and slithered through the grass, the double rifle on my lap, my butt scraping the dirt until we were within shooting distance, which was about thirty-five yards away from the bull.

Mbogo, standing quietly behind a small bush, seemed oblivious to our presence. I eased into a shooting position. After a few seconds, as if on cue, he stepped into the open, facing to my left. I quickly aimed at the heart area and fired. *Mbogo* fell.

The bull rolled over, kicked once or twice, and as we approached from the rear, emitted the characteristic soft dying bellow. Gordon had me make doubly sure by shooting into the cervical spine, but there was no need. *Mbogo* was dead.

Although the light was rapidly fading, I could see clearly into his eyes. There was no deadly stare. Perhaps I am being too imaginative and sentimental, but I would swear *mbogo* radiated contentment. The solid boss on his horns was worn smooth, and multiple scars covered his hide. This particular *mbogo* was very old. During the usual picture taking and field dressing, I couldn't help but speculate. Was he really oblivious to our presence? Why had he been such an easy target? Did I carry out his wishes?

Moriturus Te Saluto

I'm tired. My youth is behind me.
My wives and children are gone.
They serve a stronger new master,
To the herd I no longer belong.

Many years I've lived alone,
Enjoyed the quiet and peace.
But each night when the hyenas chatter,
I think how my life will cease.

Worried and torn by those vermin,
While my heart's blood ebbs away.
A more loathsome way to end my life
Would be hard to say.

On my left I see three hunters.
I smell their fear of me.
I could vanish into the long grass,
And leave not a trace to see.

But hurry you hairless monkeys.
I'll bellow my final breath
And cheat the hyenas of supper
For I chose a bullet for death.

Rep's Revenge

This story was published in
Big Game Adventures,
Fall/Winter 2005.

I had nothing to do with the beginning of this episode, but I was very much involved with ending it. As I said earlier, when Joey O'Bannon decided to expand J&R Outfitters from primarily a quail-hunting operation to include big game, he hit upon the notion of providing "fair-chase" buffalo hunting in Florida. In 1998, he obtained approximately one hundred Asian water buffalo ranging in age from one to five years. At that time the ranch was fenced with a standard five-strand barbwire cattle fence. Since a similar fence previously had contained these water buffalo, he felt safe in assuming they would remain inside the fenced area. As a general rule, this degree of restraint worked out quite well, although occasionally bulls in small groups or singles broke through the fence and went "visiting" the neighbors.

The standard approach to bringing an escaped buffalo home was for several cowboys and cattle dogs to herd it back to the ranch. If the buffalo had strayed so far that this method wasn't feasible, the buffalo was roped, "enticed" into a cattle truck, and transported home. This latter approach did provide some excitement but without any significant problems—with the following exception.

Any group always has one or two individuals who seem to create the majority of the trouble. This rule also applies to these buffalo; in fact, one specific bull became a real problem whose escapes and absentee behavior formed the basis of this tale.

The third or fourth time this very vexatious buffalo escaped, he made a new home for himself about a mile from the ranch in a very dense palmetto thicket. Three of Joey's cowboy friends, including Danny MacFarland riding a cow horse named Rep, set out to round up this bull. (In his youth, Rep, a potential race horse, became a determined bucker and was nearly impossible to ride. Joey salvaged him from the "kill truck" and aptly named him Reprieve, or Rep for short. Joey got the horse's "attention," and Rep soon became a reliable cow horse.)

The dogs bayed the bull, and Danny rode the horse toward them. At that point, things got very sticky. The bull, instead of trying to escape, charged. Danny and Rep were in thick cover and unable to get out of the way. The bull lowered his head, ran under the horse's belly, and hooked upward. Danny found himself sitting on an impaled horse. Fortunately for Danny, the bull didn't toss the horse but instead disengaged himself. For some reason, rather than press his advantage, the bull retreated. Danny had escaped from a very serious predicament, but after dismounting quickly found that Rep was fatally wounded. Score for the day: buffalo one, cowboys zero.

The next day, a larger crew attempted the capture. Again, the bull was bayed by the dogs, with two of them coming out of the encounter much worse off. A bulldog, Winston by name, decided to be a real hero and grabbed the maddened buffalo by the nose. The buffalo reacted quickly and mashed the dog between his horns and the ground. Needless to say, the dog did not survive. Shortly thereafter a very good cow dog, Rastas, was hooked in the shoulder and tossed fifteen or twenty feet up into a myrtle bush. Two weeks in the hospital with a collapsed lung was the result, but at least he survived. While the bull was engaged with the dogs, the cowboys threw several ropes around its neck. With considerable difficulty, they pulled the bull into the cattle truck and finally deposited him back at the ranch.

In short order, Joey had an eight-foot-high, nine-mile-long, secure game fence constructed. This troublesome buffalo and his wandering kin remained confined.

After this episode, the bull, now labeled as a rogue, became a recluse. He stayed in a marshy and overgrown area of the ranch and seldom mingled with the other buffaloes. On several occasions, he demonstrated an aggressive and territorial nature by mock-charging nearby vehicles and generally making a nuisance of himself. It was obvious that sooner or later this rogue bull would create a significant incident. That's when I came into the picture.

I had previously killed two Asian water buffalo with Joey and thoroughly enjoyed the hunting experience. I had made a total of six safaris to Africa, and on four of them I had primarily hunted Cape buffalo. I had initially planned to go back to Africa yearly, but the September 11 terrorist situation (along with a significant depletion of my "play money") changed my thinking. I talked to Joey about the possibility of another Florida buffalo hunt. When I heard the tales regarding this particular rogue, I said to myself, "Well, you've tried to get killed in Africa on several occasions. Why not try in Florida?" So, I told Joey we would hunt this rogue bull.

I scheduled a three-day hunt and arrived at J&R Outfitters in late February of 2002, armed with my newly engraved and re-blued Holland & Holland .470 double rifle.

To accomplish our goal, we would search the ranch in the swamp buggy, locate the rogue, and then stalk to within range for a killing shot. The first two days we saw a lot of buffaloes, many with very impressive horns, both in groups and loners.

One small group included a bull that looked like our quarry. We quickly dismounted, made a three- to four-hundred-yard stalk approaching the animals downwind, and hid behind a pine tree. These buffaloes grazed to within ten yards of our location, then suddenly became aware of our presence, snorted, and retreated a few yards. Our quarry was not among them. The wind shifted. They got our scent and decamped. We continued our search, finding several solitary black bulls that resembled the one we were after, but closer inspection proved otherwise The night shadows ushered in a feeling of disappointment.

The final morning, bright and early, we continued our quest. The morning passed. We were still empty-handed. I began to

The rogue (Rep's nemesis) and the author, Indiantown, Florida

have second thoughts about achieving my goal. Surely our luck would change.

In the early afternoon, while riding next to the game fence, Joey spied a dark shape in a nearby thicket. With the help of my binoculars, I finally identified a buffalo, malevolently staring at us. The tip of the left horn was broken off. Joey quickly exclaimed, "That's him!" About this time, the bull decided he had important business elsewhere and left.

We loaded our rifles, I with the Holland and Joey with his .470 Rigby double rifle, and stepped into the bush. As usual on our hunts for dangerous game, Joey would provide backup if necessary. We tracked the bull approximately three hundred yards before Joey spied his back, nearly hidden by the thick broomstraw. I had the same problem that I had experienced in Africa hunting Cape buffalo: I'm too damn short to see over the usual cover. All I saw was broomstraw. The rogue became aware of our presence and left running downwind. He crossed a deep canal and entered into a thick overgrown swampy area where the water level ranged from ankle to knee deep. We followed, but the buffalo got our scent and again ran off. It became obvious that, because of the wind direction and the terrain, we would not be able to close with the rogue before nightfall using our current approach. We needed another plan.

When hunting, Joey uses cow dogs to find seriously wounded buffalo that have escaped into thick cover. This approach has saved him from serious mishaps on several occasions, but he had not used dogs on unwounded buffalo for a variety of reasons, not the least of which is the risk of having a dog killed.

We were on the horns of a dilemma. The likelihood of getting close to the buffalo in this swamp with an adverse wind blowing was slim. He would escape. This was my final day and I definitely wanted to kill the rogue. Joey wanted the potentially dangerous bull eliminated. After briefly discussing the situation, Joey made a decision. "Let's turn out the dogs," he said.

Walking back to the buggy, we released three dogs: Bassinger, Jeff, and Rastas (the same dog that had been seriously injured by this buffalo). Cow dogs give little or no tongue until they have located their quarry, but they obviously smelled the bull and trailed in the direction he had run.

We followed in the swamp buggy. After driving about one half mile, we heard the dogs bay in very thick woods. Just as we started to dismount, the rogue came running toward us. He ran to within about ten steps of us, but the very thick trees and brush made shooting impossible. Luckily, he didn't see either us or the buggy, for he undoubtedly would have charged. He could easily have overturned the buggy.

After leaving the thicket, he crossed into an open marsh covered with knee-deep standing water and headed toward a large overgrown island, with the dogs in hot pursuit. We followed in the buggy as fast as possible. After running about half a mile, the rogue stopped on the other side of a wide drainage ditch covered by tall myrtle bushes and palmettos. The dogs caught up and bayed him. By this time, with his adrenaline flowing, the very mad rogue aggressively tried to hook the dogs with his horns. Luckily, none of them got too close.

We grabbed our rifles and hustled to within forty yards of the fracas. The bull decided to continue his trek to the island. When he broke out of the thicket and became visible, I brought the Holland into action. The bull ran from my right to left. I thought the first shot, taken from about thirty-five yards, was well placed in the region of the heart. It turned out later that it was too high, probably clipping the top of both lungs. A lung-shot buffalo will die eventually, but characteristic of the breed, although mortally wounded but still on his feet, he can create a world of trouble. Since he was running full tilt, I led with the double rifle as I would when shooting quail. The second shot went somewhat too far forward. Instead of hitting the heart area, it went into the neck, luckily breaking his spine. Down he came in a heap, unable to rise. The rogue was paralyzed, and another bullet into his heart quickly ended his career. It was all over!

A close examination revealed a magnificent old specimen. The tip of the left horn had been broken off in some altercation; he was blind in one eye; he had numerous scars from fighting;

and he was nearly tailless. The rogue had obviously been "through the wars."

We took the usual pictures, rounded up the dogs, and dragged the rogue out with the swamp buggy so he could be loaded onto a trailer. (After butchering, the meat was donated to a local substance abuse rehabilitation center.)

I had an outstanding hunt; the Holland worked perfectly; I felt warm and fuzzy from the knowledge that Rep had been revenged. Not the least, Joey, the dogs, and I had come through the experience unscathed.

Although the mystique of Africa isn't there, buffalo hunting in Florida can be one hell of an exciting adventure!

Selous Lion, A "Proper" Trophy?

This is a shortened version of chapter six, published in *Big Game Adventures*, Summer/Fall 2006.

In 1998, along with Joey O'Bannon, my hunting partner, I had participated in a successful lion hunt in Rungwa, Tanzania. While waiting in the blind for lions to appear, an event occurred that had a major bearing on this safari. A beautiful lioness, lithe and graceful, approached the kongoni bait and with the late afternoon sun shining on her coat, she was definitely a thing of beauty. She rose up on her hind legs and pulled a piece of flesh off the bait and began to eat.

The male appeared next on the scene. Although larger, his extensive hirsute mane detracted from his athletic appearance, at least to me. (As usual, I'm at odds with the rest of humanity regarding this observation.) At any rate, after the "tumult and shouting" was over, I wondered why the hairy male is always judged the more desirable trophy. Personally, I would be quite content with a mature male lion having a "short" mane.

For this safari, I had planned to hunt only Cape buffalo. However, through a series of circuitous events, I booked an October hunt in the Selous for both lion and buffalo with Miombo Safaris. (Lions in the Selous are not noted for their long manes, but this suited me just fine.)

Joey would accompany me and function as the professional hunter (PH). This would be his second year as a licensed Tanzanian PH. Coupled with a lifetime of hunting in Florida and keen woodsmanship, his experiences in both South Africa and Tanzania resulted in Joey developing into an outstanding big-game guide.

I made a decision to carry my .465 Holland & Holland double rifle. It fits me perfectly and is a joy to shoot. To hell with worrying about the value! If it's stolen, I'll cry then. (The rifle is insured.) My decision, no doubt, was influenced by Joey. A grateful client recently willed Joey a .470 NE Rigby double rifle, and it is a beautiful gun. Joey's dilemma was whether he should hunt with a rifle worth more than his house? His answer was a definite "Yes!"

Joey and I arrived in camp via air charter to begin our adventure. I was in for a real treat. Our head tracker, Makanyanga, had a reputation as being the best tracker in Africa. Makanyanga had guided for many of the best-known professional hunters: beginning in 1964 with Kevin Torrens, followed by Brian Hearne, Dannny McCallam, and Robin Hurt. He had hunted exclusively with Alex Walker since 1991. I soon learned that his reputation was well deserved. Makanyanga is a member of the Wakamba tribe in Kenya, the legendary elephant hunters. Fifty-plus-years old, he has seen it all . . . and then some! Clearly, Makanyanga has had as much experience with dangerous game as anyone alive. The other tracker, Pius, had hunted with me in Rungwa and was superb.

As in Rungwa, the camp staff designated me by the descriptive Swahili name, Bwana Babu (grandfather), probably reasonable, if unflattering. Joey had been dubbed Bwana Marlboro. (His western hat mimicked the Marlboro man.)

Since hunting lion was a major component of this safari, we needed to procure sufficient bait. On our first day, Makanyanga spotted a large wildebeest facing us. He put the sticks down; my shot was on target. (Sticks is a term describing three wooden rods held together with inner-tube rubber. This tripod is used to support the rifle while firing.)

During the next five days, acquiring additional lion bait became necessary. Accordingly, I killed a kongoni (Lichtenstein hartebeest), another wildebeest, and a zebra. Although we did not specifically seek trophy-quality animals, the horns from both the kongoni and wildebeest measured record-book size. One of the baits was briefly chewed by lions. We built a blind and waited one afternoon and early the next morning, but to no avail. The lions did not return.

Other than this one episode, our other baits remained untouched. We did see numerous large tracks, indicating that male lions had walked close to the baits. Either because they were too wary or too full of young impala, baiting for lions seemed to be unfruitful. Although we had an exciting time hunting buffaloes, by the eighth day I was beginning to have doubts about the likelihood of shooting a lion.

A pride of lions had been roaring nightly close to camp and Makanyanga devised a new plan. During dinner that evening, he appeared and outlined this new approach to Joey. After considerable animated discussion, they concocted the following simple scheme. Since there were plenty of lions near camp, we would sashay around early in the morning before daylight to see if we could get close to them. We would hunt lions the way they're supposed to be hunted—without using bait. Joey spelled out the idea to me. My response was an incredulous, "We're going to do what?"

To add to the difficulties of this plan, I have a very significant blind spot. It takes good light for me to be able to see well enough to shoot. Joey knew about this problem, but said, "Well, we won't get to the lions until you can see to shoot."

(Really? How in the hell could he be sure?) To add to my consternation, I knew that lions possess exceptional night vision. They could see us; we couldn't see them!

It wasn't clear to me exactly what Makanyanga and Joey had been drinking, but undoubtedly I was dealing with two lunatics. I had to decide whether to join them or to hide in camp. After remembering that my insurance premiums had been paid recently, I decided to be one of the "boys" and go along with this hare-brained scheme. Bwana Babu shoots a lion, gets killed, or both!

Anyway, about 5:30 A.M. away we went. Two double rifles, the shooting sticks, and four intrepid hunters—one with significant reservations regarding the sanity of this adventure. Makanyanga indicated that a male lion had moved off to the long grass about 5 A.M. He was not sure if there was anything left but lionesses. We went anyway.

The night was nearly dark with a quarter moon, but there was just enough light so that I could see Joey's back—although it faded

The Selous lion, a very "proper" trophy.

in and out, depending on whether he was in my blind spot. Pius brought up the rear. His primary function was to stop me from running back to camp!

Makanyanga indicated that the lions would be on the far side of the dried riverbed. Well, fine. I wasn't at all convinced that they had read their part of the script. Even if correct, my guess, it would take about two or three seconds for them to get on our side. Anyway, we began our trek.

We crept slowly, for perhaps five hundred yards, to the edge of the riverbed where we were hidden by fairly thick brush. Enough light now shone so that, in looking through the scope, I could actually see. My heart rate slowed, at least somewhat, but I was a long way from being calm.

All of a sudden, a large lioness walked out of the bushes and across an open glade on the other side of the riverbed and lay down (exactly as called for in Makanyanga's plan). She was about sixty-five yards off. We waited. After three to four minutes, the first rays of the rising sun shone on the head and body of a very large male lion lying about ninety yards away and just past the lioness. He gazed in our direction as if contemplating whether it was worth the effort to dine on the nearby monkeylike creatures.

Makanyanga planted the sticks for me, and Joey whispered, "Can you kill him?"

"Of course!" I replied, pretending to be calm. "Why do you ask?" In fact, my thoughts were much less self-assured.

After the report of the rifle and the subsequent thud as the bullet went home, the lion jumped straight up in the air about five feet. He roared and fell down. He got up just as the bullet from the second barrel hit his chest. Joey exclaimed, "He's toast."

(Actually what he said is unprintable, but conveyed the distinct impression that the lion was seriously impaired.) The lion continued to roll over. I reloaded. Joey shot; I shot again. The lion became still. The lioness had apparently exited.

Makanyanga gave his usual high-pitched warbling victory yell. I heard the truck in camp start up. In a few minutes, the rest of the contingent arrived. We drove to where the lion lay. When he was judged dead, "all hell broke loose."

I'm not sure why, but killing a lion elicits the damnedest celebration imaginable. It ain't staged. The entire crew, especially Pius, began hollering, singing, and dancing.

The lion had a short mane. Estimated to be about eight years old and covered with scars, he was a magnificent creature. I had a "proper" trophy.

I probably owed Joey and Makanyanga an apology for doubting their plan, but, true to form, I didn't admit anything. (I always heed a maxim ascribed to John Wayne: "Never admit a mistake. It's a sign of weakness.")

In reliving the experience, Joey had a confession to make. "I didn't tell you that our major worry about the late-night stalk was inadvertently getting too close to elephants in the riverbed."

I thanked Joey for keeping this concern a secret. Undoubtedly, the possibilities of being trampled by elephants, as well as being ingested by lions, would have precluded my participating in what turned out to be a very exciting event.

The celebration became even more intense. It took the entire contingent to load the lion into the truck. When we arrived at camp, I was toted around in a chair with a garland of toilet paper around my neck. The dancing involved everyone, even me. After about an hour, the entire crew was exhausted.

Later in the early afternoon, I went to the skinning shed and got frightened out of my wits by looking at the size of the lion's paws and teeth. The first bullet had entered the front of the chest, went through the heart, and exited the chest into the leg, finally lodging in the paw.

That night, shortly after 1 A.M., I was awakened by the nearly continuous vocal outpourings of three lionesses. Apparently looking for their deceased "Lord and Master," they camped on the other side of the dry riverbed, about eighty yards from my tent. Joey had informed me that "as long as I remained in the tent at night, I was safe." Well fine! Had these lionesses read the appropriate instruction manuals? I quickly loaded the Holland and sat on the edge of the bed while listening to the ladies roaring. I assumed that as long as I could hear them, I would be OK.

After about an hour, all became suddenly quiet. A loud noise made by a creature in the nearby bathroom broke the silence, which, to say the least, got my undivided attention. I pointed my rifle in that general direction and turned on the flashlight. The light outlined a bat, the cause of the ruckus, trying to extricate himself from the mosquito netting. I breathed again.

The ladies soon restarted their serenade from approximately the same location. After about an hour, they wandered off, their roaring fading into the distance. I lapsed into a restful sleep.

Hounded!

This is a shortened version of chapter thirteen, published in *Sporting Classics*, September 2010.

The hound music swelled to a high intensity as the pack gained on the leopard. Suddenly, the snarling cough of the leopard was audible as he took his stand in the Namibian brush. The next few minutes would end this affair one way or the other. A "moment of truth" for me was at hand!

How did I get into this situation? The adventure had its origin when I asked Mr. Frank Cole of Cabela's Outdoor Adventures to try to arrange a leopard hunt with dogs. I have never liked still-hunting from a blind. In my estimation, it has the same appeal as watching paint dry. Hunting a leopard with hounds . . . now that's my idea of real excitement. To each his own! Mr. Cole contacted Mr. Barry Burchell of Frontier Safaris who proposed a fifteen-day leopard hunt at Trudia Game Ranch in northern Namibia, just south of Etosha National Park. They had not hunted leopard previously on the ranch. However, tracks were abundant. It didn't take much to convince me to give it a try.

After a long but uneventful flight, I arrived at Windhoek and was met by Barry. We drove three hundred miles north to the ranch through rocky semiarid hilly land covered with low brush and stunted trees. It was late September and although the nights were cool, the temperature warmed up to ninety degrees plus by 2 P.M. Thus, most of the serious hunting would be done early in the morning. In order to avoid dealing with the problems related to transporting my firearm, I borrowed a Remington Model 700 in 7mm magnum from Barry.

When we arrived at the ranch, I met the primary actors in this episode. Mr. Roy Sparks had brought his pack of bluetick and treeing Walker hounds. Roy had hunted leopard for a number of years. He spends his entire time training dogs and pursuing predominately stock-killing leopards. A major member of his entourage is Moshile, a Xhosa tribesman and an extraordinary tracker and dog handler. The other person on the team was Alex, a tracker, who worked for Barry.

The first afternoon, we drove along some of the woods roads looking for spoor and hung two gemsbok baits. Constantly harassed by ranchers, the leopards in this area are wary. They seldom come to bait. We gave it a try anyway.

The next morning at 4:30 A.M., after a hurried cup of coffee, we began hunting in earnest. Moshile and Alex rode on the hood of the Land Cruiser and used a spotlight and the headlights to try to pick up leopard tracks as we slowly drove along the woods roads. It seems impossible, but that's what they did! They found a number of tracks several days old as well as where a leopard had marked the area with scent and scat. We covered about six miles; Moshile and Roy seemed quite satisfied that a large male leopard was using that area. We quit about 11 A.M. and returned that afternoon at 4 P.M. without the dogs. We hung several more baits in the same general area and also scouted another area for leopard sign.

The next morning was a repeat performance of the day before. We found the remains of a gemsbok killed by a large leopard about two weeks earlier. However, no fresh tracks were found and none of the baits were touched. On the fourth day, about 6 A.M., after we had passed all of the uneaten baits and had moved toward the end of the area where the leopard had been using, the situation changed abruptly. Moshile raised his hand, a signal to stop the truck. He was smiling. He had found fresh tracks! At least that's what he and Roy decided. I had a hard time making out what they were looking at even when the spoor was pointed out to me.

After quickly putting tracking collars on three of the hounds, they were released. Moshile and Alex walked in the direction where the leopard seemed to be going. Moshile carried a radio to keep in contact with us. After ten minutes, he indicated that he had found a fresh track in a dry streambed. About that time, one of the dogs opened. They were in a ravine at the base of a fairly high hill on the far side. Our side was a much lower hill thickly covered with thornbushes, scrub trees, and grass.

For the next hour, the trackers gradually moved about three-fourths of a mile up the depression, the hounds giving tongue more frequently. At this juncture, Roy turned out another hound. When he opened, Roy smiled and indicated that this dog would only bark on a fairly hot track. All the hounds began giving tongue more frequently as they unraveled the leopard's trail. We moved the vehicle twice to keep ahead of them. All of a sudden, over the radio Moshile yelled in an excited staccato voice. He had seen the leopard! At that juncture, the truck tailgate was dropped and the remaining six hounds rapidly joined the chase. (A sign on the truck, "When the tailgate drops, the B.S. stops," was prophetic.) Rather than going up the hill behind us, the leopard turned in our direction. For ten or fifteen minutes, the air was filled with a high volume of hound music. About two hundred yards to our left, the hounds bayed. The rasping snarl of the leopard, who took his stand on the ground rather than climb a tree, became quite audible. We hustled toward the engagement.

I had a problem. Although it infrequently happens, I'm subject to periods of rapid heart rate of more than one hundred sixty beats per minute. I'll be damned if this affliction didn't decide to manifest itself at this time. For a few seconds, I became quite woozy, but then adjusted rapidly. I took a deep breath, ignored the problem, and hurried toward the fracas. We got to about sixty-five yards of where the dogs had surrounded the leopard, but we couldn't see it. Mr. Spots moved about another hundred yards and again stopped. He was mad as hell and growling constantly at his tormentors. They continued their vocal outpourings.

We got within about thirty yards of him. I made out an area of yellow covered by black spots about three feet behind a black and white hound named Charlie. Because of the thick brush, I saw only the body of the leopard. Neither the head nor the tail was visible.

I eased the rifle onto the shooting sticks and waited. After a minute or so, Charlie moved, and I had a clear view of the leopard's chest. My shot was greeted with a loud growl.

The leopard lurched about five yards to the left and became completely hidden by the brush. However, the continued baying of the hounds let us know he was close-by. The three of us walked deliberately toward where the leopard had disappeared. Barry was in the middle, abreast of Roy. I was approximately two yards to their right and slightly to the rear. Barry, who is quite tall, saw the leopard lying on his left side, barely breathing, approximately eight yards away. The brush obscured my view. "He's dying," Barry exclaimed. "No need for us to shoot again."

Mr. Spots disagreed. Without uttering a sound, the leopard stood up—silent as death—and charged hellbent in Roy's direction. In an instant, the air was filled with missiles from both Roy and Barry's rifles. I saw the charging leopard just as he piled up about two yards in front of Roy. . . . The hunt was over!

Interestingly, unlike hounds that hunt raccoons and hogs in the United States, these dogs did not attack the body. They only looked at the leopard, smelled some of his blood, but showed no interest in chewing on the carcass. Maybe they had learned that mixing it up with even a supposedly dead leopard could be hazardous to their health.

While describing the final events, Barry confided to me that he had made a big mistake, dictated primarily by his desire not to puncture the leopard's skin with too many holes. I'll bet he won't refrain from shooting a "dying" leopard in the future. (By the way, I'm not sure when it happened, but my fast heart rate had disappeared. It did add an unwanted distraction.)

Moshile easily picked up the heavy leopard, draped him around his shoulders and walked back to the truck, followed by the tired hounds. He deposited Mr. Spots in an open area so that we could take pictures. Most animals, at least in my experience, when dead lose much of their persona. Certainly, a dead elephant is a very depressing sight. Not so this leopard; even in death, he was majestic.

He was measured to be 7 feet, 5 inches long, and Roy estimated his weight at about 165 pounds. He was a very large male leopard. Later, when he was skinned and the chest opened, we found that my bullet had penetrated through the edge of the heart. His chest was full of blood. How he lived long enough to charge remains a mystery. The hounds came through the fracas generally unscathed. Several had fairly deep scratches and one had been either bitten or clawed on his leg. However, the bleeding had stopped and he seemed oblivious of the situation. No other serious damage was incurred.

That's about all. To sum it up, it might be possible to have a more exciting experience hunting leopard. . . but I don't see how.

Rhino, The Last Rung in My Big Five Ladder

This is a shortened version of chapter fourteen to be published in *African Hunting Gazette.*

For the past forty-five minutes, I had crouched immobile behind a low thornbush on the edge of a twenty-acre grass-covered meadow watching five rhinos graze. Moving their enormous heads from side to side, they cut a swath through the field, ingesting an impressive amount of green groceries. A slight wind was blowing in our direction; the quarry was completely unaware of our presence. When first spotted, they were approximately seventy yards off and had come no closer during their recent machinations.

In the last three minutes, this situation changed. Two of the rhinos, one having the largest horn, grazed in our direction, moving from my left to right. The smaller one came to within twenty yards of our location while the larger was approximately fifty yards away. For reasons known only to them, both rhinos suddenly stopped. They were not agitated, just frozen. The larger rhino was partially obscured by the closer.

I held the dart gun on "ready." Carl had set the pressure for a distance of approximately fifty yards. Barry's hands tightened on his .470 Krieghoff Classic double rifle—just in case! Lady Luck smiled. After two to three minutes (it seemed a lot longer) the large rhino walked forward, giving me an unobstructed view. The "moment of truth" had arrived. I sighted the red dot on its right shoulder and squeezed the trigger. Following the whooshing sound as the dart flew, I could see the red tip impaled on the rhino's shoulder.

Startled by the sound, both rhinos charged forward full speed, but luckily, not in our direction. They were joined by their companions and rapidly ran downhill. I breathed a sigh of relief and felt elated. Perhaps my final quest was over?

******

Just why am I here? Six months prior to this event, I had little interest in hunting a southern white rhinoceros. On two occasions, I had seen them in the wild: in Timbavati while I was hunting an elephant, and on the Zuka Game Ranch in KwaZulu-Natal. Neither of these encounters whetted my appetite to hunt these apparently docile behemoths. However, last fall when I killed a very large male leopard at the Trudia Game Ranch in northern Namibia, I realized that I had killed four of the African Big Five, and all of record-book quality. I needed only a rhinoceros to complete the Grand Slam.

The major impediment to my shooting a rhinoceros was the kill fee, which is at least $50,000. This was out of the question. On the other hand, I could afford the substantially less cost of darting one of these "Pleistocene hold-overs." Through Cabela's Outdoor Adventures, Frank Cole arranged for a hunt with Barry Burchell (Frontier Safaris, Port Elizabeth, South Africa). The hunt was to include darting a rhino, hunting caracal with Barry's hounds, and introducing my daughter, Ruth Ann, to big-game hunting.

Accordingly, we arrived in Port Elizabeth after the obligatory twenty-four-hour air travel. The facilities of the game ranch were very impressive. Located approximately fifty miles inland from the Eastern Cape, the spectacular hilly terrain was sparsely covered with small bushes and short trees. The weather, early winter, was dry and the temperature ideal. The first day, while we were getting over the jet lag, Ruth Ann killed her first trophy, a very impressive kudu bull.

The next morning, we drove thirty miles to the Lalibela Game Reserve through a heavy fog and met Carl van Zyl who was to be our primary guide. The veterinarian, a delightful individual, arrived and showed me the "ins and outs" of using his dart gun. This gun had a long thin barrel and a red-dot sight. The maximum range was fifty yards. He made it very clear that, due to the parabolic trajectory of the dart, the precise distance to the quarry must be known. (If the rhino was twenty yards away and the gun was set at fifty yards, the dart would go over its back. Conversely, if the rhino was fifty yards away and the gun was set at twenty yards, the dart would hit the dirt before reaching the rhino.) I practiced several times, and managed to hit a small cardboard box.

We piled into a Land Cruiser and went hunting for rhino. We first encountered a female rhino with a young calf. She didn't seem too perturbed at our presence, but it was obvious that she expected us to move on, which we did. After about an hour, we located five grown rhinos in a grass-covered meadow and crawled slowly to the edge. One rhino had a trophy-quality large horn. Frankly, at that juncture, I could have borrowed Barry's .470 Krieghoff and killed the rhino without further ado. It would not have been a particularly challenging event, to say the least. However, since I was on a darting mission, the next forty-five minutes were filled with excitement and anticipation as I sat still and waited.

Let's return to the hunt. After the rhinos left the field, they soon disappeared from our view. Carl whistled for the crew to bring the Land Cruiser. They picked up both Ruth Ann and the veterinarian who had hidden behind a tree approximately seventy-five yards to our rear to watch the spectacle. We all boarded the Land Cruiser and followed the path made by the rhinos as they ran downhill into a ravine. We drove to the ravine and spotted the darted rhino, seemingly crouched in thick bush. (The total distance traveled was approximately seven hundred and fifty yards.)

We gingerly approached the downed behemoth, but it became clear that the animal could not move. Its respirations were shallow and rapid and its skin felt quite hot. The veterinarian quickly began taking horn measurements, drawing blood samples, administering antibiotics, etc. The rest of the crew chopped down the nearby brush so that the rhino could be photographed. The dart was still in place; it had been driven in exactly perpendicular to the surface. (This is important so that the sedating agent could be injected directly into the muscle and not into the very thick skin.) After fifteen minutes of these activities, the dart was pulled out, and we were ready to begin the final step.

With all of us aboard, the Land Cruiser was turned around and made ready to exit. The veterinarian administered the antidote and hotfooted it back to the truck. The rhino seemed to shake itself somewhat and attempted to rise. We made a circle and returned higher up on the hill. By that time, approximately five minutes had elapsed. The rhino was up and walking around unsteadily, but headed in the direction of his departed buddies. Ten minutes later, we saw him grazing with the group as though nothing had happened.

In discussing the rhinoceros darting program with Carl, he indicated that they had only one other rhino that they had darted previously. The one I chose had never been darted. They would not dart any animal more frequently than once a year. He also indicated that this darting episode went about as smoothly as he had experienced.

The next day, I received a certificate of the horn measurements. A fiberglass replica of the horn constructed using these measurements would be sent later.

The next few days on Barry's ranch were spent hunting and game viewing. Ruth Ann shot a very nice bushbuck and a large springbok. One morning after a very exciting and music-filled race, the hounds treed a large male caracal. We had fulfilled all of our goals.

After a day of rest, we began the tiresome and boring part of the trip—the long flight home. While in the air, I relived this experience and mulled over the future. As of now, I have hunted in four African countries and taken the "Big Five." Would I return, or call it quits? What is the answer? Undoubtedly, there is a Cape buffalo that needs my close attention in the future.

In comparison with hunting the other Big Five, this safari clearly was not as high a level of excitement as I had experienced before. But I must say, in spite of what I had previously thought, darting was not without some hazard and certainly was far more of a challenge than killing this rhino would have been. An added positive feature has to be that our rhino was happier regarding the chosen alternative. Of that I'm certain. At any rate, I've climbed the final rung in the African Big Five ladder.

Last Hour Leopard

This is a shortened version of chapter sixteen to be published in *Safari* magazine.

About 7:30 A.M., Barry stopped the Land Cruiser and shrugged his shoulders. As on the prior fifteen days, we had spent the last three hours checking baits and looking for fresh leopard spoor, all to no avail. Although Joey and I had experienced a thoroughly enjoyable safari, the primary goal of shooting a leopard was not to be. While drinking a cup of coffee, we attempted to put a "happy face" on the situation. We promised ourselves that although this hunt was unsuccessful, we would soon return to fulfill the mission.

At that moment, Alex called. He was with Esau in the other truck examining the roads on the other side of the ranch. In as an excited tone as possible in Afrikaans, he indicated that they had seen fresh leopard tracks near an old cistern. We should come immediately!

I need to put into perspective the events that led up to this moment. In September 2006, through Cabela's Outdoor Adventures, I had booked a leopard hunt with hounds on the Trudia Game Ranch in northern Namibia. Barry Burchell of Frontier Safaris was the professional hunter. On nine previous safaris, I had traveled to Africa with Joey, my Florida quail-hunting partner. However, on this occasion Joey, as a PH, was hunting Cape buffalo in Tanzania.

To say the least, my leopard hunt had a high level of excitement from day one. The trackers found leopard spoor daily. The hunt culminated on the fourth day in a very exciting four-hour chase that ended with my killing a very large (7 feet, 5 inches) male leopard that had been bayed by the pack of hounds and had put up quite a fight. I wanted to repeat the experience, take Joey with me, and let him shoot a leopard. Although as a PH, Joey had been on a number of successful leopard hunts shooting from a blind with clients, he had never killed a leopard himself. Also, he had not hunted leopard with hounds.

In order to comply with Joey's schedule, the fifteen-day safari had to take place in May 2008. Joey brought his .500 double rifle. After the obligatory eighteen-hour plane ride, we were met in Windhoek by Barry. During the drive to the game ranch, he informed us that due to the recent rains, leopard tracks might be very hard to find. Up until February, there had been a severe drought. In fact, some of the plains game were beginning to suffer. However, the rains came, and for the next two months it had rained nearly every day for a total of twenty-nine inches. (The normal annual rainfall in northern Namibia is fourteen inches.) Although it hadn't rained in two weeks, green grass was everywhere, covering most of the desertlike terrain and making leopard tracks virtually impossible to find. Well, we'll do the best we can.

The next morning, we began our daily routine at 5 A.M. Riding the roads with Corporal, our tracker, perched on the hood of the Land Cruiser, we began looking for tracks. We methodically covered the game ranch as well as three additional cattle ranches that the owners had asked Barry to help eliminate the stock-killing leopards. In addition, we put out a variety of baits. On the third day, we found leopard tracks in a dried riverbed. The trackers, Corporal and Mike, along with the dogs, followed the leopard spoor for approximately three miles. They found where he had been drinking and evidence of several recent kills, but weren't able to make contact with Mr. Spots.

After these morning activities each day, we returned to camp, had a light brunch, rested, and then spent the entire afternoon looking for leopard signs as well as hunting plains game. Joey killed a very large impressive kudu as well as a gemsbok and a warthog. On the seventh day, we found fresh leopard tracks at an adjoining ranch.

The dogs took the trail. We followed for approximately six miles. We found where the leopard had lain, but lost the spoor in a rocky area about 12 P.M. It had become too hot for the dogs to smell the faint scent. We continued this general game plan for the next seven days. In addition, on a number of occasions, Corporal and Mike took the dogs through areas that looked promising, but again, we were unable to come to close quarters with a leopard. Both the trackers and dogs were becoming quite tired.

We had approached each day with a "hope that springs eternal within the human breast." However, in spite of all the other exciting events, it looked like our prime goal of getting Joey a leopard was not to be achieved.

Alex's urgent call changed everything! It took us about twenty minutes to get to the location. The four trackers, Corporal, Alex, Mike, and Esau, along with about fifteen hounds, went to work. They showed me where a large male leopard had walked near an old water cistern. The spoor was distinct enough so that even my untrained eye could delineate it. We were situated on a low hill covered with grass, small trees, and brush. There was a ravine in front, and on the other side, a fairly steep hill. In fact, it was in this area that I had shot my leopard eighteen months ago.

Very methodically, the four trackers and the dogs scoured the area. The spoor was not sufficiently fresh for the dogs to open, but the trackers found where the leopard had left the area. They followed his trail for approximately one and one half miles in a westward direction. Then the leopard turned around and walked along the ravine in our direction. The trackers found enough spoor to follow his meanderings. Mike came to where we waited and showed me a very fresh piece of leopard scat, which he had picked up in the ravine. The trackers and hounds followed the spoor eastward in the ravine.

About this time, the dogs began to open sparingly, indicating that the scent was becoming fresher. After about two miles, the leopard crossed and went up the side of the hill. The hounds began to bark more frequently as the track became hotter. We positioned ourselves and waited, all the time expecting that the leopard would go over the hill and hide in the rocky terrain. However, he turned and once more came back in our direction.

About one mile from us, Corporal saw the leopard jump out of a tree. The hounds were not nearby and it took about five minutes for them to pick up the trail. Although the scent was fresh, the temperature was quite hot by that time (11:30 A.M.) and the hounds could not move as fast as I had expected. However, they were in full cry and slowly coming in our direction. Joey quietly, prophetically remarked, "I believe the leopard is close-by."

About that time, three hundred yards to our front, the Jack Russell terrier (which is used to route leopards out of caves and holes) started to bark. It turned out that he was looking up at the leopard in a tree! In a few minutes, all the dogs and the trackers arrived at the tree. Corporal let us know that they had found the leopard. We got there as fast as possible. The leopard was in a tree about halfway up the steep hill.

About the time Joey got ready to shoot, the leopard sailed out of the tree, but did not attempt to fight the hounds, and ran off. He went over the top of the hill and down the other side for about three hundred yards and treed again. By that time the dogs, trackers and I'm sure, the leopard, were exhausted, but the pack let us know that they were again looking at the leopard. We got there in time. Joey's double rifle brought a successful conclusion to the chase. (I've never seen anyone happier or more excited.)

The leopard was transported on Alex's shoulders to the Land Cruiser and we moved him to an open area to take pictures. Mr. Spots was placed on a downed tree trunk, which happened to be the same tree that we had used to take the pictures of my leopard eighteen months before.

It was a majestic animal, weighing 145 pounds and measuring 7 feet and ½ inch. Why did he climb several trees rather than staying on the ground and fighting the hounds as most male leopards do? One possibility is that his stomach was full from a recent meal.

Perhaps he was more inclined to sleep rather than battle with the hounds. We drove back to camp, had a brief celebration, and bid the staff farewell. Still highly elated, we began the arduous journey homeward.

If there ever was a situation in which "All's Well That Ends Well," this was it.